JAVA Network Security

The ITSO Networking Series

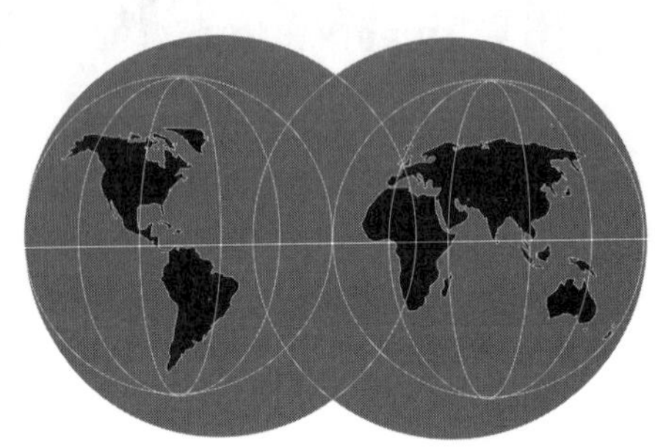

TCP/IP Tutorial and Technical Overview
by Murphy, Hayes, and Ender

Asynchronous Transfer Mode (ATM)
by Dutton and Lenhard

High-Speed Networking Technology
by Dutton and Lenhard

www.security: How to Build a Secure World Wide Web Connection
by Macgregor, Aresi, and Siegert

Internetworking over ATM: An Introduction
by Dorling, Freedman, Metz, and Burger

Java Network Security
by Robert Macgregor, Dave Durbin, John Owlett, Andrew Yeomans

JAVA Network Security

ROBERT MACGREGOR ■ DAVE DURBIN ■ JOHN OWLETT ■ ANDREW YEOMANS

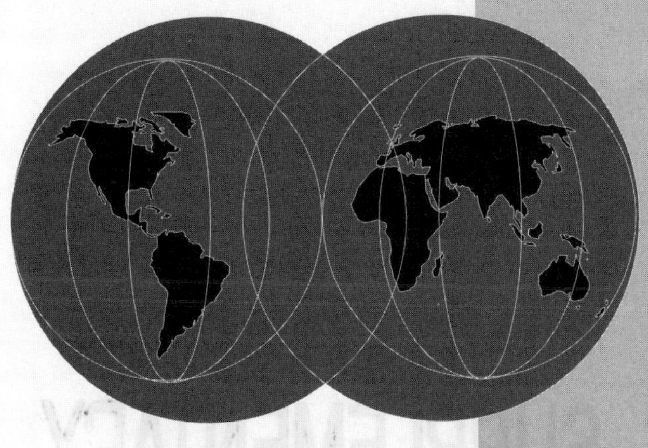

PRENTICE HALL PTR, UPPER SADDLE RIVER, NEW JERSEY 07458

For information about redbooks:
http://www.redbooks.ibm.com/redbooks

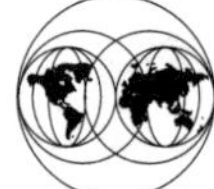

Send comments to:
redbooks@vnet.ibm.com

Published by

Prentice Hall PTR
Prentice-Hall, Inc.
A Simon & Schuster Company
Upper Saddle River, NJ 07458

Prentice Hall books are widely used by corporations and government agencies for training, marketing, and resale. The publisher offers discounts on this book when ordered in bulk quantities.
For more information, contact

Corporate Sales Department,
Phone 800-382-3419; FAX: 201-236-7141
E-mail (Internet): corpsales@prenhall.com

Or Write: Prentice Hall PTR
Corp. Sales Department
One Lake Street
Upper Saddle River, NJ 07458

Printed in the United States of America

1 0 9 8 7 6 5 4 3

ISBN 0-13-761529-9

Prentice-Hall International (UK) Limited, *London*
Prentice-Hall of Australia Pty. Limited, *Sydney*
Prentice-Hall Canada Inc., *Toronto*
Prentice-Hall Hispanoamericana, S.A., *Mexico*
Prentice-Hall of India Private Limited, *New Delhi*
Prentice-Hall of Japan, Inc., *Tokyo*
Simon & Schuster Asia Pte. Ltd., *Singapore*
Editora Prentice-Hall do Brasil, Ltda., *Rio de Janeiro*

Contents

Preface

Java is fashionable, but is it reliable? Java is entertaining, but is it secure? Java is useful, but is it safe?

The purpose of this book is to answer those questions, from the point of view of people who *want* to use Java, but want to do so reliably, securely and safely. That makes it different from much recent writing on Java which focuses, perfectly legitimately, on how Java can be broken and how to avoid those dangers. We focus on how Java can be made secure and how to exploit its strengths. The goal is to be a practical help to the various groups of people involved in making a Java-based application or Web site into an industrial-strength commercial proposition.

These various groups of people have different needs and different skills, which we have tried to meet in the different parts of the book. The first part is aimed at the intelligent non-specialist who has to oversee system management or application development, or incorporate Java into the security policy. Only a basic understanding of computers and a limited exposure to Java is assumed, but all the themes of Java security are introduced in a context which stresses over and over again how Java security must be seen as an integral part of system security.

The second part goes into more detail of how Java security works, and is aimed more at system and network administrators and programmers, who need to know more of what is going on. Perhaps, though, only the programmers will ever read the tables in Chapters 4 and 5.

The third part looks at the broader context in which Java operates, including some extensions to Java security and some aspects of its future. At the time of writing, the Java Development Kit is at JDK 1.1 level, though most people's browsers are still at an earlier level. Accordingly, the book is written primarily from the point of view of JDK 1.1, in the knowledge that current practical Internet applications must be usable from JDK 1.0 browsers, and in the knowledge that JDK 1.2 with its domains of protection is not long away.

The Team That Wrote This Book

This book was produced by a team of specialists from the IBM Installation Support Centre, Hursley, on behalf of the Systems Management and Networking ITSO Center, Raleigh.

Dave Durbin is a specialist in Java and in Cryptolope technology at IBM's Internet Centre of Competence serving Europe, the Middle East and Africa from the Installation Support Centre in Hursley, England. He first became involved in Internet development in 1986 and has been a frequent technical speaker on Java ever since the 1Alpha1 release in 1995. Dave graduated from the University of Edinburgh, Scotland, in the late 1980s and worked as an object-oriented programmer in the Life Insurance industry before joining IBM in Edinburgh. He moved to Hursley at the beginning of 1997.

Rob Macgregor is a systems specialist at the IBM Installation Support Centre, Hursley. He has long experience in the fields of distributed systems management and network security, on which subjects he writes and teaches IBM classes extensively. He also provides technical support and advice for customers. Prior to joining the ISC in 1997, Rob was an assignee to the Raleigh ITSO Center, producing redbooks and skills-transfer materials.

John Owlett is an Internet security specialist, also at the ISC. He first became fascinated with logical data security while he was a visiting associate professor at Aarhus University, Denmark, in the 1970s. Later he had the opportunity to put the ideas into practice as a systems manager for IBM's large internal computer center at Portsmouth, England. Dr. Owlett has been involved with Java since early in 1995, the year he joined the Internet Centre of Competence based in Hursley.

Andrew Yeomans specializes in UNIX, AIX, firewalls and security, advising customers and teaching these subjects across Europe. He joined the IBM Internet Centre of Competence in 1996 from IBM's Scientific and Technical group, where he managed the security of their UNIX systems. He joined IBM in 1991, following 15 years in software development and consultancy in high-quality color image processing, page composition, hand-held terminals and word processing.

Acknowledgements

This book had its genesis when IBM's Internet Division asked Rick Lacks of the International Technical Support Organization in Raleigh, North Carolina, to arrange for a "redbook" on the subject and he assigned the project to Rob Macgregor, then a member of his team. The others, all members of the Internet Centre of Competence in Hursley, christened the project JamJar; echoes of this working title can be seen in some of the examples in the book.

Thanks to the following people for their invaluable advice and guidance provided in the production of this book:

- Our editors, Shawn Walsh and Gail Wojton ("the fair editrix") of the ITSO Center at Raleigh
- Pete Lawther of the University of Sunderland and of the Installation Support Centre at Hursley, who wrote Appendix A
- Simon Phipps of the Centre for Java Technology at Hursley, for his help in our early discussions of the project

Bibliography

Building Internet Firewalls, D. Brent Chapman and Elizabeth D. Zwicky (O'Reilly & Associates) 1-56592-124-0

Firewalls and Internet Security, William R. Cheswick and Steven M. Bellovin (Addison-Wesley) 0-201-63357-4

Web Spoofing: An Internet Con Game, Edward W. Felten, Drew Dean, and Dan S. Wallach (Technical Report 540-96, Department of Computer Science, Princeton University)

Practical UNIX and Internet Security, Simson Garfinkel and Gene Spafford (O'Reilly & Associates) 1-56592-148-0

Vice President's Statement on Encryption, October 1, 1996 (http://www.bxa,doc.gov/encrypt.htm)

Java Security: Hostile Applets, Holes, and Antidotes, Gary McGraw and Edward W. Felten (John Wiley & Sons) 0-471-17842-X

TCP/IP Illustrated: Volume 1 - The Protocols, W. Richard Stevens (Addison-Wesley) 0-201-63346-9

The Java Virtual Machine, John Meyer & Troy Downing (O'Reilly & Associates) 1-56592-194-1

Using Assembly Language, 2nd Edition, Allen L. Wyatt (Que Corporation) 0-88022-464-9

Part 1. Introduction to Java and Security

Chapter 1. An Overview of Java Security

The purpose of this chapter is not only to introduce the themes of the book to those who will later read the more detailed chapters that follow, but also to act as a brief overview for the intelligent non-specialist who does not need all the details. This is because the focus of the book is on helping people to deploy Java in a secure way. There are many people involved in that – managers, administrators, developers, systems programmers, users – all of whom play a part.

1.1 What Java Does

What Java does is to solve the problem of executable content. What's that? Well, the early sites on the Worldwide Web were static: pictures and text. That was revolutionary enough. The richness of the pages was a revelation to anyone used to the usual staid appearance of information downloaded from a server; the hypertext links, which made cross-referencing easy, made it a more useful information source than an encyclopedia; and the amount of information available was staggering. But if you wanted a program to run, you had to send a data file to the server where that program was – you filled in a form on the screen, clicked the send button, and waited for the result.

Some programs are better run on the client than on a server. So why couldn't part of the content of the Web pages be executable? Why couldn't a page comprise some text, some pictures, and some programs that run on the client? There were two reasons:

1. It would be dangerous from a security point of view. There are enough viruses on the Web anyway. With executable content, you might not even realize that you were downloading potentially dangerous code.
2. The programs might not run on a particular operating system. One of the joys of the Web was that you could choose whatever client system was right for you and download pages running on a completely different system.

   But executable content is not just cute – it is extremely valuable:

   - Executable content can make a Web page much more exciting. This is what Java became well known for in its early days: dancing cartoon characters, bouncing heads, ticker tapes. You can't do these if all the programs must run on the server. Some of the early examples were indeed just cute – they showed what the technology could do, not why it was important – but appearance, excitement, and even cuteness are important in attracting customers to a business site.

- Many dialogues with a customer are unbearably slow if you have to communicate with a Web server at each interaction. With executable content, the dialogue – an insurance proposal, a request for a credit card, a browse through a catalogue, or whatever – can be completed on the client machine, and the resulting transaction sent across the Web.

Java makes executable content possible while solving the problems noted above by having three components:

1. A Java Virtual Machine (JVM) designed to prevent the downloaded code (usually called an applet) from tampering with the client system. The applet runs in a protected space, known informally as the sandbox, and has only limited and always strictly controlled access to the surrounding system. This is to meet requirement 1 above.
2. A set of bytecodes – virtual machine instructions – which are interpreted by the JVM. You have to have these to prevent the applet from jumping outside the sandbox, but they have a benefit of their own. Since they are machine-independent, if you have a JVM for your workstation, then you can run any applet from any server, satisfying requirement 2 above.
3. A high-level object-oriented language in which to write the classes that make up the applets. This is a language similar in many ways to C++ with some functions (such as pointers) omitted because they could be used to escape from the sandbox.

There is now a Java Development Kit (JDK) – comprising JVM, compiler, and basic classes – for most operating systems, and most Web browsers contain a JVM, so executable content is now real.

So far, we have concentrated on executable content and on the downloaded code known as an applet. Java high-level language, however, has wider uses than just applets. It is a general-purpose language, a well designed object-oriented language, in which you can write any program you like.

A Java program which is loaded locally, rather than from the Web, is called an application. Because it has not come over the Web, it is not constrained by the sandbox and can access the local machine, just like a program written in any other language. In this book we always clearly distinguish between applets and applications.

All you have to do is write an application once in Java, and you can run it anywhere that has a JVM. This makes it very useful for people writing applications which will be used by a wide variety of users – quite independently of whether they will ever be downloaded from the Web.

1.2 Java Is Not an Island: Java as a Part of Security

> *"Chubb lock to the door..., and those preposterous English windows which a child could open" - Sherlock Holmes, A Scandal in Bohemia*
>
> (A.Conan Doyle, 1891)

The geographical Java certainly is an island: a separate part of Indonesia. But Java the computer system is not something separate from the other components that make up the total system. So it is essential that the security of Java is seen as being one part of the security of the whole. This is hardly a new message. More than 100 years ago, Conan Doyle was ridiculing an approach to physical security that fitted a top-grade door lock and left the windows unsecured.

What this means for Java security is that it must be *holistic*, *adequate* and *perpetual.*

First, Java security must be holistic. An attacker who wishes you harm (rather than one who wants to prove his own cleverness) will focus on the weak links in the security, so the security of a system that uses Java must be reviewed as a whole, following the flows of data and application, and considering the potential for attack or accident at each point. Specifically, if Java is being used to pass applets over a shared network like the Internet, then you have to consider:

- Private network protection, using a firewall and allied security policies
- Private data protection, using encryption to shield data as it flows over the public network

- User authentication, using digital signatures, or protected passwords

Secondly, Java security must be adequate. It has to be strong enough for the purpose in hand: Java must not be the weak link. But there is no need to spend extra to make it far and away the strongest link, unless either:

- Your potential attackers don't just want to crack your system, they want to crack your *Java* system, or
- Your users have a particular fear of Java, and you need to reassure them (security has to match levels of threat and worry, as well as, levels of potential loss)

So, if you cannot put fastenings on your sash windows, you don't need that Chubb lock on the front door.

Thirdly, Java security must be perpetual. This book will help you build a secure Java system to face today's perils of accident and attack. But those perils will change. So you must review your Java security – as a part of your overall security of course – regularly, to stay one jump ahead of potential attackers.

How well does Java meet those needs? Three points:

1. **Java architecture permits secure design**. Java's use of a "sandbox" provides the capability of separating your computer from the applets you download. This is described in much more detail later. The point here is that the problems with Java that have been reported are problems with the *implementation*, not problems with the *design*.
2. **Java implementations respond to error reports**. The attack applets we describe later were all reported by applet hunters; they come, not from incidents of loss on the Internet, but from laboratory studies of how Java can be used and abused. The applet hunters have been as responsible as they are clever, and have alerted the Java implementors to the problems before telling the public. So normally you will hear of an implementation loophole at the same time as hearing of the fix. Thus any risk of using Java gets gradually less as loopholes are closed.
3. **Nothing in Java should permit complacency**. Installers and users of Java must be as willing to respond as the implementors. That is, users must recognize that loopholes will be found and must be closed without delay.

In summary, provided that you have an implementation that is free of known errors, and that you install, maintain and review Java carefully, you can reach levels of security which are appropriate for any business purpose.

1.2.1 Safety and Security

To enthusiastic object-oriented programmers, it is the Java *language* that is important. It contains a number of important differences from C++ which reduce the chance of writing a rogue program by accident, as well as making it more difficult to write a rogue program by design.

But, from a security point of view, it is the Java *virtual machine* that matters. The business benefits of Java are the security and portability of the JVM, and these come from the bytecodes, not from the Java source language.

So, we shall be more concerned with bytecode programs, which are different from Java source programs. All valid Java source programs can be compiled to bytecode programs, but there are bytecode programs that have no corresponding Java source. And, of course, it is possible to generate Java bytecode programs from other high-level languages. The first other language was NetREXX, a variant of the REXX language, and others have followed.

This difference between high-level and bytecode is both bad and good:

- It is bad because people can circumvent the design features of the Java language. This was designed to produce well-behaved bytecode programs, a design that has limited security strength if an attacker can write directly in bytecode.
- It is good because you can foil the decompilers. These take bytecode and generate Java source code – source code which is very readable because of the large amount of information a Java class file contains. To prevent people decompiling your valuable copyright code, you can modify the compiled class file so that there is no decompiled version. (We discuss this in detail in "Decompilation Attacks" on page 60.

So the good features of the high-level Java language should be seen as *safety* features, not as *security* features.

1.2.2 Java as an Aid to Security

Sometimes, discussions of Java and security focus only on the perils of Java, as though there was only a downside to using it, from a security point of view anyway. But this is not the whole story. Java can be a great help to the security of a system, and can strengthen weak links, primarily because *code distribution is a risky process.*

Many applications need code running on the client in cooperation with code running on the server – for example, graphical front ends, or dialers to connect to the telephone network – and this code has to be installed there somehow. The distribution of this code is often a weak link in an online system, and it is usually *much* easier to attack this than to waste time trying to decrypt messages flowing over the Internet.

What is the danger? If this code can be tampered with, then, for example, a dialer number can be changed so that the client dials the attacker's site rather than the proper server. The client will never realize this because the attacker, acting as a "man in the middle" forwards all traffic between client and server, reading it as it goes. Or a virus can be introduced, or a host of other horrible possibilities.

The options for code distribution are:

- To send a physical diskette or CD-ROM to the client
- To have the client download the code over an existing network
- To use Java

The safest of the three is Java. It isn't always suitable – the client must already have a network connection that is fast enough for the purpose – but it is by far the easiest to update with a new release, it is less easily intercepted than a physical distribution and, unlike a normal download, it is checked on arrival. Moreover, it can be signed.

The checking and signing of Java applets is central to Java security and (very) much more will be said about them in later chapters. In this introductory chapter, it is enough to describe briefly the three components of applet checking:

1. The *Class Loader* is responsible for bringing together all of the different parts of the program so that it can be executed.
2. The *Class File Verifier* (which includes the bytecode verifier) checks that the program obeys the rules of the Java Virtual

Machine (but note that this does not necessarily mean that it obeys the rules of the Java language).

3. The *Security Manager* imposes local restrictions on the things that the program is allowed to do. It is perfectly possible to customize this to allow applets limited access to carefully controlled resources, but in practice the browser vendors have implemented a version of the highly restrictive default that Sun supplies. This allows no access to the local file system, and network access only to the location from which the applet, or its Web page, came.

The way forward for allowing wider access is via the signed applets of JDK 1.1. You may wish, for example, to print something from an applet. You are unlikely to want your security manager to allow anyone to do that, but you might allow access to especially trustworthy people. So you download the applet; discover that it is encrypted with someone's private key; check the accompanying public-key certificate to make sure it is valid, and identifies someone especially trustworthy; decrypt the applet with that public key, and then allow it the necessary access.

One important thing that distinguishes Java from other forms of executable content is that it has *both* the web of trust that signatures bring *and* the three security components to validate the downloaded code. These precautions are taken, not because Java users are less trustful than others, but because even the most trusted of code suppliers sometimes make mistakes, or can have their systems compromised. Without the validation, a web of trust can become a web of corruption if any one trusted site is successfully cracked.

1.2.3 Java as a Threat to Security

So, in the absence of implementation errors, either on the part of the browser vendors *or on the part of computer operators, administrators and systems programmers*, Java should be safe. The browser vendors have a good reputation for responding to reports of flaws in their implementations, and one of the key purposes of this book is to help you avoid any slips in your installation.

If something does go wrong, then the most severe threat you face is *system modification*, the result of what are sometimes called "attack" applets. This is worse than someone's being able to read data from your system, because you have no idea what has been left behind. There could be a virus on your computer, or on any computer to which you are connected. Alternatively, some of your business data could have been modified so that it is no longer valid.

This is exactly the sort of thing that Java is intended to prevent, and its defences against attack applets are strong. They are equally strong against the next, still severe, threat of *privacy invasion*, in which read access rather than update access is gained. This does not leave you having to reinstall all your software and reassemble all your business data, but the loss can be serious enough. In addition to the exposure of business data, if your private key is compromised, then it can be used to sign electronic payments in your name.

Because Java has the strongest security for executable content, it has been seen as a challenge by security specialists, who find both the intellectual challenge exciting and want to help close any loopholes in Java implementations. Up to the date of writing, all the reported attack applets were developed by such specialists, not by malicious or criminal attackers.

There are another couple of, much less severe, threats against which Java does not have strong defences. The very essence of Java is that a program from a server will come down and run on your client with little, if any, intervention from you. What if the program is not one you want to run... if it is stealing your cycles?

The most extreme form of cycle stealing is a *denial of service* attack. The applet can use so much of the client's machine time that it cannot perform its normal function. This is the Java equivalent of flooding a company with mail or with telephone calls; like those nuisances it cannot readily be prevented – all you can do is find out who is responsible and take action after the event.

Less extreme examples of cycle stealing are the irksome, *nuisance*, applets. These run unhelpful programs intended to show how clever the author is and embarrass the owner of the client machine. They can even pretend to be you (psyche stealing?), for example by sending e-mail that appears to come from you.

1.2.4 Java as Something to Be Secured

This is a different point of view again. From this point of view, Java applets are seen neither as aids to strengthening security weak links, nor as potential weak links themselves, but as assets that need to be protected. They can cost a lot to write and are valuable. They must not be copied and their use should be charged for.

This is an area which is still in its infancy. As was described earlier in this chapter, Java is a well-behaved language, and a Java class file can be decompiled to give a thoroughly intelligible Java program. So the same person who developed the Mocha decompiler has also developed the Crema obfuscator, which smudges the information in the class file so that the decompiler will no longer work. There is more on this subject in "Beating the Decompilation Threat" on page 67.

However, the long term goal has to be to charge for the use of valuable Java applets. The most promising approach at the moment is the work on Cryptolopes, whereby the bulk of the applet is downloaded in encrypted form. Enough is unencrypted that the user can see what he is being offered, and request the decryption key, thereby agreeing to pay. This approach is discussed in Chapter 13, "Java and Cryptolopes" on page 201.

1.2.5 Writing Secure Java

The sort of applet described in the previous section – one that is an asset because it performs significant business function – is likely to need to communicate with the server it came from, and to do so securely. All sensitive communication over the Internet needs proper cryptographic protection, and so JDK 1.1 contains an application programming interface (API) for security.

There are two keys parts of this for writing applets that use cryptography. One of the reasons for the division is that some cryptographic functions are seen as being dangerous in the wrong hands. No government wants to provide organized crime, or terrorist groups, with a cheap effective way of communicating that the police cannot decrypt. Exactly how to prevent this is not so clear, so there are many different export and import rules for cryptographic products. The cryptographic interfaces are divided into two parts, JCA and JCE, which reflect the divide between exportable and unexportable cryptography. We discuss this in more detail in "Cryptography to the Rescue!" on page 31.

1.2.6 Staying One Jump Ahead

To get ahead, the owners of a client or a Web site need to develop an overall security policy of which Java is a part, and implement it with care. They need to use the latest information on what is known about Java security. This is bound to change; realistically, Java is so young that it cannot be otherwise.

So how do they find the very latest information? Two key sources are the CERT Coordination Center, which is on the Web at http://www.cert.org/ and Sun Microsystems's list of frequently asked questions about applet security at http://java.javasoft.com/sfaq. This gets you ahead. Staying ahead means that the security policy should include regular checks of these sites, and regular reviews of which are the right sites to check.

Another part of staying ahead involves balancing security with stability. If an implementation error is discovered in the browser you use, and you see on the Web sites a description of the problem together with news of a new beta version of the browser to fix the problem, do you change to the new beta at once? Systems managers are traditionally very cautious about beta code: they want to see a lot of testing before they put it live on their production systems. This caution is one of the most important causes of the very high availability levels of modern systems, so systems managers are not about to change.

Traditionally, a change to include new function is forced to wait until it passes thorough testing, while a security change may be allowed through with less testing. It's a business decision, and it's worth including guidance in the security policy. The only way in which Java is different from all other areas of security, where similar business decisions must be made, is that news of a loophole can be spread worldwide extremely quickly, so the presumption should be that security fixes must go on quickly.

1.2.7 The Vigilant Web Site

The cure for abuse is proper use, not non-use. Executable content has such a great value to computer systems and to computer business that we need to do it properly, not to ban it.

Proper use of Java involves vigilance on everybody's part, including:

- Vigilance on the part of the systems administrators who need to be sure that they can trust their sources
- Vigilance on the part of the network administrators who need to protect against network attacks such as the man-in-the-middle

- Vigilance on the part of applet developers who need to be sure that the tools they are using do not corrupt their class files: their workstations may not be production machines, but they must be properly protected

There is something of an irony in remarks one sometimes hears about how Java should be turned off, made by people who are happy to download a code patch or a driver from a Web site. It is similar to those who are deeply concerned about sending their credit card information over the Web, but would willingly hand a credit card to a waiter in a restaurant.

If Java is used with vigilance, then its unique combination of web of trust and code validation makes it more secure than forms of executable content which depend on the web of trust alone. And, of course, dramatically more secure than downloading natively executable code from the Web.

Chapter 2. Attack and Defense

Many claims have been made for the security of Java. A lot of these claims have been rather exaggerated, but underlying them is the fact that security was designed-in at an early stage in the development of the language. Saying that Java has strong security is like challenging the world to find the holes in it, which is exactly what has happened. Some very clever (and very devious) people have been applying their brain-power to the problem of breaking down the Java defenses.

In this chapter we give a high-level view of how Java defends itself and then summarize the different ways in which it can be attacked.

2.1 Java Is Not Just a Language

Most of the books on the subject deal with Java as a programming language. As a programming language it has much to recommend it. Its syntax is very like C, but with many of the features that hurt your brain removed. It is strongly object-oriented, but it avoids the more obscure corners of the O-O world.

For most programming languages the question of "how secure is it" does not arise. It's the application that needs to implement security, not the language it is written in. However, Java is many other things in addition to being a programming language:

- A set of object-oriented frameworks, primarily for GUI building and networking
- An operating system
- A client/server management mechanism
- A unifying force that cuts across operating system and network boundaries

It is not surprising that Java has become so widely accepted, so quickly. Before we look at the security issues, let us review some Java fundamentals.

2.2 Components of Java

There are a number of different components to Java:

- **Development environment**
  The *Java Development Kit* (JDK) contains the tools and executable code needed to compile and test Java programs. However, unlike a normal language, the JDK includes object frameworks for creating graphical user interfaces, for networking and for complex I/O. Normally these things are provided as additions, either by the operating system or by another software package. Of course, fully-featured development environments do exist for Java, but the core language includes a lot of what they would normally have to provide.

- **Execution environment**
  Java's execution environment is neither that of a compiled language nor an interpreted language. Instead it is a hybrid, implemented by the *Java Virtual Machine* (JVM). Java is often said to be platform-independent, but first the JVM must be ported to each platform to provide the environment it needs. The JVM implementation is responsible for all of the built-in security of Java, so it is important that it is done properly.

- **Interfaces and architectures**
  Java applications live in the real world. This means that they must be able to interact with non-Java applications. Some of these interactions are very simple (such as the way that a Java applet is invoked in a Web page). Others are the subject of more complex architectural definitions, such as the JDBC interface for relational database support. The mechanism for adding encryption to Java security, the *Java Cryptography Architecture* (JCA), falls into this latter category.

2.2.1 The Development Environment

Once you have installed the JDK, you can start creating Java source code and compiling it. Java is like any other high-level programming language, in that you write the source code in an English-like form. The source code then has to be converted into a form that the machine can understand before it can be executed. To perform this conversion for a normal language, the code is usually either compiled (converted once and stored as machine code) or interpreted (converted and executed at runtime).

Java combines these two approaches. The source code has to be compiled with a Java compiler, such as *javac*, before it can be used. This is a conventional compilation, but the output that it produces is not machine-specific code, but instead is *bytecode*, a system independent format. We will take a closer look at how bytecode is constructed in “Java Bytecode” on page 69.

In order to execute, the compiled code has to be processed by an interpreter, which is part of the Java execution environment (known as the Java virtual machine, or JVM). The JVM is a runtime platform, providing a number of built-in system services, such as thread support, memory management and I/O, in addition to the interpreter.

2.2.1.1 Class Consciousness

Java is an object-oriented language, meaning that a program is composed of a number of object classes, each containing data and methods. One result of this is that, although a program may consist of just a single class, when you have compiled it into bytecode only a small proportion of the code that gets executed is likely to be in the resulting *.class* file. The rest of the function will be in other classes that the main program references. The JVM uses *dynamic linking* to load these classes as they are needed. As an example, consider the simple applet contained in the following two Java source files:

```
import java.awt.BorderLayout;
import java.awt.event.ActionEvent;
import java.awt.event.ActionListener;
import jamjar.examples.Button;
public class PointlessButton extends java.applet.Applet implements
java.awt.event.ActionListener {
  Button  donowt = new Button( "Do Nothing" );
  int     count = 0;
/**
 * The button was clicked.
 */
  public void actionPerformed(java.awt.event.ActionEvent e) {
    donowt.setLabel( "Did Nothing " + ++count + " time" + ( count == 1? "": "s" ) );
  }
  public void init( ) {
    setLayout( new BorderLayout( ) );
    this.add( "Center", donowt );
    donowt.addActionListener( this );
  }
```

Figure 1. Applet Source Code, PointlessButton.java

```
package jamjar.examples;
import java.awt.Color;
import java.awt.event.MouseEvent;
import java.awt.event.MouseListener;
/**
 * This class was generated by a SmartGuide.
*/
public class Button extends java.awt.Button implements MouseListener {
/**
 * @param title java.lang.String
 */
  public Button(String title) {
    super( title );
    addMouseListener( this );
    setBackground( Color.white );
  }
/**
 * Set the color of the button to red when the mouse enters
 */
  public void mouseEntered( MouseEvent m ) {
    setBackground( Color.red );
  }
/**
 * Reset the color of the button to white when the mouse exits
 */
  public void mouseExited( MouseEvent m ) {
    setBackground( Color.white );
  }
/**
 * Three do nothing methods.
 * Needed to implement the MouseListener interface
 */
  public void mouseClicked(java.awt.event.MouseEvent e) {}
  public void mousePressed(java.awt.event.MouseEvent e) {}
  public void mouseReleased(java.awt.event.MouseEvent e) {}
}
```

Figure 2. Invoked Class File, Button.java

The first listing, pointlessButton.java, is an applet that places a button on the Web page. It is not a very useful button, but we like it. Instead of using the standard AWT *Button* class it uses a class of our own, also called Button (see the second listing), but in a locally-written package. This works like a normal button, except that it changes color when you move the mouse pointer over it. Figure 3 shows two copies of the applet running in a Web page.

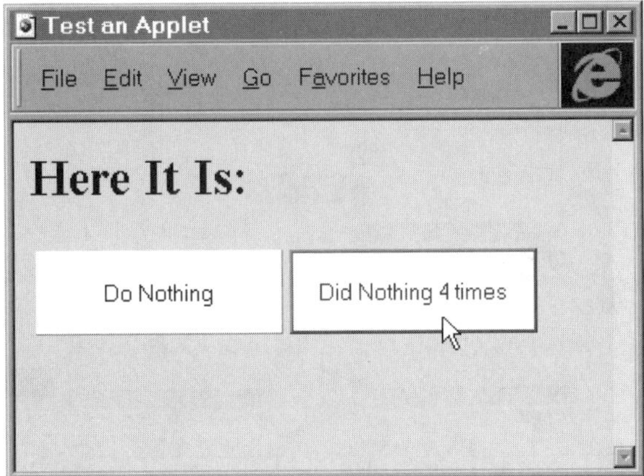

Figure 3. Running the pointlessButton Applet

The total size of the bytecode for this example is only 2 KB. However, the two classes cause a lot of other code to be dynamically installed, either as a result of inheritance (defined by the `extends` keyword in the class definition) or by instantiation (when a class creates an instance of another class with the `new` keyword). Figure 4 shows the hierarchy of classes that could potentially be loaded to run our simple applet (this is a simplified view, because it does not consider classes that may be invoked by classes above the lowest level of the hierarchy).

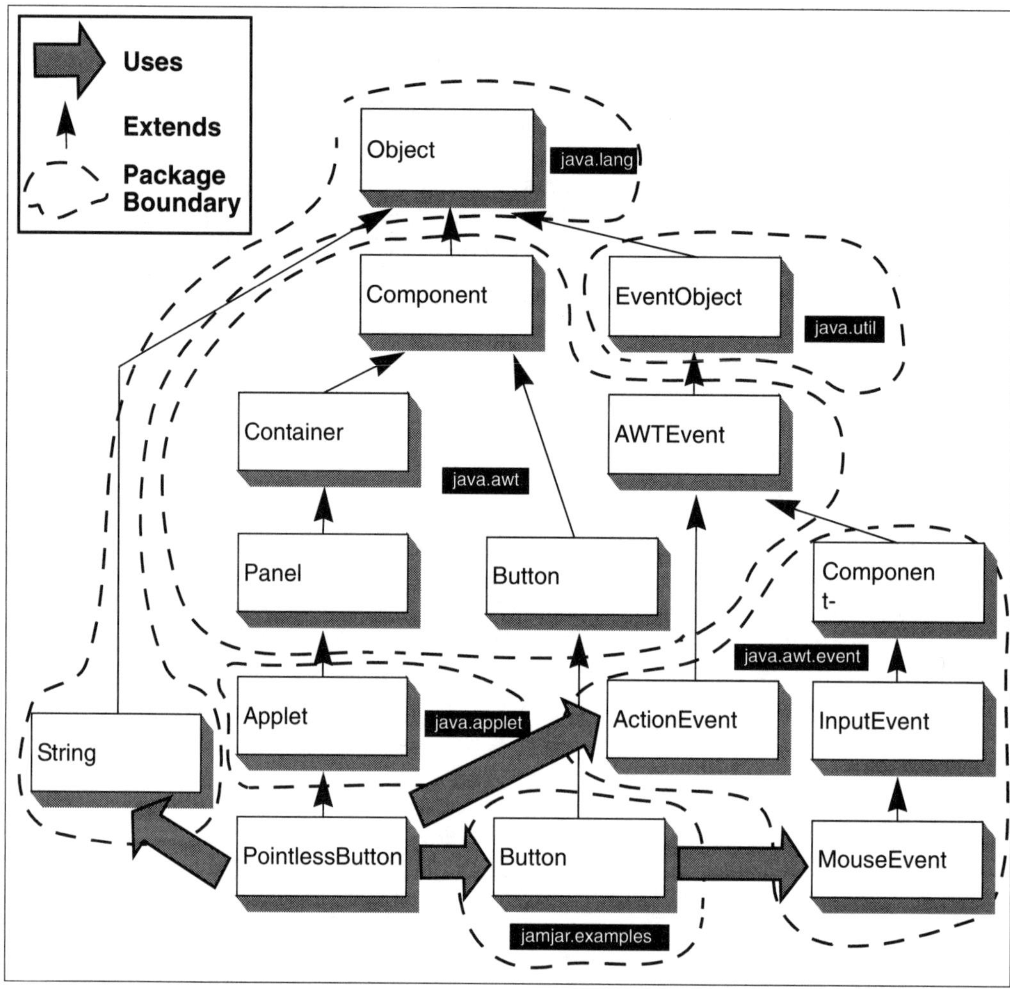

Figure 4. Classes Loaded for the pointlessButton Applet

This diagram illustrates a number of things about Java classes:

1. The classes are arranged in *packages* which are collections of related classes. The language defines a large number of these, which have to be implemented by every JVM implementation. You can add your own class packages by defining new classes that inherit from one of the basic classes. In our example, all but two of the classes are provided as standard. Normally, Java class loaders

impose a direct relationship between a package name and the location of the directory in which it expects to find the class files for the package. So, in our example, the classes contained in the *jamjar.examples* package will be found in directory {codebase}/jamjar/examples (codebase is the base directory on the server from which the applet is loaded, specified in the applet tag).[1]

2. Classes are defined as *extending* existing classes. This means that they can inherit the properties (variables and methods) of the higher (or *super*) class. They can also selectively override the properties of the super class. They also add new properties of their own.
3. Java identifies classes using the fully-qualified class name, that is, the combination of the package name and the class name. This allows you to have duplicated class names, such as our two Button classes. If two classes in different packages do have duplicate names, the programmer must take care to use the right one. Two things that help with this are: importing classes by name, instead of importing the whole package, and placing the trusted classes at the start of the class path.

2.2.1.2 VABs and Beans

Java is unusual in the breadth of function that its built-in class frameworks provide; however, for a project of any complexity you are likely to employ graphical tools, such as a *visual application builder* (VAB) to link together predefined components, thereby reducing the code you have to write to the core logic of the application. Examples of VABs include IBM VisualAge for Java and Lotus Development's BeanMachine.

A *component* in this context is a package of Java classes that perform a given function. The JavaBeans definition describes a standard for components, known as *Beans*. Basically a Bean is a package of code containing both development and runtime components that:

- Allows a builder tool to analyze how it works ("introspection").
- Allows a builder tool to customize its appearance and behavior.
- Supports "events," a simple communication metaphor than can be used to connect beans.

[1] In fact we are guilty of using an improper name construction here. If your package will be used together with packages from other sources, you should follow the naming standard laid down in the *Java Language Specification*, Gosling, Joy and Steele. In our case this would lead to a package name something like com.ibm.JamJar.examples. If you want to know more about the Java language specification, refer to http://java.sun.com/docs/books/jls/.

- Supports “properties,” or settable attributes, used both when developing an application and programmatically when the application is running.
- Supports persistence, so that a bean can be customized in an application builder and then have its customized state saved away and reloaded later.
- Provides interfaces to other component architectures, such as ActiveX and LiveConnect.

From this list you can infer that, although a Bean is mostly made up of Java classes, it can also include other files, containing persistent information and other resources such as graphical elements, etc. These elements are all packed (or *pickled*) together in a JAR (Java Archive) file.

From a security viewpoint, VABs and Beans do not affect the underlying strengths and weaknesses of Java. However, they may add more uncertainty, in that your application now includes sizeable chunks of code that you did not directly write. Their ability to provide interfaces to other component architectures may also cause problems, as we discuss in “Interfaces and Architectures” on page 27.

2.2.2 The Execution Process

We have said that the Java virtual machine operates on the stream of bytecode as an interpreter. This means that it processes bytecode while the program is running and converts it to "real" machine code that it executes on the fly. You can think of a computer program as being like a railroad track, with the train representing the execution point at any given time. In the case of an interpreted program it is as if this train has a machine mounted on it, which builds the track immediately in front of the train and tears it up behind. It’s no way to run a railroad.

Fortunately, in the case of Java, the virtual machine is not interpreting high-level language instructions, but bytecode. This is really machine code, written for the JVM instruction set, so the interpreter has much less analysis to do, resulting in execution times that are very fast.The JVM often uses "Just in Time" (JIT) compiler techniques to allow programs to execute faster, for example, by translating bytecode into optimized local code *once* and subsequently running it directly. Advances in JIT technology are making Java run faster all the time. IBM is one of many organizations exploring the technology. Check the

IBM Tokyo research lab site at http://www.trl.ibm.co.jp for project information.

Before the JVM can start this interpretation process, it has to do a number of things to set up the environment in which the program will run. This is the point at which the built-in security of Java is implemented. There are three parts to the process:

1. The first component of applet checking is the *applet class loader*. This separates the classes it loads to avoid attack: local classes are separated from remote classes, and classes from different applets are separated from each other. The search order is then Java built-in classes first, local classes next, remote classes last. So, if, by accident or design, an applet contains a class of the same name as a built-in or local class, it will *not* overwrite it.
2. The second component is the *class file verifier*. This runs when the applet is loaded, and aims either to confirm that the bytecode program will stay within the sandbox, or to reject it. It is a multipass process which begins by making sure that the syntax is valid, checks for stack overflow or underflow, and runs a theorem prover that looks to see that access and type restrictions are observed.
3. The third component is the *security manager*, which checks sensitive accesses at runtime. This is the component that will not allow Java applets illicit access to the file system, or to the network, or to the runtime operating system.

2.2.2.1 The Class Loader

So how do these classes get loaded? When the browser finds an <applet> tag in a page, it starts the Java virtual machine which, in turn, invokes the applet class loader. This is, itself, a Java class which contains the code for fetching the bytecode of the applet and presenting it to the JVM in an executable form. The bytecode includes a list of referenced classes and the JVM works through the list, checks to see if the class is already loaded and attempts to load it if not. It first tries to load from the local disk, using a platform-specific function provided by the browser. In our example, this is the way that all of the core java classes are loaded. If the class name is not found on the local disk, the JVM again calls the class loader to retrieve the class from the Web server, as in the case of the JamJar.examples.Button class (above).

2.2.2.2 Where Class Loaders Come From

The class loader is just another Java class, albeit one with a very specific function. An application can declare any number of class loaders, each of which could be targeted at specific class types. The same is *not* true of an applet. The security manager prevents an applet from creating its own class loader. Clearly, if an applet can somehow circumvent this limitation it can subvert the class loading process and potentially take over the whole browser machine.

The JVM keeps track of which class loader was responsible for loading any particular class. It also keeps classes loaded by different applets separate from each other.

2.2.2.3 The Class File Verifier

At first sight, the job of the class file verifier may appear to be redundant. After all, bytecode is only generated by the Java compiler, so if it is not correctly formatted and valid, surely the compiler needs to be fixed, rather than having to go through the overhead of checking each time a program is run?

Unfortunately, life is not that simple. The compiled program is just a file of type ".class" containing a string of bytes, so it could be created or modified using any binary editor. Given this fact, the Java virtual machine has to treat any code from an external source as potentially damaged and therefore in need of verification.

In fact, Java divides the world into two parts, Trusted and Untrusted. Trusted code includes the "local" Java classes which are shipped as part of the JVM and sometimes other classes on the local disk (detailed implementation varies between vendors). Everything else is untrusted and therefore must be checked by the class file verifier. As we have seen, these are also the classes that the applet class loader is responsible for fetching. Figure 5 illustrates this relationship.

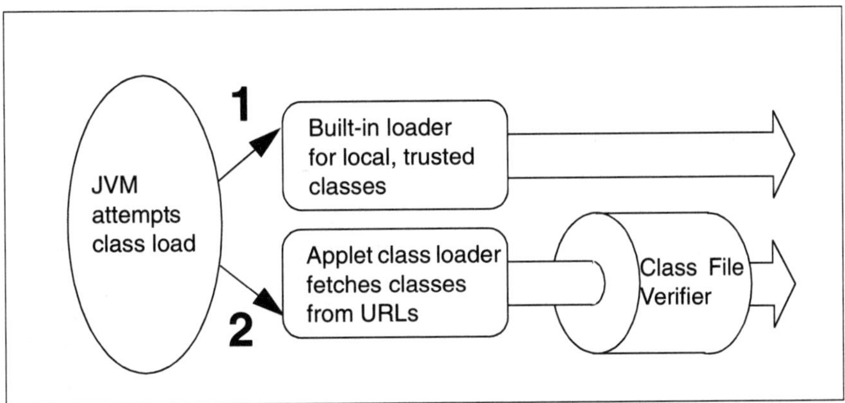

Figure 5. Where the Class File Verifier Fits

We will look in detail at the things that the class file verifier checks in "The Class File Verifier" on page 86.

You can see that, for an applet, the class loader and the class file verifier need to operate as a team, if they are to succeed in their task of making sure that only valid, safe code is executed.

From a security point of view the accuracy of the job done by the class file verifier is critical. There are a large number of possible bytecode programs, and the class file verifier has the job of determining the subset of them that are safe to run, by testing against a set of rules. There is a further subset of these verifiable programs: programs that are the result of compiling a legal Java program. Figure 6 illustrates this. The rules in the class file verifier should aim to make the verifiable set as near as possible to the set of Java programs. This limits the scope for an attacker to create bytecode that subverts the safety features in Java and the protection of the security manager.

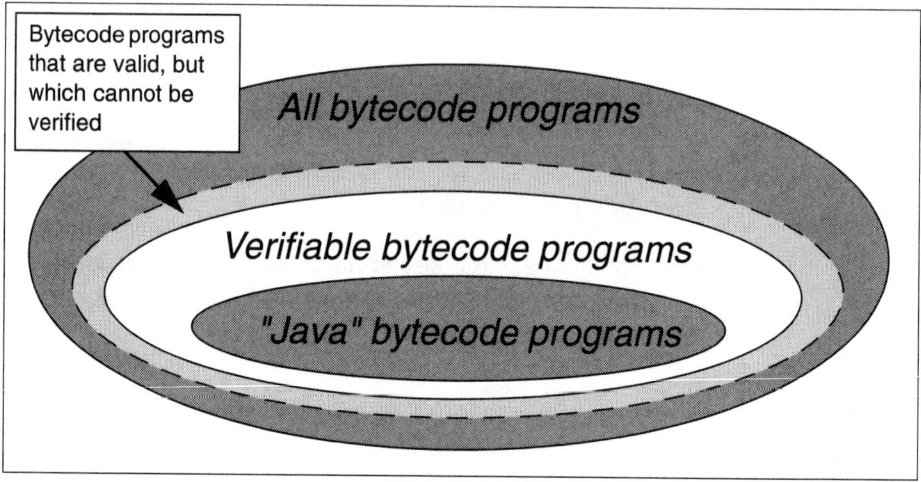

Figure 6. Decisions the Class File Verifier Has to Make

2.2.2.4 The Security Manager

The third component involved in loading and running a Java program is the security manager. This is similar to the class loader in that it is a Java class (java.lang.SecurityManager) that any application can extend for its own purpose.

The SecurityManager class provides a number of *check* methods associated with specific actions that may be risky. For example, there is a *checkRead* method which receives a file reference as an argument. If you want your security manager to prevent the program from reading that particular file, you code checkRead to throw a security exception.

Although any application could implement SecurityManager, it is most commonly found when executing an applet, that is, within a Web browser. The security manager built into your browser is wholly responsible for enforcing the *sandbox restrictions*: the set of rules that control what things an applet is allowed to do on your browser machine. Any flaw in the coding of the security manager, or any failure by the core classes to invoke it, could compromise the ability to run untrusted code securely.

2.2.2.5 The Sandbox Restrictions

The main objectives of the sandbox are to:

- Prevent damage to the browser system caused by updating files or running system commands.
- Prevent the uninvited retrieval of data by reading files or extracting environmental information.
- Prevent the browser machine from being used as a platform to attack other systems.
- Prevent the trusted built-in Java classes on the browser from being overridden or corrupted.

This last objective is the key to all of the others. This is because the security manager is, itself, a built-in class so if an attacker can corrupt or bypass it, all control is lost.

The Security Manager is part of the local browser code, so the implementation of the sandbox restrictions is the responsibility of each browser vendor. However, they all have the same objectives, so the result is a set of restrictions that is common across most vendors' implementations:

- No local disk access
- Very limited environmental information
- The "phone home" rule: the only host that an applet can establish a network connection to is the one from which it was loaded
- No linkage to local code
- No printing

We will look at the sandbox restrictions in more detail in "What the Security Manager Does" on page 97.

2.2.3 Interfaces and Architectures

We have discussed two parts of the world of Java, the development environment and the execution environment. The third part is where the world of Java meets the rest of the world, that is, the capabilities it provides for extending Java function and integrating with applications of other types. The simplest example is the way that a Java applet is created and integrated into a Web page by writing the program as a subclass of the Applet class and then specifying the class name in an <applet> HTML tag. In return, Java provides classes such as *URL* and a number of methods for accessing a Web server.

2.2.3.1 Don't Go Native! Seek Purity!

Another simple way to extend Java is by the use of *native* methods. These are sections of code written in some other, less exciting, language which provides access to native system interfaces. For example, imagine an organization with a helpdesk application which provides a C API for creating new problem records. You may well want to use this so that your new Java application can perform self-diagnosis and automatically report any faults it finds. One way to do so is to create a native method to interpret between Java and the helpdesk application's API. This provides simple extensibility, but at the cost of portability and flexibility, because:

- The native method has to be compiled for a specific system platform.
- It must be pre-installed and cannot be installed dynamically like a Java applet.
- It cannot be invoked from an applet, because the sandbox restrictions prevent it.

The Java purist will deprecate this kind of application. In fact, although the quest for *100% Pure Java* sounds like an academic exercise, there are a number of real-world advantages to only using well-defined, architected interfaces, not the least of which is that the security aspects have (presumably) already been considered.

2.2.3.2 Some of the Roads to Purity

As projects using Java have matured from being interesting exercises in technology into mission-critical applications, so the need has arisen for more complex interactions with the outside world. The Java applet gives a very effective way to deliver client function without having to install and maintain code on every client. However, the application you create this way still needs access to data and function contained in existing "legacy" systems.[2] With JDK 1.1 JavaSoft have introduced a number of new interfaces and architectures for this kind of integration. The objective is to enable applications to be written in 100% Pure Java, while still delivering the links to the outside world that real requirements demand.

Some of the more notable interfaces of this kind are:

[2] "Legacy" seems to be the current word-of-the-month to describe any computer system that does not fit the brave new architecture under discussion. It is an unfortunate choice, in that it implies a system that is outdated or inadequate. You may have a state-of-the-art relational database that is critical to the running of your business, but to the Web-based application that depends on the data it contains, it is still a "legacy system".

- **JavaBeans**. As we discussed above, these not only provide easier application development, but also provide integration with other distributed object architectures. From a security point of view this capability opens a back door which an attacker could exploit. The Java security manager provides strict and granular controls over what a Java program may do. But these controls are dependent on the integrity of the Java Virtual Machine and in particular the trusted classes it provides. A Java applet cannot meddle with the trusted classes directly, but a Bean can provide linkage to a different type of executable content, with less stringent controls. This could be used to corrupt the JVM trusted classes, thereby allowing an attack applet to take over.
- **Remote Method Invocation** (RMI). This allows a Java class running on one system to execute the methods of another class on a second system. This kind of remote function call processing allows you to create powerful distributed applications with a minimal overhead. For example, an applet running on a browser system could invoke a server-side function without having to execute a CGI program or provide its own sockets-based protocol. The security concerns for RMI are, in fact, similar to the CGI case. The server code is not subject to the applet sandbox restrictions, so the programmer needs to be wary of unintentionally giving the client more access than he or she intends.
  For example, consider a Java application that accesses a database of personal information, consisting of a server-side application communicating with a client applet. When writing the application, the programmers will naturally assume that the only code involved is what they write. However, the Java code that initiates the connection does not have to be their friendly applet, it could be the work of a cracker. The server application must be very careful to check the validity of any requests it gets and not rely on client-side validation.
- **Object Request Brokers** (ORBs). RMI provides a way to remotely execute Java code. However, for many years the O-O world has been trying to achieve a more generic form of remote execution. That is, a facility that allows a program to access the properties and methods of a remote object, regardless of the language in which it is implemented or the platform on which it runs. The facility that provides the ability to find and operate on remote objects is called an *object request broker*, or ORB. One of the most widely-accepted standards for ORBs is the Common Object Request Broker Architecture (CORBA) and packages are becoming available that

provide a CORBA-compatible interface for Java (for example, VisiBroker for Java from VisiGenic Corp, which is soon to be part of the core Java classes). Figure 7 on page 30 illustrates the relationship between a Java application or applet and a remote object. Clearly, in an implementation of this kind the Java program relies on the security of the request brokers. It is the responsibility of the ORB and the inter-ORB communications to authenticate the endpoints and apply access control. The official standard for inter-ORB communications is the *Internet Inter-ORB Protocol* (IIOP).

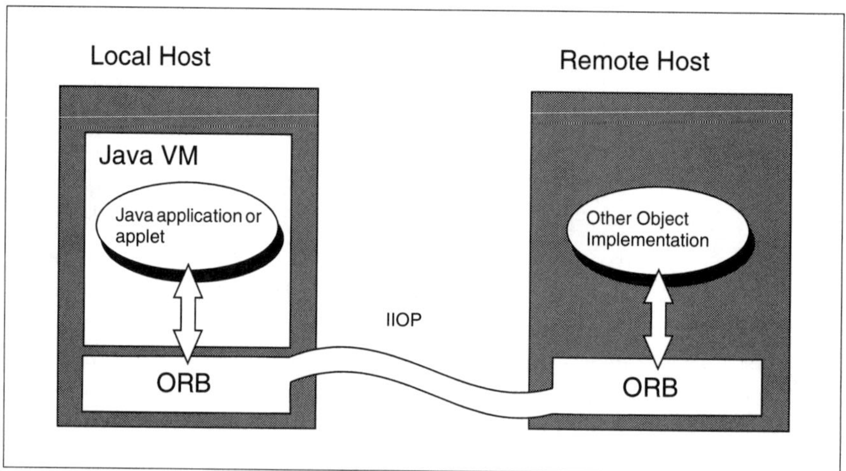

Figure 7. Interacting with an ORB

- **JDBC.** This ought to stand for "Java Database Connectivity," but actually it is a name in its own right (when you are changing the world, who needs vowels?). JDBC is an API for executing SQL statements from Java. Most relational databases implement the ODBC API (which does stand for something: Open Database Connectivity), originated by Microsoft. JBDC thoughtfully includes an ODBC bridge, thereby giving it instant usefulness. From a security point of view, there are some concerns. You should beware of giving access to more data than you intended. For example, imagine an applet which invokes JDBC on the Web server to extract information from a database. It is important that the server application is written to allow only the SQL requests expected from the applet, and not the more revealing requests that an attacker could make.

2.2.4 Cryptography to the Rescue!

The interfaces that we have briefly described above illustrate a big issue in Java. The applet environment, fenced in as it is by the sandbox restrictions, is a relatively safe platform (only "relatively" safe, because it relies on software controls that have been found to contain bugs and because it provides limited protection from nuisances such as denial of service attacks). However, in the real world we need to extend the security model to allow more powerful applications and interfaces.

The security model needs to answer questions such as the following:

- Where did this piece of Java code come from?
- What type of things should the code be allowed to do?
- If someone appears to be using an applet I provide, how can I find out who they are?
- How can I protect the confidentiality of the data my Java application is handling?

The answers to questions of this kind lie in cryptography and JDK 1.1 introduces the *Java Cryptography Architecture* (JCA) to define the way that cryptographic tools are made available to Java code.

2.2.4.1 Cryptographic Tools in Brief

The derivation of the word "cryptography" is from Greek and means literally "secret writing." Modern cryptography is still involved in keeping data secret, but the ability to authenticate a user (and hence apply some kind of access control) is even more important.

Although there are many cryptographic techniques and protocols, they mostly fall into one of three categories:

Bulk encryption This is the modern equivalent of "secret writing." A bulk encryption algorithm uses a key to scramble (encrypt) data for transmission or storage. It can then only be unscrambled (or decrypted) using the same key. Bulk encryption is so called because it is effective for securing large chunks of data. Some common algorithms are DES, IDEA and RC4.

Public key encryption This is also a technique for securing data but instead of using a single key for encryption and decryption, it uses two related keys, known as a *key pair.* If data is encrypted using one of the keys it can only be decrypted using the other, and vice versa. Compared to bulk encryption, public key is computationally expensive and is therefore not suited to large amounts of data. The most commonly-used algorithm for public key encryption is the RSA system.

Hashing A secure hash is an algorithm that takes a stream of data and creates a fixed-length digest of it. This digest is a unique "fingerprint" for the data. Hashing functions are often found in the context of *digital signatures*. This is a method for authenticating the source of a message, formed by encrypting a hash of the source data. Public key encryption is used to create the signature, so it effectively ties the signed data to the owner of the key pair that created the signature.

We describe the process of creating a digital signature in "The Security Classes in Practice" on page 115.

2.2.4.2 Java Cryptography Architecture

JCA is described as a *provider architecture*. It is designed to allow different vendors to provide their own implementation of the cryptographic tools and other administrative functions. This makes a very flexible framework which will cater for future requirements and allow vendor independence.

The architecture defines a series of classes, called *engine classes*, that are representations of general cryptographic functions. So, for example, there are several different standards for digital signatures, which differ in their detail implementation but which, at a high level, are very similar. A single engine class (java.security.Signature) represents all of the variations. The actual implementation of the different signature algorithms is done by a *provider class* which may be offered by a number of vendors.

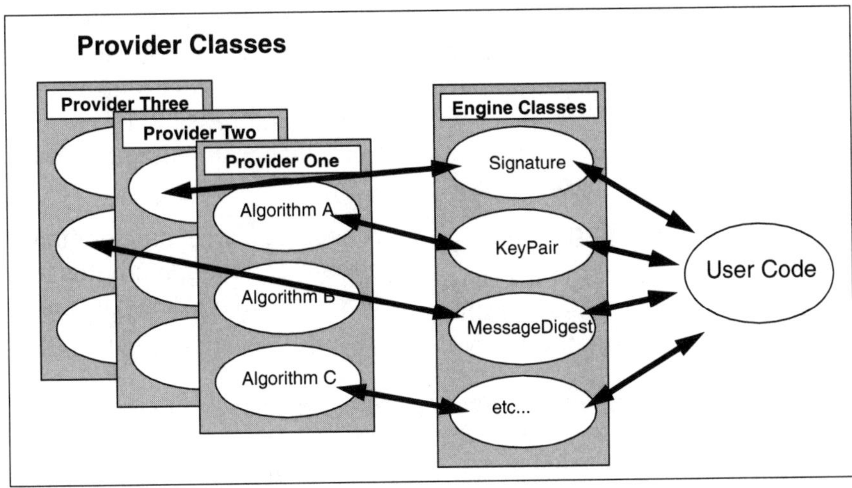

Figure 8. Provider and Engine Classes

The provider architecture has the virtue of offering a standard interface to the programmer who wants to use a cryptographic function, while at the same time having the flexibility to handle different underlying standards and protocols. The providers may be added either statically or dynamically. Sun, the default provider, provides:

- Digital signatures using DSA
- Message digests using MD-5 and SHA-1

Support for the management of keys and access control lists were not in the initial release of JDK 1.1, but will be provided later.

We discuss the JCA in more detail in "Introducing JCA: the Provider Concept" on page 113.

2.2.4.3 US Export Rules for Encryption

Unfortunately, only a subset of the cryptographic possibilities are implemented in JDK 1.1. It includes all of the engine classes needed for digital signatures, plus a provider package, but nothing for bulk or public key encryption. The reason for this is the restrictions placed by the US government on the export of cryptographic technology.

The National Security Agency (NSA) is responsible for monitoring communications between the US and the rest of the world, aiming to intercept such things as the messages of unfriendly governments and organized crime. Clearly, it is not a good thing for such people to have access to unbreakable encryption, so the US Government sets limits on the strength of cipher that a US company can export for commercial purposes.[3] This applies to any software that can be used for "general purpose" encryption. So, the SUN provider package that comes with JDK 1.1 can include the full-strength RSA public key algorithm, but it can only be used as part of a digital signature process and not for general encryption.

Finally, in 1996, the US government relaxed the export rules. The promise is that any strength of encryption may be exported, so long as it provides a technique for *key recovery*, that is, a way for the NSA to retrieve the encryption key if they need to break the code.

The JavaSoft response to the current restrictions was to define two, related, packages for cryptography in Java. JCA is the exportable part, which contains the tools for signatures and is partially implemented in JDK 1.1. The not-for-export part is the *Java Cryptography Extensions* (JCE) which include the general purpose encryption capabilities. These consist of engine classes for bulk and public key encryption, plus an extension to the Sun provider package that offers the DES bulk encryption algorithm.

The eventual aim is to develop a full strength, exportable cryptographic toolkit with key recovery built into it.

2.2.5 Signed Applets

Using JCA, it is possible for a Java application or applet to create its own digital signatures. This allows you to write more sophisticated programs, but a more common scenario is where you want an applet to do something that the sandbox restrictions normally forbid. In this case, the browser user needs to be convinced that the applet is from a trustworthy source. The way this is achieved is by digitally signing the applet.

The signature on an applet links the code to the programmer or administrator who created or packaged it. However, the user has to be able to check that the signature is valid. The signer enables this by

[3] Cipher strength is controlled by the size of the key used in the encryption algorithm. Current export rules limit the key size for bulk encryption to 40 bits, which can now be cracked in a matter of hours with quite modest computing facilities. Each extra bit doubles the key space, so a key size of 64 bits is 16 million times tougher than 40 bits. A similar rule applies to public key encryption, where an export-quality 512-bit modulus is inadequate, but a 1024-bit modulus is expected to remain effective for the next ten years, at least for commercial use.

providing a *public key certificate.* We discuss this in detail in Chapter 9, "Java Gets Out of Its Box" on page 119.

2.2.5.1 The Other Side of the Coin: Access Control

When you receive an applet that has been digitally signed you know where it came from and you can make a judgement of whether or not it is trustworthy. Next, you want to exercise some *access control.* For example, an applet may want to use your hard disk to store some configuration information. You probably have no objection to it doing so, but that does not mean that you are happy for it to overwrite *any* file on the system. This is the difference between a *binary* trust model ("I trust you, do what you like") and a *fine-grained* trust model ("tell me what you want to do and I'll decide whether I trust you").

Other types of executable content, such as browser plug-ins and ActiveX currently use the binary model. By contrast, signed Java operates on top of the very tight sandbox restrictions. This means that fine-grained controls can be implemented. At the time of writing, the standards for controlling access were still being evolved. We discuss the different approaches in "JAR Files and Applet Signing" on page 119.

2.3 Attacking the World of Java

In the early days of most software developments, security is a long way down the list of priorities. This makes Java very unusual, in that security has been an important consideration from the very beginning. No doubt, this is because the environment to which the infant language has been exposed in its formative years is a cruel and unforgiving one: the Internet. In this section we take a cracker's-eye view; what opportunities do we have to abuse a Java applet, to make it do our dastardly deeds for us?

2.3.1 Perils in the Life of an Applet

The Java applet that runs in your Web browser has had an unusually long and interesting life history. Along the way it has passed through a number of phases, each of which is in some way vulnerable to attack. Figure 9 illustrates the points of peril in the life of an applet.

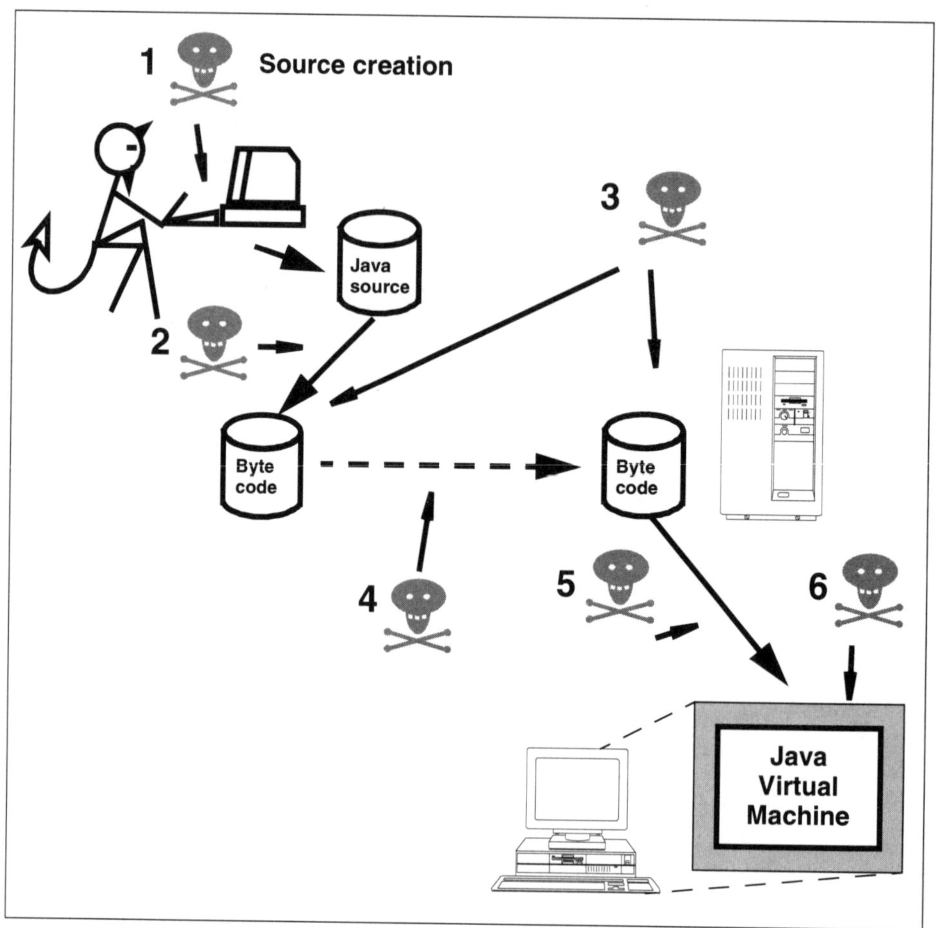

Figure 9. Perils in the Life of an Applet

Let us look at the points of vulnerability in some detail:

1. You may think that all of the programmers you know are angels, but there is no way to tell if really there is a devil inside. In the case of a Java applet you are another step away from the person who wrote the code. So, when you buy a software product from a well-known company, you can be fairly sure that the contents of the shrink-wrap will not do you any harm. When you receive *any* code from the Internet you have to be wary of where it really comes from. In the case of a Java applet, the risk is in some ways worse, because you may not even be conscious that you have received the program at all. We will show some examples of the kind of things that a hostile applet can do in "Malicious Applets" on page 104 and we will

discuss the code signing capabilities of JDK 1.1 in Chapter 9, "Java Gets Out of Its Box" on page 119.

2. The Java compiler, javac, takes source code and compiles it into class files (in bytecode format) that can be executed by the Java virtual machine. It is quite common for a developer to have multiple versions of javac on his or her computer. For example, the Java development kit for various system platforms is available for download from Javasoft and other computer manufacturers. Very often, a developer will have a current and one or more beta versions installed. javac is also provided as part of many application development tools.

   Normally you expect that the bytecode generated by a compiler would reflect the source code you feed in. However, a compiler can easily be hacked so that it adds its own, nefarious, functions. Even worse, a compiler could produce bytecode output that *cannot* be a translation of normal Java source code. This would be a way to introduce code to exploit some frailty of the Java code verification process, for example.

   Although a hacked compiler is the most obvious example of a compromised programming tool, the same concern also applies to other parts of the programmer's arsenal, such as editors, development toolkits and pre-built components.

For the Applet Developer

Can You Trust Your Tools?

Naturally, you want to be at the leading edge of development, using the latest and greatest tools for your Java development. However, this enthusiasm needs to be moderated by some caution. You must make sure that the tools you use come from a reputable source. You should also report any odd behavior to the manufacturer. It is probably only a bug, but it could be the manifestation of a hacker's work.

3. If an attacker can get update access to the class files, wherever they are stored, they can subvert the function of the applet. For example, by modifying business data used in the applet or inserting rude messages. One obvious point of attack is where the class files are stored on the Web server. If an attacker can get update access to the directory they are in, they can be corrupted. Java class files should therefore be protected in much the same way as CGI programs, for example. Some basic principles for protection are:

- Don't allow update permissions for the user ID that the Web server runs under. Many successful attacks on Web servers rely on finding holes in the logic or implementation of CGI programs and tricking them into executing arbitrary commands.
- Make sure that the server has been properly hardened to reduce the risk of someone gaining access beyond the normal Web connection. You should remove unwanted network services and user IDs, enforce password restrictions and limit access using firewall controls. You should also make sure that you have the fixes for the latest security advisories installed.

4. One side-effect of Java's portability is that a Webmaster can get applet code from any number of different sources. The code could just generate some entertaining animation or cool dialogs. Alternatively it could be a fully-fledged application, containing thousands of lines of source code.

   Any applets you import in this way should be treated with suspicion. This raises a moral question: how responsible should you feel if your Web site somehow damages a client connecting to it, even if you are not ultimately responsible for the content that caused the damage? Most reasonable people will agree that there is a duty of care which should be balanced against your desire to build the world's most dynamic and attractive Web site. Indeed it would be a good idea to check whether your agreements with others mean that you have a formal *legal* duty of care. You do not want a thoughtlessly-included applet to result in your being sued.

For the System Administrator

Checking Your Sources

So, you're the administrator of a Web site and you want to include some applet code from somewhere else. You want to be sure that the applet is safe, but how can you check it?

For simple applets you should try to get the code in source form, so that you can inspect it and compile it yourself. This means that you need to understand the Java language. Your job already requires you to have a superhuman knowledge of computer systems and the Web; adding Java to your knowledge base must be a trivial matter for a person of such skill.

In fact the problem is not so great as it first appears. It is much easier to read a computer program and understand what it is doing than to write it in the first place. In "Malicious Applets" on page 104 we will discuss some of the things that you should watch for.

Applets that are only provided in compiled form are more of a problem. Very often they are too large to do a practical visual check and anyway, if they are commercially-produced, the writer is unlikely to want to share his coding tricks with the world at large. You can, of course, check the external behavior, but that gives no clue to what browser holes it may be probing or background threads it may be spinning. There are tools like javap and Mocha which allow you to at least get an idea of what an applet is doing; refer to "Decompilation Attacks" on page 60 for more information.

JDK 1.1 introduces *signed applets* which allow you to check who the real originator of an applet is and know that it has not been altered on its way to you. You still have to make a judgment of who to trust, but at least you are basing the judgment on sound data.

5. The next journey in the life of an applet is when it is loaded into the browser virtual machine across the network from the server. Although it could, potentially, be intercepted in mid-flight and modified, a much more likely form of attack would involve some type of *spoofing*. What this means is that the attacker fools the browser into thinking that it is connecting to rocksolid.reliable.org, when really the applet is coming from nogood.badguys.com. The most sophisticated form of spoofing is the *Web spoof*, where the attacker acts as a filter for all of the traffic between the browser and anywhere else, passing most requests straight through, but intercepting particular requests and modifying them or replacing

them with something more sinister (see Figure 10 on page 40). Note that it does not have to be this way around. It is equally possible for a Web spoof to screen everything going to and from a server, rather than a client system.

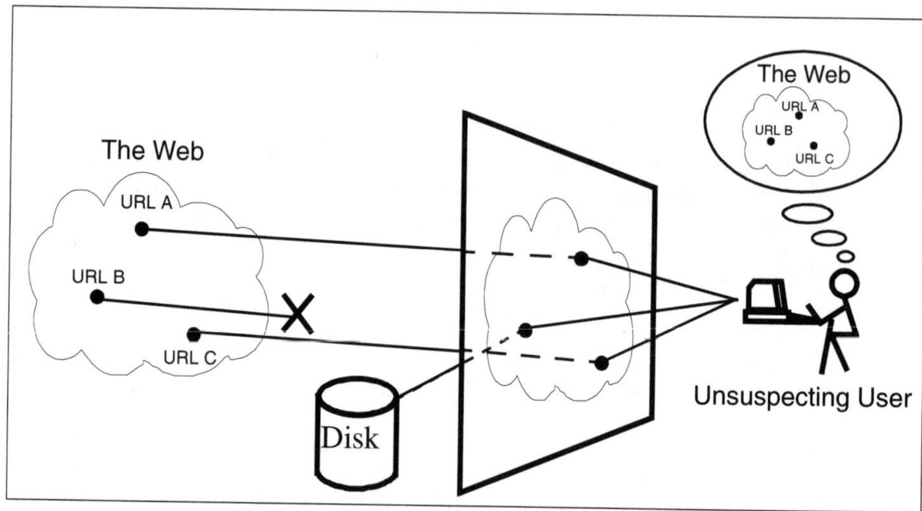

Figure 10. A Web Spoof

Spoofing is not just a problem for Java applets, of course. Any Web content can be attacked in this way. With Java this gives the attacker an opportunity to execute a malicious applet or try to exploit security holes in the browser environment. However, compared to the risk of downloading and installing a conventional program in this kind of environment, the risk is small.

For the Network Administrator

Guarding against Spoofing

If you are a network administrator responsible for a site in which browsers or servers live, how do you protect yourself from an attacker that spoofs as a legitimate address? The first thing is to ensure that your systems and firewalls do not accept any of the common methods that can induce them to believe that a network node is really somewhere else. The ICMP redirect and IP source route functions are good examples. Refer to Chapter 11, "Firewalls: In and Out of the Net" on page 169 for more firewall discussions.

You may consider that you do not want any of the browsers in your site to be able to run applets from outside the firewall. A number of firewall implementations now provide screening for Java in general or for specific classes.

Signed applets can again help with this problem. An attacker may be able to substitute subversive class files to attack the browser, but it is much more difficult to forge the class signature.

6. Finally the applet arrives at the browser; class files are loaded and verified and the virtual machine goes to work. If the installation is working as designed, the worst peril that can befall you as a user is that the applet may annoy you or eat excessive system resources (see Chapter 4, "Class of 1.1" on page 55 for a description of class loader and security manager controls). There are two things that can go wrong with this idyllic picture:

   - There may be bugs in the Java implementation.
   - You may have installed a hacked version of the browser code.

   Of these two, the first is more likely. There have been a number of well-publicized security breaches found in the Java virtual machine components. The best description of how these operate can be found in *Java Security, Hostile Applets, Holes, and Antidotes*, by Felten and McGraw. You can also find more up-to-date online information at the sites listed in Appendix A, "Sources of Information about Java Security" on page 211. The best way to protect yourself is to make sure you are aware of the latest breaches and install the fixes as they arrive.

   The possibility of installing a browser that has been tampered with is a real one, although there are considerable practical hurdles for an attacker to overcome in creating such a thing. If you do as we recommend (above) and install the latest fixes, you will inevitably be running a downloaded version of the browser. There is some small risk that this could be a hacked version, but no examples of this have yet been detected.

For the Web User

Should I Switch Java Off?

The Big Question that all browser users ask about Java is this: should I allow it to run or not? In the final analysis, this is a personal decision. As we have described, there is some peril in allowing Java applets to run in your system, because you cannot be sure of where they have come from or whether they exploit security holes in your browser. You may decide that this risk is too high to take.

If you take this view, you should also review your other Web usage. If you download any executable program from the Web it is potentially far more dangerous to the health of your system than any Java applet.

Many companies and software producers are writing applications that use Java applets for their client component. These are usually designed for intranet, rather than Internet use, so the likelihood of attack is (presumably) much lower.

2.3.2 Vulnerabilities in Java Applications

A Java applet is an obvious vehicle to mount an attack, because it can install itself uninvited and probe for weaknesses. And, of course, this is why so much thought has gone into the construction of the sandbox and the JDK 1.1 code-signing capabilities.

A Java application, on the other hand, is a much less obvious target. There are many ways in which such an application could be implemented, for example:

- On a Web server using CGI to interface with Web pages or applets
- As a stand-alone application on a server, interfacing with client code using socket connections
- As a stand-alone application on a server, using remote object request services (like RMI or CORBA) for communication

To a cracker, the fact that the application is written in Java rather than any other language is not really important. The strategies that he or she would use to search for vulnerabilities are the same. For example:

- Many successful attacks rely on driving the application with data that it is not equipped to handle. In particular, if the application uses a command line interface, it should be very careful to screen out escape sequences that an attacker could use to execute arbitrary commands.
- Applications frequently have to give themselves temporary higher privileges to use system functions or get special access (such as user IDs for database control). If an attacker can crash the application at this critical point, or link to it from another running program he or she can use the special privileges illegally.

As we said earlier, vulnerabilities of this kind apply to applications written in Java the same as any other application programming environment. However, Java does include safety features that make it harder for an attacker to find a flaw. These safety features work at two levels:

Java source The Java language uses strong type constraints to prevent the programmer from accessing data in an inconsistent way. You can cast objects from one type to another, but only if the two classes are related by inheritance; that is, one must be a superclass of the other. This does not operate symmetrically, which means you can always cast from a subclass to its superclass, but not always vice versa. Referring again to Figure 4 on page 20, you could access an instance of the Button class as an Object, but you could not access a Button as a Panel.

Furthermore, Java prevents you from having direct access to program memory. In C it is common to use a pointer to locate a variable in memory and then to manipulate the pointer to process the data in it. This is a frequent source of coding errors, due to the pointer becoming corrupted or iterating beyond the end of the data. Java allows a variable to be accessed *only* through the methods of the object that contains it, thereby removing this class of error.

Bytecode The Java virtual machine is type-aware. In other words, most of the primitive machine instructions are associated with a particular type. This means that the JVM also applies the type constraints that the compiler imposes on the Java source. In fact, this job is split between the class file verifier, which handles everything that can be statically checked and the JVM, which deals with runtime exceptions. Contrast this with other languages, in which the compiler produces microprocessor machine code. In this case the program is just handled as a sequence of bytes, with no concept of the data types that are being represented.

The JVM is also, at a basic level, strongly compartmentalized, mirroring the object orientation of the Java source. This means that each method in the code has its own execution stack and only has access to the memory of the class instance for which it was invoked.

2.4 Summary

This first part of the book has been a tour through the many aspects of Java security. You should now have a good high-level understanding of the issues involved and the mechanisms that are at work. In the next section we look under the covers, at the detailed operation of the Java virtual machine and the security classes.

Part 2. Under The Hood

Chapter 3. The Java Virtual Machine

> *"... a special machine for the suppression of one class by another"*
>
> (V.I.Lenin)

This part of the book is aimed primarily at people who wish to understand the inner workings of the Java security model. The level of detail is deliberately high and you should ensure that you are seated comfortably with some soothing music and a scratch pad to hand.

You should probably consult your doctor before attempting to read the whole of Part 2 at once.

Understanding how the various components of the JVM cooperate to provide a secure execution environment for Java code will enable you to implement your own extensions to the JVM in order to provide a more tailored security policy.

3.1 The Java Virtual Machine, Close Up

Later chapters in Part 2 examine the various components of the JVM in detail. In this chapter we identify the key components of the JVM and in particular, those which are found in Web browsers.

Figure 11 shows a simplified representation of the JVM. Those components which are highlighted are generally only found in Web browsers rather than in the stand-alone implementations required to execute Java applications.

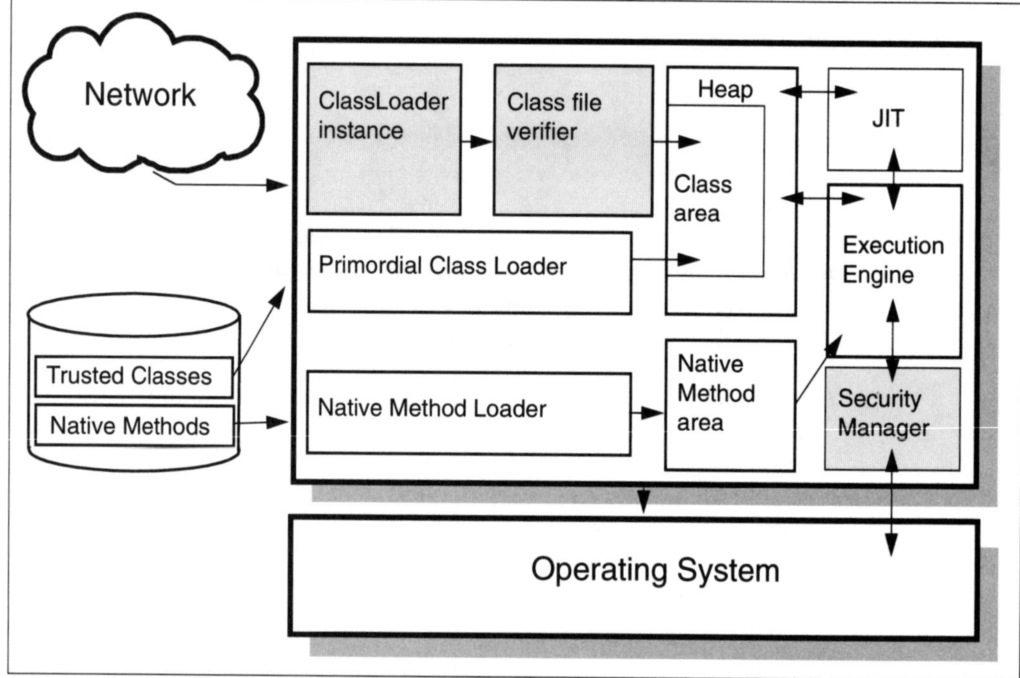

Figure 11. Components of the JVM

As you will see, the additional components are required to provide the additional security needed when loading and executing Java bytecode which has been loaded from an untrusted source such as a Web server.

3.1.1 The Class Loader

Before the JVM can run a Java program, it needs to locate and load the classes which comprise that program into memory. In a traditional execution environment, this service is provided by the operating system which loads code from the filing system in a platform-specific way.

The operating system has access to all of the low level I/O functions and has a set of locations on the filing system which it searches for programs or shared code libraries. On PC and UNIX systems this is some combination of PATH settings which specify a list of directories to be searched for files. In mainframe environments the same function is provided by the LINKLIST.

In the Java runtime environment things are complicated a little by the fact that not all class files are loaded from the same type of location. In general classes can be divided into three categories:

- **Classes forming the core Java API**

  These are the classes shipped with the JVM which provide access to network, GUI and threading functions. They are shipped with the JVM implementation and are part of the Java specification. As such they are regarded as highly trusted classes and are not subject to the same degree of scrutiny at runtime as classes brought into the JVM from an external source.

- **Classes installed in the local filing system**

  While not a part of the core Java class set, these classes are assumed to be safe since the user has at some point installed them onto his or her machine and presumably accepted the associated risks. In many cases these classes are treated in the same way as those classes in the core Java API.

- **Classes loaded from other sources**

  In a Web browser, these would be the classes constituting an applet loaded from a remote Web server. These are the least trusted classes of all as they are being brought into the safe environment of the JVM from potentially hostile sources and often without the specific consent of the user. For this reason, these classes must be subjected to a high degree of checking before being made available for use in the JVM.

Given the diverse range of possible sources for class files and the different checking requirements of the JVM it is clear that different mechanisms will be required to locate and load classes. The class loader comes in various flavors, each responsible for locating and loading one type of class file.

Users may also implement their own class loaders to load classes from particular locations or to impose more rigorous checking of class files loaded from normally trusted sources. This allows you to implement highly flexible security policies.

3.1.2 The Class File Verifier

As mentioned above, some of the class files loaded by the JVM will come from untrusted sources. These files need to be checked prior to execution to ensure that they do not threaten the integrity of the JVM.

The class file verifier is invoked by the class loader to perform a series of tests on class files which are regarded as potentially unsafe.

These tests check all aspects of a class file from its size and structure down to its runtime characteristics. Only when these tests have been passed is the file made available for use.

3.1.3 The Heap

The heap is an area of memory used by the JVM to store Java objects during the execution of a program. Precisely how objects are stored on the heap is implementation specific and this adds another level of security since it means that a hacker can have no idea of how the JVM represents objects in memory. This in turn makes it far more difficult to mount an attack that depends on accessing memory directly.

When an object is no longer used, the JVM marks it for garbage collection and at some point the memory on the heap is freed up for reuse.

3.1.4 The Class Area

The class area is where the JVM stores class-specific information such as methods and static fields. When a class is loaded and has been verified, the JVM creates an entry in the class area for that class.

Often the class area is simply a part of the heap. In this case classes may also be garbage-collected once they are no longer used. Alternatively, the class area may be a separate part of memory and will require additional logic on the part of the JVM implementor to clean up classes which are not being used.

When a JIT compiler (see section 3.1.10) is present, the native code generated for class methods is also stored in the class area.

3.1.5 The Native Method Loader

Many of the core Java classes, such as those classes representing GUI elements or networking features, require native-code implementations to access the underlying OS functions. Programmers may also implement their own native methods, assuming of course that they don't want their code to be portable. These native methods are composed of a Java wrapper – which specifies the method signature – and a native-code implementation – often a DLL or shared library.

Core Java classes aren't hindered by the fact that they use native-code; they're part of the JVM implementation for a particular operating system. Applets and applications, on the other hand, are more useful if they are portable, but they are portable only if they eschew native methods.

The native method loader is responsible for locating and loading these shared libraries into the JVM. Note that it is not possible for the JVM to perform any validation or verification of native code and installing such code exposes you to all of the risks associated with running untrusted programs on your machine.

3.1.6 The Native Method Area

Once native code has been loaded, it is stored in the native method area for speedy access when required.

3.1.7 The Security Manager

Even when untrusted code has been verified, it is still subject to runtime restrictions. The security manager is responsible for enforcing these restrictions. In a Web browser, the security manager is provided by the browser manufacturer and is the component of the JVM which prevents applets from reading or writing to the file system, accessing the network in an unsafe way, making inquiries about the runtime environment, printing and so on.

By default, in a stand-alone JVM implementation there is no security manager (since there is no mechanism to load classes from an untrusted source). It is, however, possible for an application writer to implement a security manager to enforce a particular security policy.

3.1.8 The Execution Engine

The execution engine is the heart of the JVM. It is the virtual processor which executes bytecode. Memory management, thread management and calls to native methods are also performed by the execution engine.

3.1.9 The Trusted Classes

The trusted Java classes are those classes which ship as part of the JVM implementation. This includes all classes in packages which start "java." and "sun." as well as any vendor-provided classes used to implement the platform-specific parts of core classes (such as the GUI components).

They are often stored in the filing system (usually in a ZIP archive called classes.zip) but may be held as part of the JVM executable itself.

3.1.10 The Just In Time (JIT) Compiler

Since Java bytecodes are interpreted at runtime in the execution engine, Java programs generally execute more slowly than the equivalent native platform code. This performance overhead occurs because each bytecode instruction must be translated into one or more native instructions each time it is encountered.

The performance of Java is still significantly better than that of other interpreted languages because the bytecode instructions were designed to be very low level – the simplest instructions have a one-to-one correlation with native machine code instructions.

Nevertheless, Sun saw that there would be a need to improve the execution performance of Java and to do so in a way which did not compromise either the "write once run anywhere" goal and did not undermine the security of the JVM.

Since all bytecode instructions are ultimately translated to native machine code, the principal ways of speeding performance involve making this translation as quick as possible and performing it as few times as possible.

On the other hand, the security and portability of Java is dependent on the bytecode and class file format which enable code to be run on any JVM and to be rigorously tested to ensure that it is safe prior to execution. Thus, any translation must occur after a class file has been loaded and verified.

Two options present themselves:

1. Translate the whole class file into native code as soon as it is loaded and verified.
2. Translate the class file on a method-by-method basis as needed.

The first option seems quite attractive but it is possible that many of the methods in a class file will never be executed. Time to translate these methods is therefore wasted. The second option was the one selected by Sun. In this case, the first time a method is called, it is translated into native code, which is then stored in the class area. The class specification is updated so that future calls to the method run the native code rather than the original bytecode.

This meets our requirement that bytecode should be translated as few times as is necessary – once when the code is executed and not at all in the case of code which is not executed.

The process of translating the bytecode to native code on the fly is known as just in time (JIT) compilation and performed by the JIT compiler. Sun provided a specification for how and when JIT compilers should execute and vendors were left to implement their own JIT compilers as they chose.

JIT compiled code executes much more quickly than regular bytecode – between 10 to 50 times faster – without impacting portability or security.

3.2 Summary

You now have a good idea of how the various components of the JVM work together. The next four chapters examine the principle elements of the Java security architecture – the class file structure, the class loader, the bytecode verifier and the security manager – in greater detail.

Chapter 4. Class of 1.1

> *"... My ancestors were country squires, who appear to have led much the same life as is natural to their class" - Sherlock Holmes The Adventure of the Greek Interpreter*
>
> (A. Conan Doyle)

In this chapter we will explore a number of topics:

- The relationship between Java class files and conventional object and executable files
- The threat presented by the class file format
- How bytecodes aid security

In addition, we will:

- Describe the contents of a Java class file
- Describe ways in which to reduce the threat of decompilation

4.1 The Traditional Development Life Cycle

As you have seen earlier, Java is a compiled language. That is, source code is written in a high-level language and then converted through a process of compilation to a machine-level language, the Java bytecode, which then runs on the Java Virtual Machine. Before we look more closely at Java bytecode, we'll quickly review the differences between high- and low-level languages, the compilation process and runtime behavior of a more traditional environment.

On the PC, program files are recognized in two ways. The first is by the file extension (.EXE, .COM) and the second is by the file format itself. Executable files contain some information in a header which informs the operating system that this file is a program and has certain requirements in order to run. These requirements include such things as the address at which the program should be loaded, other supporting files which will be required and so on.

When DOS or Windows attempts to run a program file, it loads the file and ensures that the header is legitimate, that is, that it describes a real program. The header also indicates where the starting point of the program itself is. The program is stored in the program file as machine code instructions. These instructions are numeric values which are read and interpreted by the processor as it executes. Having validated the header, the operating system starts executing the code at this address.

From the above description, it should be clear that anyone with a good understanding of the header format and of the machine code for a particular operating system could construct a program file using little more than an editor capable of producing binary files. (Such an individual would be well advised to seek urgent medical attention.)

Of course this is not how programs are produced. The closest that anyone gets to this is writing assembly code. Assembly language programming is very low level. Its statements, after macro expansion, usually translate into one or at most two machine language instructions. The assembly source code is then fed through an assembler which converts the (almost) human readable code into machine code, generates the appropriate header and finally outputs an executable file.

Most programs, however, are written in a high-level language such as C, C++, COBOL and so forth. Here it is the task of the compiler to translate high-level instructions into low-level machine code in the most optimal way. The resultant machine code output is generally very efficient, although – depending on the compiler – it may be possible to write more efficient assembler language. Because different compilers manage the translation and optimization process in different ways, they will produce different output for the same source code. In general it is true to say that the higher level the source language, the more scope there is for variation in the resultant executable file since there will be more than one possible translation of each high-level statement into low-level machine code.

During the compilation process, high-level features such as variable and function names are replaced by references to addresses in memory and by machine code instructions, which cause the appropriate address to be accessed (in the case of variables) or jumped to (in the case of functions).

In the case of both assembly language and high-level language programming, the output of the assembly or compilation phase is generally not immediately executable. Instead, an intermediate file (known as an object module or object file[1]) is produced. One object file is produced for each source file compiled, regardless of the content or structure of the source code. These object modules are then combined using a tool called a linker which is responsible for producing the final executable file (or shared library). The linker ensures that references to a function or variable in one object module from another object module are correctly resolved.

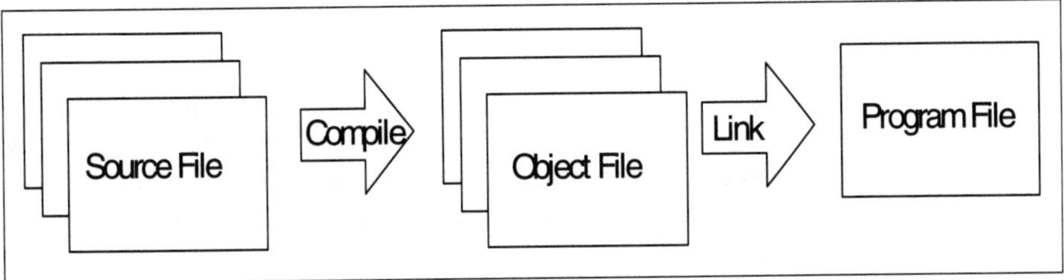

Figure 12. Program Compilation and Linking

In summary then:

- An object file contains the machine code which is the actual program plus some additional information describing any dependencies on other object files.
- An executable file is a collection of object files with all inter-file dependencies resolved, together with some header information which identifies the file as executable.

4.2 The Java Development Life Cycle

Moving back to the world of Java, we see that it is a high-level programming language and that bytecode is the low-level machine language of the Java Virtual Machine. Java is an object-oriented language; that is, it deals primarily with objects and their interrelationships. Objects are best thought of in this context as a collection of data (*fields* in Java parlance) and the functions (*methods*) which operate on that data. Objects are created at runtime based on templates (*classes*) defined by the programmer.

A Java source file may contain definitions for one or more classes. During compilation each of these classes results in the generation of a single class file. In some respects, the class file is the Java equivalent of an object module rather than an executable program file; that is, it contains compiled machine code, but may also contain references to

[1] An unfortunate nomenclature and nothing at all to do with object-oriented programming. If the source file is the subject of the compilation process then the resultant file must be the object.

methods and fields which exist in other classes and hence in other class files.

Class files are the last stage of the development process in Java. There is no separate link phase as linking is performed at runtime by the Java Virtual Machine. If a reference is found within one class file to another, then the JVM loads the referenced class file and resolves the references as needed.

The astute reader will deduce that this demand loading and linking requires the class file to contain information about other class files, methods and fields which it references, and in particular, the names of these files, fields and methods. This is in fact the case as we shall see in the next section.

Even more astute readers may be pondering some of the following questions.

- Is it possible to compile Java source code to some machine language other than that of the JVM?
- Is it possible to compile some other high-level language to bytecode for the JVM?
- Is there such a thing as an assembler for Java?
- What is the relationship between the Java language and bytecode?

The simple answer to the first three questions is yes.

It is possible with the appropriate compiler (generally referred to as a native code compiler) to translate Java source code to any other low-level machine code, although this rather defeats the “write once run anywhere” proposition for Java programs since the resultant executable program will only run on the platform for which it has been compiled.

It is also possible to compile other high-level languages into Java bytecode, possibly via an interim step in which the source code is translated into Java source code which is in turn compiled. Bytecode compilers already exist for Ada, COBOL, BASIC and NetREXX (a dialect of the popular REXX programming language).

Finally, *Jasmin* is a freely available Java assembler which allows serious geeks to write Java code at a level one step removed from bytecode.

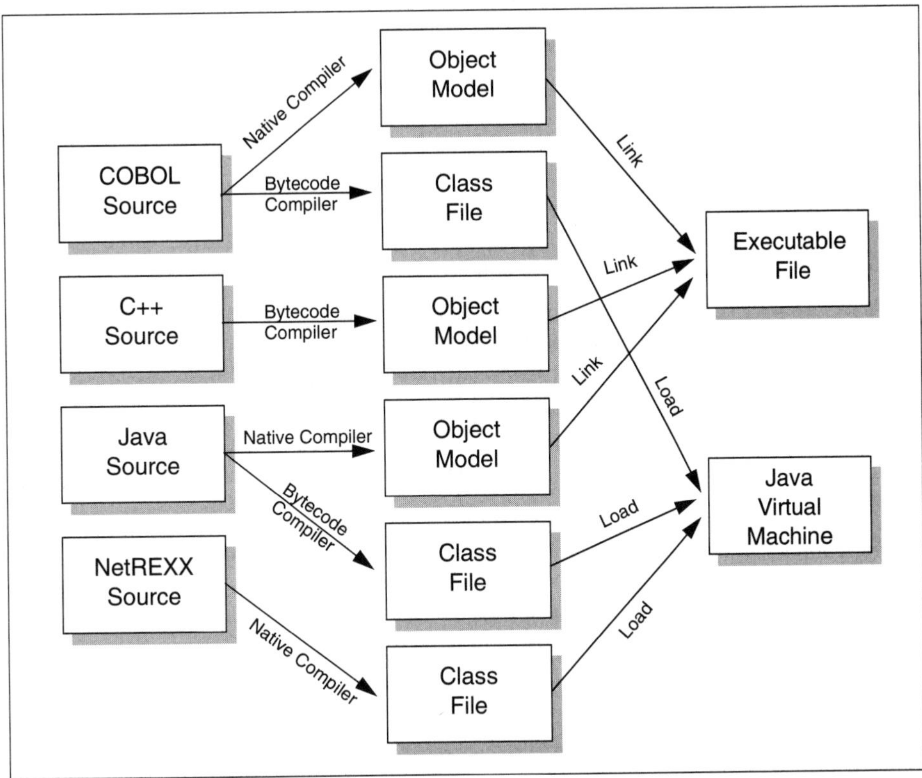

Figure 13. Compiler Models

4.3 The Java Class File Format

The class file contains a lot more information than its cousin, the executable file. Of course, it still contains the same type of information, program requirements, an identifier indicating that this is a program and executable code (bytecode) but it also contains some very rich information about the original source code.

The high level structure of a class file is shown in Table 1.

Table 1. Class File Contents

Field	Description
Magic number	Four bytes identifying this file as a Java class file. Always set to 0xCAFEBABE

Field	Description
JVM minor version	The minor version number of the JVM on which this class file is intended to run
JVM major version	The major version number of the JVM on which this class file is intended to run
Constant pool	See below
Class name	The name of this class
Super class name	The name of the superclass in the Java class hierarchy
Interfaces	Description of the interfaces implemented for this class
Fields	Description of the class variables defined for this class
Methods	Description of the methods declared by this class
Source file name	The file from which this class file was compiled

Much here is as we would expect. There is information to identify the file as a Java class file, as well as the virtual machine on which it was compiled to run. In addition, there is information describing the dependencies of this class in terms of classes, interfaces (a special type of Java class file), fields, and methods. There is much more information than this however, buried within the constant pool: information which includes variable and method names within both this class file and those on which it depends.

In addition to managing dynamic linking, the JVM must also ensure that class files contain only legal bytecode and do not attempt to subvert the runtime environment, and to do this, still more information is required in the class. More details of how this works are in Chapter 5, "The Class Loader and Class File Verifier" on page 77.

The main thing to understand at this point is that the inclusion of all of this information makes the job of a hacker much simpler in many ways.

4.3.1 Decompilation Attacks

One of the areas seldom discussed when considering security implications of deploying Java is that of securing Java assets. Often considerable effort is put into developing software and the resultant intellectual property can be very valuable to a company.

Hackers are a clever (if misguided) bunch and there are many reasons why they might want to get "inside" your code. Here are a few:

- To steal a valuable algorithm for use in their own code
- To understand how a security function works to enable them to bypass it
- To extract confidential information (such as hard-coded passwords and keys)
- To enable them to alter the code so that it behaves in a malicious way (such as installing Trojan horses or viruses)
- To demonstrate their prowess
- For their entertainment (much as other people might solve crosswords)

The chief tool in the arsenal of the hacker in these cases is the decompiler. A decompiler, as its name suggests, undoes the work performed by a compiler. That is, it takes an executable file and attempts to re-create the original source code.

Advances in compiler technology now make it effectively impossible to go from machine code to a high-level language such as C. Modern compilers remove all variable and function names, move code about to optimize its execution profile and, as was discussed previously, there are many possible ways to translate a high-level statement into a low-level machine code representation. For a decompiler to produce the original source code is impossible without a lot of additional information which simply isn't shipped in an executable file.

It *is,* however, very easy to recover an assembly language version of the program. On the other hand, the amount of effort required to actually understand what such a program is doing makes it far less worthwhile to the hacker to do. (Nevertheless, it is done. Much pirated software is distributed in a "cracked" format, that is, with software protection disabled or removed.) So, it is fair to say that it is impossible to completely protect any program from tampering.

When JDK 1.02 was shipped, a decompiler named Mocha was quickly available which performed excellently. It was able to recover Java source code from a class file. It was so successful that at least one person used it as a way of formatting his source code! In fact the only information lost in the compilation process and unrecoverable using Mocha are the comments. If meaningful variable names are used (such as “accountNumber”, or “password”) then it is readily possible to understand the function of the code, even without the comments.

The current version of Mocha is unable to decompile Java 1.1 class files but this is not because the class files contain any less information, merely because the format has changed slightly. It is only a matter of time before a functional decompiler for Java 1.1 class files is developed.

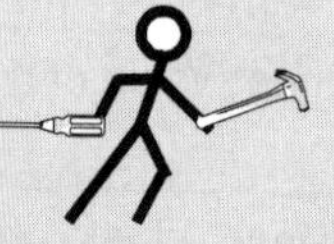

For the System Administrator

Should You Have a Decompiler in Your Toolkit?

If you can read Java source code, it is a good idea to have a decompiler available, to check the function of Java class files that you receive, particularly if they come from an unknown origin.
The only problem with this is that you are stepping into a legal and moral minefield. Decompilers are downloadable from a number of sources and also are in some commercial Java development packages. However there have been strong attempts to prevent them being available in this way, because it allows unscrupulous people to steal the source code of proprietary products.
The authors’ view is that, until signed, verifiable Java is more generally available, there is a place for the decompiler as a tool for checking what is really going on inside a class file.

4.4 The Constant Pool

We said earlier that the constant pool contained a great deal of information. In fact it contains a strange mixture of items. The constant pool combines the function of a symbol table for linking purposes as well as a repository for constant values and string literals present in the source code. It may be considered as an array of heterogeneous data types which are referenced by index number from other sections of the class file such as the Field and Method sections. In addition, many Java bytecode instructions take as arguments numbers which are in turn used as indexes into the constant pool. Table 2 shows the types of entries in the constant pool, as defined by the current JVM.

Table 2. Constant Pool Entry Types

Type Name	Used For	Contains
UTF8	String in UTF8 format (a shorthand for writing Unicode strings)	An array of bytes making up the string
Integer	A constant 32-bit signed integer value	The numeric value of the integer
Long	A constant 64-bit signed integer value	The numeric value of the long
Float	A constant 32-bit floating point value	The numeric value of the float
Double	A constant 64-bit double precision floating point value	The numeric value of the double
String	A Java string literal	Reference to the UTF8 representation of the string
ClassRef	Symbolic reference to a class	Reference to a UTF8 representation of the class name
FieldRef	Symbolic reference to a field	Reference to a ClassRef for the class in which the field occurs and a NameAndType for this field
MethodRef	Symbolic reference to a method	Reference to a ClassRef for the class in which the method occurs and a NameAndType for this method
InterfaceMethodRef	Symbolic reference to an interface method	Reference to a ClassRef for the interface in which the field occurs and a NameAndType for this method
NameAndType	Shorthand representation of a field or method signature and name	Reference to a UTF8 representation of the name and another to the signature[a]

a. The signature of a field is simply its type. The signature of a method is both its return type and the types of any parameters which it takes. Method signatures are represented by a pair of parentheses with the parameter types enclosed and separated by semicolons. The parentheses are followed by the return type of the method. See Appendix B, "Signature Formats" on page 217 for a full description of Java type representations.

As an example of a constant pool, let's take a look at the PointlessButton example we met earlier. Table 3 shows a dump of the constant pool for the PointlessButton class. The information in this table was generated using the DumpConstantPool application, which is on the CD accompanying this book.

Table 3. Constant Pool Example

Index	Type	Value
1	UTF8	bytes = "PointlessButton"
2	Class	name = (1) "PointlessButton"
3	UTF8	bytes = "java/applet/Applet"
4	Class	name = (3) "java/applet/Applet"
13	NameAndType	name = (8) "donowt", type = (7) "Ljamjar/examples/Button;"
14	FieldRef	class = (2) "PointlessButton", name and type = (13) "donowt", "Ljamjar/examples/Button;"
17	UTF8	bytes = "Did Nothing "
18	String	value = (17) "Did Nothing "
24	MethodRef	class = (20) "java/lang/String", name and type = (23) "valueOf", "(Ljava/lang/Object;)Ljava/lang/String;"
25	UTF8	bytes = "<init>"
33	NameAndType	name = (31) "append", type = (32) "(I)Ljava/lang/StringBuffer;"
34	MethodRef	class = (16) "java/lang/StringBuffer", name and type = (33) "append", "(I)Ljava/lang/StringBuffer;"
52	MethodRef	class = (49) "java/awt/Button", name and type = (51) "setLabel", "(Ljava/lang/String;)V"
53	UTF8	bytes = "Code"
54	UTF8f	bytes = "()V"
55	NameAndType	name = (25) "<init>", type = (54) "()V"
56	MethodRef	class = (4) "java/applet/Applet", name and type = (55) "<init>", "()V"value = (37) " times"

The full table has 83 entries, not bad for such a simple program. Looking at this data you can see that there is a wealth of information here. As an example of how a method is represented, let's look at entry number 56. This is a MethodRef entry and as such it has two further references to track down. The first is the Class entry, (4) which in turn references a UTF8 entry (3) for the class name: java.applet.Applet.

The second is the NameAndType entry, which surprisingly enough identifies the method name and the type of the method. The NameAndType entry (55) references a UTF8 entry (25) for the method name: <init>, and another UTF8 entry (54) for the type: ()V.

The name used here is a little special; <init> is not a valid name in itself, but it is used by the JVM to represent a constructor for a class. The type entry ()V indicates a method which takes no parameters (empty parentheses) and returns no value (V following the parentheses indicates a return type of void - Java's term for no value).

From this little jaunt through the constant pool we see that the pointlessButton class calls the java.applet.Applet default constructor. Following a similar process, we can identify all of the other fields and methods utilized in this class. Furthermore, by finding *where* entry number 56 is referenced in the bytecode, we can build a clear picture of what this code does.

This is precisely what the javap utility shipped with the JDK does. By examining the constant pool and other parts of the class file structure, it is able to produce a high-level picture of the class file. Here's the output of javap when run against pointlessButton:

```
Compiled from PointlessButton.java
public class PointlessButton extends java.applet.Applet implements
java.awt.event.ActionListener
    /* ACC_SUPER bit set */
{
    jamjar.examples.Button donowt;
    int count;
    public void actionPerformed(java.awt.event.ActionEvent);
    public PointlessButton();
    public void init();
}
```

As we already knew, pointlessButton extends java.applet.Applet and as such it must call the Applet constructor - the method reference we saw by tracing through the constant pool.

If this were all that javap did then it would still be a useful tool for examining class files for which we didn't have the source code in an attempt to reuse them or work out what they were doing. But it's not all. By using additional option switches it is possible to get richer information, including even the disassembled bytecode. The following is the result of running javap with the c (disassemble) and p (include private fields) options enabled.

```
Compiled from PointlessButton.java
public class PointlessButton extends java.applet.Applet implements
java.awt.event.ActionListener
```

```
    /* ACC_SUPER bit set */
{
    jamjar.examples.Button donowt;
    int count;
    public void actionPerformed(java.awt.event.ActionEvent);
    public PointlessButton();
    public void init();
Method void actionPerformed(java.awt.event.ActionEvent)
   0 aload_0
   1 getfield #14 <Field PointlessButton.donowt Ljamjar/examples/Button;>
   4 new #16 <Class java.lang.StringBuffer>
   7 dup
   8 ldc #18 <String "Did Nothing ">
  10 invokestatic #24 <Method
java.lang.String.valueOf(Ljava/lang/Object;)Ljava/lang/String;>
  13 invokespecial #28 <Method
java.lang.StringBuffer.<init>(Ljava/lang/String;)V>
  16 aload_0
  17 dup
  18 getfield #30 <Field PointlessButton.count I>
  21 iconst_1
  22 iadd
  23 dup_x1
  24 putfield #30 <Field PointlessButton.count I>
  27 invokevirtual #34 <Method
java.lang.StringBuffer.append(I)Ljava/lang/StringBuffer;>
  30 ldc #36 <String " time">
  32 invokevirtual #39 <Method
java.lang.StringBuffer.append(Ljava/lang/String;)Ljava/lang/StringBuffer;>
  35 aload_0
  36 getfield #30 <Field PointlessButton.count I>
  39 iconst_1
  40 if_icmpne 48
  43 ldc #41 <String "">
  45 goto 50
  48 ldc #43 <String "s">
  50 invokevirtual #39 <Method
java.lang.StringBuffer.append(Ljava/lang/String;)Ljava/lang/StringBuffer;>
  53 invokevirtual #47 <Method
java.lang.StringBuffer.toString()Ljava/lang/String;>
  56 invokevirtual #52 <Method java.awt.Button.setLabel(Ljava/lang/String;)V>
  59 return
Method PointlessButton()
   0 aload_0
   1 invokespecial #56 <Method java.applet.Applet.<init>()V>
   4 aload_0
   5 new #58 <Class jamjar.examples.Button>
   8 dup
   9 ldc #60 <String "Do Nothing">
  11 invokespecial #61 <Method
jamjar.examples.Button.<init>(Ljava/lang/String;)V>
  14 putfield #14 <Field PointlessButton.donowt Ljamjar/examples/Button;>
  17 aload_0
  18 iconst_0
  19 putfield #30 <Field PointlessButton.count I>
  22 return
Method void init()
   0 aload_0
   1 new #64 <Class java.awt.BorderLayout>
   4 dup
   5 invokespecial #65 <Method java.awt.BorderLayout.<init>()V>
   8 invokevirtual #71 <Method
java.awt.Container.setLayout(Ljava/awt/LayoutManager;)V>
```

```
  11 aload_0
  12 ldc #73 <String "Center">
  14 aload_0
  15 getfield #14 <Field PointlessButton.donowt Ljamjar/examples/Button;>
  18 invokevirtual #77 <Method
java.awt.Container.add(Ljava/lang/String;Ljava/awt/Component;)Ljava/awt/Componen
t;>
  21 pop
  22 aload_0
  23 getfield #14 <Field PointlessButton.donowt Ljamjar/examples/Button;>
  26 aload_0
  27 invokevirtual #81 <Method
java.awt.Button.addActionListener(Ljava/awt/event/ActionListener;)V>
  30 return
}
```

Here we have the complete code for all of the methods albeit in Java "assembly" language. By appropriate use of a binary editor it would be a relatively simple matter for a hacker to subvert the function of this code. For example, simply changing the value of String (3) "Did Nothing" in the constant pool we could cause the button to print a rude message when pressed. This is a trivial example but hopefully illustrates the vulnerability of class files.

4.4.1 Beating the Decompilation Threat

The very real threat of decompilation is not going to go away. Decompilers work by recognizing patterns in the generated bytecode which can be translated back into Java source code statements. The field and method names required to make this source code more readable are readily available in the constant pool as we have seen.

To date, there have been two main approaches to thwarting would-be decompilers, code obfuscation and bytecode hosing.[2]

The principle of obscuring (or obfuscating) source code to make it more difficult to read is not new. In the UNIX world – where incompatibilities between platforms and implementations make it necessary to distribute many applications in source format – "shrouding" is common. This is the process of replacing variable names with meaningless symbols, removing comments and white space and generally leaving as little human readable content in the source code without impacting its compilability.

After the release of Mocha, the author released Crema, a further appalling coffee pun, which was designed to thwart Mocha. It did this by replacing names in the constant pool with illegal Java variable names and reserved words (such as "if" and "class"). This had no

[2] For the benefit of Non-US readers, if something is "hosed" it is seriously damaged, In this case deliberately.

affect on the JVM, which merely used the names as tags to resolve references without attributing any meaning to them. Nor did it actually prevent decompilation. It *did* however mean that the decompiled code was more difficult to read and understand and also would not recompile as the Java compiler would object to the illegal names.

Bytecode hosing is more subtle and is aimed at preventing the decompiler from recognizing patterns within the bytecode from which it could recover valid source. It does this by breaking up recognizable patterns of bytecodes with "do nothing" instruction sequences (such as the NOP code or a PUSH followed by a POP). A good example of a bytecode hoser is HoseMocha.

Of course, this approach can be defeated since once a hacker has established what types of do-nothing sequences are being generated by a bytecode hoser, he or she can modify the behavior of the decompiler to ignore such sequences. Furthermore, attempts to decompile hosed bytecode will generally result in broadly readable code interspersed with unintelligible passages rather than completely unreadable code.

In addition to this, bytecode hosers present a more insidious problem to Java users. As we have already seen, the principal method of optimizing Java performance is in the JVM and in particular through the use of just in time (or JIT) compilation. And how do JITs work ? Yup, you guessed it, they recognize patterns in the generated bytecode which can be optimized into native code. Breaking up these patterns through the use of a bytecode hoser can seriously impact the performance of JIT compilers.

For this reason, it is safe to assume that Java compilers will not follow the same evolutionary path as their native compiler cousins in terms of generating wildly differing output for the same source code since this too would thwart JIT compilers.

This is a well understood dilemma in security circles, the trade off between security and performance/price/ease of use.

The only safe course of action is to assume that ALL Java code will at some point be decompiled.

For developers this means ensuring that no sensitive information is distributed in the class file either algorithmically or as hard-coded values. This can be accomplished by building client/server type applications with a Java presentation layer which can be run anywhere and a secured server side where sensitive information or algorithms can be stored. This may also involve extending the development and testing process to ensure that distributed Java code is “safe”.

Finally you may decide that the existing method of protecting distributed code, that of legal sanction under copyright laws, is sufficient to deal with any serious threat to Java-based intellectual property...in which case we have some real estate you may be interested in buying.

4.5 Java Bytecode

In the next chapter we look at how the Java class loader and class file verifier provide a level of security against rogue class files. This section prepares us for that chapter by looking more closely at bytecode.

4.5.1 A Bytecode Example

Though you may not realize it, you have already seen an example of bytecode or at least the human readable format. The output generated by the javap command when we ran it with the -c flag contained a disassembly of each of the methods in the class file. The code snippet in Figure 14 was taken from the actionPerformed method of our pointlessButton class. It was compiled from three lines of Java source code:

```
public void actionPerformed(java.awt.event.ActionEvent e) {
donowt.setLabel( "Did Nothing " + ++count + " time" + ( count == 1? "": "s" ) );
}
```

```
Method void actionPerformed(java.awt.event.ActionEvent)
   0 aload_0
   1 getfield #14 <Field PointlessButton.donowt Ljamjar/examples/Button;>
   4 new #16 <Class java.lang.StringBuffer>
   7 dup
   8 ldc #18 <String "Did Nothing ">
  10 invokestatic #24 <Method java.lang.String.valueOf(Ljava/lang/Object;)Ljava/lang/String;>
  13 invokespecial #28 <Method java.lang.StringBuffer.<init>(Ljava/lang/String;)V>
  16 aload_0
  17 dup
  18 getfield #30 <Field PointlessButton.count I>
  21 iconst_1
  22 iadd
  23 dup_x1
  24 putfield #30 <Field PointlessButton.count I>
```

Figure 14. Decompiled Method (Part 1 of 2)

```
  27 invokevirtual #34 <Method java.lang.StringBuffer.append(I)Ljava/lang/StringBuffer;>
  30 ldc #36 <String " times">
  32 invokevirtual #39 <Method
java.lang.StringBuffer.append(Ljava/lang/String;)Ljava/lang/StringBuffer;>
  35 aload_036 getfield #30 <Field PointlessButton.count I>
  39 iconst_1
  40 if_icmpne 48
  43 ldc #41 <String "">
  45 goto 50
  48 ldc #43 <String "s">
  50 invokevirtual #39 <Method
java.lang.StringBuffer.append(Ljava/lang/String;)Ljava/lang/StringBuffer;>
  53 invokevirtual #47 <Method java.lang.StringBuffer.toString()Ljava/lang/String;>
  56 invokevirtual #52 <Method java.awt.Button.setLabel(Ljava/lang/String;)V>
  59 return
```

Figure 15. Decompiled Method (Part 2 of 2)

Notice the #nn references in the bytecode such as instruction 30:

```
ldc #36 <String " times">
```

The #36 here refers to entry number 36 in the constant pool, the text after the #36 is a comment for the benefit of the reader showing that entry #36 in the constant pool is a String with value " times".

The next thing that you should notice about this code is that even at this level, there are still references made to Methods and Fields. From this you may infer that Java is object-oriented even at the bytecode level and you would be correct.

We are not going to analyze all of this code, there are other books which serve to teach bytecode. Instead we will compare this code fragment with 80x86 equivalent code and draw some conclusions about the measures that exist within bytecode itself to protect the JVM against subversion.

Let's look at the following fragment :

```
13 aload_0
14 dup
15 getfield #30 <Field pointlessButton.count I>
18 iconst_1
19 iadd
20 dup_x1
21 putfield #30 <Field pointlessButton.count I>
```

Table 4 explains what each of these instructions does.

Table 4. Bytecode Byte-by-Byte

Instruction	Effect	Stack after instruction
aload_0	Push a copy of local variable 0 onto the stack. This variable is equivalent to the "this" keyword in Java source code; it holds a reference to the current object. In this case, that object is an instance of pointlessButton.	this (pointlessButton) [end of stack]
dup	Duplicates the item on the top of the stack.	this (pointlessButton) this (pointlessButton) [end of stack]
getfield #30	Pops the top item from the stack. Checks that it is a pointlessButton reference. Gets the count field with type I (integer) from it. Pushes the count field onto the stack.	this.count (int) this (pointlessButton) [end of stack]
iconst_1	Pushes the integer constant 1 onto the stack.	1 (int) this.count (int) this (pointlessButton) [end of stack]
iadd	Pops the top two values from the stack. Adds them. Pushes the result (as an integer).	this.count + 1 (int) this (pointlessButton) [end of stack]
dup_x1	Duplicates the value on top of the stack and inserts it under the second item from the top.	this.count + 1 (int) this (pointlessButton) this.count + 1 (int) [end of stack]
putfield #30	Store the value on top of the stack in the pointlessButton.count field of the object second from the top of the stack.	this.count + 1 (int) [end of stack]

The net of this sequence of operations is to have incremented the count field of the current object by one and left a copy of it on the stack (for use in the next instruction which prints the count).

The equivalent 80x86 code looks like this:

```
MOV BX, thisPointlessButton   ; Set BX to the base address of this button
MOV SI, count_field           ; Set SI to the offset of the count in button class
MOV CX, [ BX + SI ]           ; Get the count field in register CX
INC CX                        ; increment the CX register
MOV [ BX + SI ], CX           ; Store the result in BX+SI (the count field)
```

There are a few differences here which we'll examine in turn.

- **Stack-based architecture vs register-based architecture**

  The JVM has a stack-based architecture. This means that its instructions deal with pushing values onto, popping values from, and manipulating values on a stack.

  The 80x86 processor range from Intel are register-based. They have a number of temporary storage areas (registers) some of which are general purpose, others of which have a particular function.

  The advantage of making the JVM stack based is that it is easier to implement a stack-based architecture using registers than vice versa. Thus, porting the JVM to Intel platforms is easy compared with porting a register-based virtual machine to a stack-based hardware platform.

  In addition, there are benefits in a stack-based architecture when it comes to establishing what code actually does – more of this in the next chapter.

- **Object-oriented vs non-object-oriented**

  As we have already mentioned, the Java bytecode is object-oriented. This makes for safer code since the JVM checks at runtime that the type of fields being accessed or methods invoked for an object are genuinely applicable to that object.

  In the 80x86 code snippet, we have variable names to make it clearer what the code is doing but, there are no checks to make sure that the value loaded into the base register really is a pointer to an object of type pointlessButton and that the offset loaded into SI represents the count field of that object.

  There is no object-level information at all stored in 80x86 machine code, regardless of the high-level language from which it was compiled!

  This is so important we'll restate it: even if you write programs in Java, once you compile them to 80x86 machine code, all object information is lost and with it a degree of security since the runtime engine cannot test for the validity of method and/or field accesses.

- **Type Safety**

  While on the subject of type information, another difference to notice is the inclusion of type information in JVM bytecode instructions. The instruction `iadd`, for example, pops the top two values from the stack, adds them and pushes the return value. The i- prefix indicates that the instruction operates on and returns an integer value. The JVM will actually check that the stack contains two integers when the `iadd` instruction is to be executed. In fact this check is performed by the bytecode verifier, prior to runtime execution.

Contrast this with the 80x86 instructions which contain no type information. In this case, it is possible that the data loaded into the CX register for incrementing is an integer. It is also possible that it is part of a telephone number, an address, or a recipe for apple pie. There are simply no checks performed on data type. This is fine if you can trust your compiler and there is no likelihood of programs being attacked en route to their execution environment. As we have seen, however, in a networked environment, these assumptions cannot be made so lightly.

Not all bytecodes are typed; with a maximum of 256 distinct bytecode values there simply aren't enough to go around. Where a bytecode instruction is typed, the type on which it can operate is indicated by the prefix of the instruction. Table 5 lists the type prefixes and Table 6 shows the bytecodes in detail.

Table 5. Type Prefixes for Bytecodes

Prefix	Bytecode type	Prefix	Bytecode type
i	Integer	b	Byte
f	Floating point	s	Short
l	Long	c	Character
d	Double precision floating point	a	Object reference

Table 6. Bytecode Table

Bytecode	int	long	float	double	byte	char	short	object ref	Function
?2c	X								Convert value of type <?> to character
?2d	X	X	X						Convert value of type <?> to double
?2i		X	X	X					Convert value of type <?> to integer
?2f	X	X		X					Convert value of type <?> to float
?2l	X		X	X					Convert value of type <?> to long
?2s	X								Convert value of type <?> to short
?add	X	X	X	X					Add two values of type <?>
?aload	X	X	X	X	X	X	X	X	Push an element of type <?> from an array onto the stack

Bytecode	int	long	float	double	byte	char	short	object ref	Function
?and	X	X							Perform logical AND on two values of type <?>
?astore	X	X	X	X	X	X	X	X	Pop a type <?> from the stack and store in an array of type <?>
?cmp		X							Compare two long values. If they're equal push 0, if the first is greater push 1, else push -1
?cmpg			X	X					Compare two IEEE values of type <?> from the stack. If they're equal push 0, if the first is greater push 1 if the second is greater push -1. If either is NaN (not a number) push 1
?cmpl			X	X					Compare two IEEE values of type <?> from the stack. If they're equal push 0, if the first is greater push 1 if the second is greater push -1. If either is NaN (not a number) push 1
?const	X	X	X	X				X	Push constant value <n> of type <?> onto the stack
?div	X	X	X	X					Perform a division using two values of type <?> and store the quotient
?inc	X								Increment the top of the stack (possibly by a negative value)
?ipush					X		X		Push sign extender byte or short value onto stack
?load	X	X	X	X					Push a value of type <?> from a local variable
?mul	X	X	X	X					Perform multiplication of two values of type <?>
?neg	X	X	X	X					Negate a value of type <?>
?newarray								X	Create a new array of object references
?or	X	X							Perform logical OR on two values of type <?>
?rem	X	X	X	X					Perform a division using two values of type <?> and store the remainder
?return	X	X	X	X				X	Return a value of type <?> to the invoking method
?shl	X	X							Perform arithmetic shift left on type <?>
?shr	X	X							Perform arithmetic shift right on type <?>

Bytecode	int	long	float	double	byte	char	short	object ref	Function
?store	X	X	X	X				X	Pop a value of type <?> and store in a local variable
?sub	X	X	X	X					Perform a subtraction using two values of type <?>

There are a few seeming anomalies about this table. For example, the ?cmp and ?newarray instructions are typed and yet only apply to a single type (long in the case of ?cmp and object references in the case of ?newarray). Interestingly enough there is no equivalent of the ?cmp instruction for integers. These oddities can be explained away in terms of future expansions to the instruction set. However there are other peculiarities which are not as easily explained.

Consider the fact that there are no typed arithmetic instructions for byte or short values. This, coupled with the lack of support for short and byte values in the constant pool, might lead you to believe that the underlying support in the JVM for these types is less than full. You would be right.

The JVM's processor stack is 32 bits wide. Values which are longer (doubles or longs) or shorter (bytes or shorts) than this are treated specially within the JVM. Double and long values occupy two spaces each on the stack and thus require special instructions to deal with them. Bytes and shorts on the other hand are treated as integers within the JVM for arithmetic and logical operations. If you are dealing with pure Java source code then this is not a problem as the Java compiler will take care of generating the appropriate instructions on your behalf. If you start to work with bytecode which has not been generated from the Java compiler then things become a little different and it is quite possible that variables of byte or short types may end up containing values larger than their maximum permissible ones.

This is a symptom of one of the general difficulties with the JVM. There is no one-to-one relationship between Java source code and bytecode. On the one hand, the lack of a tight binding between the source language and bytecode enables cross-compilation from other source languages as we discussed previously.

On the other hand it does mean that there has to be a lot more work performed to ensure that the bytecode being executed is safe. There is some concern that the lack of a rigid relationship between the Java language and Java bytecode may be the source of some as yet undiscovered nastiness which could emerge to overthrow the entire Java security model. The next chapter looks at some of the measures which have been taken to prevent this type of nastiness.

Chapter 5. The Class Loader and Class File Verifier

> *"My dear fellow, you know my methods" -Sherlock Holmes, The Adventure of the Stockbroker's Clerk*
>
> (A. Conan Doyle)

In this chapter we explore a number of topics:

- How the components of the Java virtual machine work together to implement the Java security model
- How the class loader locates and loads class files
- How the class file verifier ensures that class files are legal prior to execution

In addition, we discuss issues to keep in mind when designing your own ClassLoader.

5.1 Overview of the Java Security Model

Before examining the components of the security model in detail, we'll take a high-level look at the whole process involved in loading and running a class.

Figure 16 illustrates the steps involved in loading a class into the JVM.

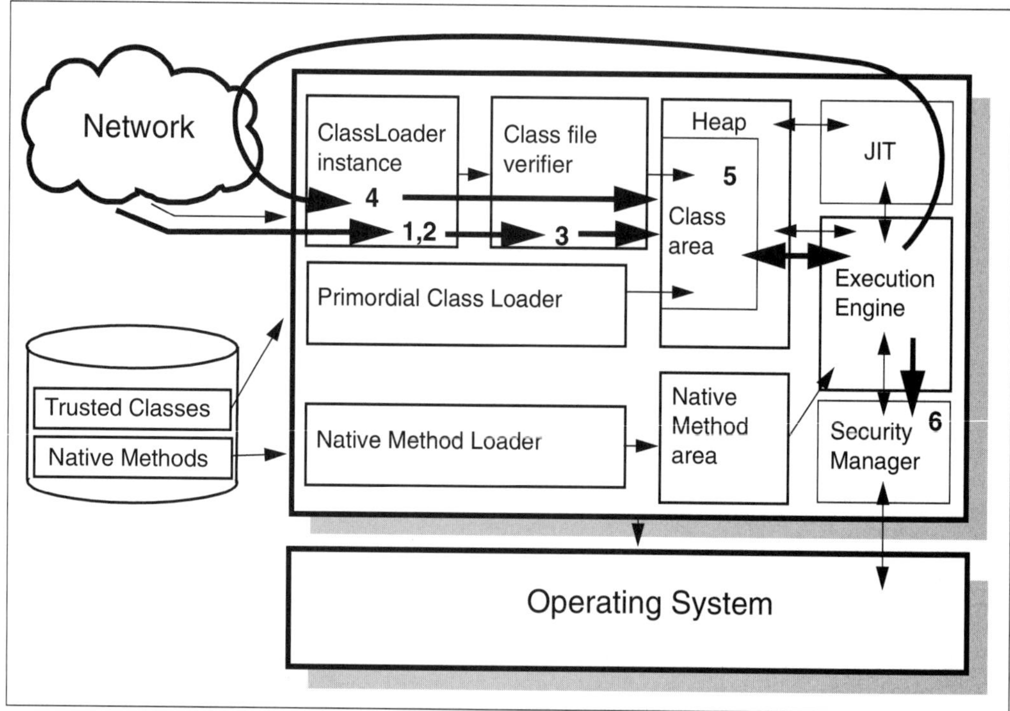

Figure 16. Steps in Loading a Class

1. When an applet or application requests a class file, the execution environment, whether it be a browser or the Java VM running from a command line, invokes a class loader to locate and load the class.[1]
2. The class loader receives the class as an array of bytes and converts it into a Class object in the class area of the JVM. The class area may be a part of the JVM heap (where all other objects are created and stored) or a separate region of memory.
3. Depending on the class loader which loaded the class file, the JVM may also run the class file verifier. The verifier is responsible for making sure that class files contain only legal Java bytecodes and that they behave in a consistent way (for example, they do not attempt to underflow or overflow the stack, forge illegal pointers to memory or in any other way subvert the JVM). More details of this are in "The Class File Verifier" on page 86.

[1] Throughout this chapter we refer to "class loaders" by which we mean the general mechanism by which class files are located and loaded into a JVM and "ClassLoader" by which we mean the specific Java ClassLoader class or classes derived from it.

4. Assuming that the class passes verification, the JVM is handed a loaded class. It then links the class by resolving any references to other classes within it. This may result in additional calls to the class loader to locate and load other classes.
5. Next, static initialization of the class is performed; that is, static variables and static initializers are run. Finally, the class is available to be executed.
6. In the context of an applet executing within a Web browser, there will always be an instance of the SecurityManager constructed. This may also be true in a Java application. When a SecurityManager is present, calls which could result in the system's integrity being violated (such as file read and write requests, network access requests, or requests to access the environmental variables) are presented to the SecurityManager for validation. If the SecurityManager refuses access, it does so by throwing a SecurityException. Since access to these key system functions is controlled by API calls within the trusted classes, there is no way to avoid the SecurityManager other than by replacing these classes.

5.2 Class Loaders

A class loader has a number of duties. Class loaders are the gatekeepers of the JVM, controlling what bytecode may be loaded and what should be rejected. As such they have two primary responsibilities:

1. To separate Java code from different sources, thus preventing malicious code from corrupting known good code
2. To protect the boundaries of the core Java class packages (trusted classes) by refusing to load classes into these restricted packages

The class loader has another, useful, side effect. By controlling how the JVM loads code, all platform-specific file I/O is channelled through one part of the JVM, thus making porting the JVM to different platforms a much simpler task.

Let's look a little more closely at these two aims and why they are necessary. First, Java code can be loaded from a number of different sources. These include but are not limited to:

- The trusted core classes which ship with the JVM (java.lang.*, java.applet.* etc.)

- Classes stored in the local file store and locatable via the CLASSPATH environmental variable
- Classes retrieved from Web servers (as parts of applets)

Clearly, we would not want to overwrite a trusted JVM class with an identically named class from a Web server since this would undermine the entire Java security model (the SecurityManager class is responsible for a large part of the JVM runtime security and is a trusted local class; consider what would happen to security if the SecurityManager could be replaced by an applet loaded from a remote site). The class loader must therefore ensure that trusted local classes are loaded in preference to remote classes where a name clash occurs.

Secondly, where classes are loaded from Web servers, it is possible that there could be a deliberate or unintentional collision of names (although the Sun Java naming conventions exist to prevent unintentional name collisions). If two versions of a class exist and are used by different applets from different Web sites then the JVM, through the auspices of the class loader, must ensure that the two classes can coexist without any possibility of confusion occurring. Class type confusion is a key way of attacking the JVM and is discussed later in this chapter.

The last point, that the class loader must protect the boundaries of the trusted class packages merits further explanation. The core Java class libraries that ship with the JVM reside in a series of packages which begin "java.", for example, java.lang and java.applet. Within the Java programming language, it is possible to give special access privileges to classes which reside in the same package; thus, a class which is part of the java.lang package has access to methods and fields within other classes in the java.lang package which are not accessible to classes outside of this package.

If it were possible for a programmer to add his or her own classes to the java.lang package, then those classes would also have privileged access to the core classes. This would be an exposure of the JVM and consequently must not be allowed.

The class loader must therefore ensure that classes cannot be dynamically added to the various core language packages. It achieves this by examining the name of the class which it is being asked to load and refusing to load those which start with "java."

5.2.1 How Class Loaders Are Implemented

The JVM architecture diagram (Figure 16 on page 78) shows two class loaders. In fact, the JVM may have many class loaders operating at any point in time, each of which is responsible for locating and loading classes from different sources.

One of the class loaders, the primordial class loader, is a built-in part of the JVM; that is, it is written in C or whatever language the JVM is written in and is an integral part of the JVM. It is the root class loader and is responsible for loading trusted classes; these are classes from the core Java classes and those classes which can be found in the CLASSPATH and usually in the local filestore.

Classes loaded by the primordial class loader are regarded as special insofar as they are not subject to verification prior to execution; that is, they are assumed to be well formed, safe Java classes. Obviously if would-be attackers could somehow inveigle a malicious class into the CLASSPATH of a JVM they could cause serious damage.[2]

In addition to this primordial class loader, application writers (including JVM implementors) are at liberty to build more class loaders to handle the loading of classes from different sources such as the Internet, an intranet, local storage or perhaps even from ROM in an embedded system. These class loaders are not a part of the JVM; rather, they are part of an application running on top of the JVM, written in Java and extending the java.lang.ClassLoader class.

The most obvious example of this is in the context of a Web browser which knows how to load classes from an HTTP (Web) server. The class loader which does this is generally known as the applet class loader and is itself a Java class which knows how to request and load other Java class files from a Web server across a TCP/IP network.

In addition, application writers can implement their own class loaders by subclassing the ClassLoader class (note that such behavior may be disallowed by the SecurityManager in an applet; we discuss more of this in the next chapter).

It is clear then that there can be many types of class loader within a Java environment at any one time. In addition, there may be many instances of a particular type of class loader operating at once.

[2] This was the basis of one of the attacks discovered by the Secure Internet Programming team at Princeton University. Their attack, "Slash and Burn", is described more fully in *Java Security, Hostile Applets, Holes and Antidotes,* Gary McGraw and Ed Felten.

To summarize the above;

- There will always be one and only one primordial class loader. It is part of the JVM, like the execution engine.
- There will be zero or more additional ClassLoader derivatives, written in Java and extending the ClassLoader abstract class. In a Web browser environment there will be at least one additional class loader: the applet class loader.
- For each additional ClassLoader type, there will be zero or more instances of that type created as Java objects.

Let's look at this last point more closely. Why would we want to have multiple instances of the same class loader running at any one time?

To answer this question we need to examine what class loaders do with a class once it has been loaded.

Every class present in the JVM has been loaded by one and only one class loader. For any given class, the JVM "remembers" which class loader was responsible for loading it. If that class subsequently requires other classes to be loaded, the JVM uses the same class loader to load those classes.

This gives rise to the concept of a name space: the set of all classes which have been loaded by a particular instance of a class loader. Within this name space, duplicate class names are prohibited. More importantly, there is no cross name space visibility of classes; a class in one name space (loaded by a particular class loader) cannot access a class in another name space (loaded by a different class loader).

Returning to the question "Why would we want to have multiple instances of a given ClassLoader derivative?", consider the case of the applet class loader. It is responsible for loading classes from a Web server across the Internet or intranets. On most networks (and certainly the Internet) there are many Web servers from which classes could be loaded and there is nothing to prevent two Webmasters from having different classes on their sites with the same name.

Since a given instance of a class loader cannot load multiple classes with the same name, if we didn't have multiple instances of the applet class loader we would very quickly run into problems when loading classes from multiple sites. Moreover, it is essential for the security of the JVM to separate classes from different sites so that they cannot inadvertently or deliberately cross reference each other. This is achieved by having classes from separate Web sites loaded into separate name spaces which in turn is managed by having different instances of the applet class loader for each site from which applets are loaded.

5.2.2 The Class Loading Process

The ability to create additional class loaders is a very powerful feature of Java. This becomes particularly apparent when you realize that user- written class loaders have first refusal when it comes to loading classes; that is, they take priority over the primordial class loader. This enables a user-written class loader to replace any of the system classes, including the SecurityManager. In other words, since the class loader is Cerberus to the JVM's Hades, you had better be sure that when you replace it, you don't inadvertently install a lapdog in its place.

We have already stated that a class loader which has loaded a particular class is invoked to load any dependent classes. We also know that a class loader generally has responsibility for loading classes from one particular source such as Web servers.

What if the class first loaded requires access to a class from the trusted core classes such as java.lang.String? This class needs to be loaded from the local core class package, not from across a network. It would be possible to write code to handle this within the applet class loader but it is unnecessary. We already have a class loader in the shape of the primordial class loader which knows how to load classes from the trusted packages.

This leads us to our second observation about class loaders: they frequently interoperate, one class loader asking another to load a class for it.

To illustrate how this works, consider the PointlessButton applet. As a reminder, PointlessButton uses a second class, JamJar.examples.Button which represents a push button on the browser display. Pushing the button results in nothing happening and a display being updated to inform you how many times nothing has happened to date.

When a Web browser encounters the pointlessButton applet in a Web page the following sequence of events occurs:

1. The browser finds the <APPLET> tag in the Web page and determines that it needs to load PointlessButton.class from the Web server. It creates an instance of the applet class loader (specific to this Web site) to fetch the class.
2. The applet class loader first asks the primordial class loader to load PointlessButton.class. The primordial class loader which only knows about the trusted classes fails to locate the class and returns control to the applet class loader.
3. The applet class loader connects to the Web site using the HTTP and downloads the class.
4. The JVM begins executing the PointlessButton applet.
5. PointlessButton needs to create an instance of JamJar.examples.Button, a class which currently has not been loaded. It requests the JVM to load the class.
6. The JVM locates the applet class loader which loaded PointlessButton and invokes it to load JamJar.examples.Button.
7. The applet class loader again first asks the primordial class loader to load the JamJar.examples.Button class and again the primordial class loader fails to find it and returns control to the applet class loader which is able to load the class from the Web server.
8. JamJar.examples.Button creates a java.lang.String object as the title of the button. The String class has not yet been loaded so again the JVM is requested to load the class.
9. The applet class loader which loaded both PointlessButton and JamJar.examples.Button is now invoked to load the java.lang.String class.
10. The applet class loader requests the primordial class loader to load the String class. This time, the primordial class loader is able to locate and load the class since it is part of the trusted classes package. Since the primordial class loader was successful, the applet class loader needs look no further and returns.

There are a couple of interesting points to note here.

First, at step 7, if we were using a regular java.awt.Button class then the primordial class loader would have been able to find the class in the trusted packages and the search would have stopped.

Secondly, there are actually many references to the java.lang.String class in the code. However, only the first reference results in the class being loaded from disk. Subsequent requests to the class loader will result in it returning the class already loaded. Since it is the primordial class loader which loads the String class, if there are multiple applets on a single page, only the first one to request a String class will result in the primordial class loader loading the class from disk.

Note also the order in which the applet class loader searches for classes. An applet class loader could always search the Web server from which it loaded the applet first for any subsequent classes and this would cut out some calls to the primordial class loader. This would have been incredibly bad practice for two reasons:

- Most of the class load requests for an applet will be for trusted classes from the java.* packages.
- More importantly, if classes were sought on the Web server before being sought in the trusted package, it would allow subversion of built-in types, enabling malicious programmers to substitute their own implementations of core, trusted classes such as the SecurityManager or even the applet class loader itself.

For this reason all commercially available browsers have applet class loaders which implement the following search strategy:[3]

1. Ask the primordial class loader to load the class from the trusted packages.
2. If this fails, request the class from the Web server from which the original class was loaded.
3. If this fails, report the class as not locatable by throwing a ClassNotFound exception.

This search strategy ensures that classes are loaded from the most trusted source in which they are available.

5.2.3 Why You Might Want to Build Your Own Class Loader

If it is done correctly, a user-built class loader can significantly enhance the security of an application deployed on an intranet, particularly if it is used in conjunction with a firewall and other local security measures.

Note that at the time of writing, Web browsers use the security manager to prohibit the creation of new derivatives of ClassLoader, although this may change with the new Java security model and the

[3] This is common practice but note that it is *not* enforced by the JVM architecture. Class loader writers are at liberty to implement any search strategy they choose for locating classes.

various permissions APIs which are being implemented. Chapter 7, "Playing in the Sandbox" on page 97 examines the security manager in more detail.

Some of the situations in which a user-written class loader could be used are:

- To restrict searches for trusted classes to a particular directory or path other than the CLASSPATH
- To allow the JVM to load classes from a particular source such as from EPROM or a non-TCP/IP network
- To specify paths which should be searched in advance of the CLASSPATH
- To provide auditing information about access to classes

In each of these cases you will need to build your own class loader and implement your own search strategy for locating classes.

It is beyond the scope of this book to show you how to write your own extension to ClassLoader and there are other resources, both books and on-line, which will teach you the specifics. For the serious codeheads out there, there is a sample ClassLoader included on the CD accompanying this book which implements a simple audit trail for class libraries.

5.3 The Class File Verifier[4]

Once a class has been located and loaded by a class loader (other than the primordial class loader), it still has another hurdle to cross before being available for execution within the JVM. At this point we can be reasonably sure that the class file in question cannot supplant any of the core classes, cannot inveigle its way into the trusted packages and cannot interfere with other safe classes already loaded.

We cannot, however, be sure that the class itself is safe. There is still the safety net of the SecurityManager which will prevent the class from accessing protected resources such as network and local hard disk, but that in itself is not enough. The class might contain illegal bytecode, forge pointers to protected memory, overflow or underflow the program stack, or in some other way corrupt the integrity of the JVM.

[4] **Important note**: The class file verifier is sometimes referred to as the bytecode verifier, but as we show in this section, running the bytecode verifier is only one part of the class file verification process.

As we have said in earlier chapters, a well behaved Java compiler produces well behaved Java classes and we would be quite happy to run these within the JVM since the Java language itself and the compiler enforce a high degree of safety. Unfortunately we cannot guarantee that everyone is using a well behaved Java compiler. Nasty devious hacker types may be using home made compilers to produce code designed to crash the JVM or worse, subvert the security thereof. In fact, as we saw in Chapter 4, we can't even be sure that the source language was Java in the first place!

In addition to this there is the problem of release-to-release binary compatibility. Let's say that you have built an applet which uses a class called TaxCalculator from a third party. You have constructed your applet with great care and have purchased and installed the TaxCalculator class on the server with your applet code.

At this point you are certain that the methods you call in TaxCalculator are present and valid but what happens if/when you upgrade TaxCalculator? Of course you *should* make sure that the API exposed by TaxCalculator hasn't changed and that your class will still work, but what if you forget? In practice it is quite possible that TaxCalculator has changed between versions and methods or fields which were previously accessible have become inaccessible, been removed or changed type from dynamic to static fields. In this case, when your applet is downloaded to a browser and it tries to make method calls or access fields within TaxCalculator those calls may fail.

This is because the binary (code) compatibility between the classes has been broken between releases. These problems exist with *all* forms of binary distributable libraries. On most systems this results in at best a system message and the application refusing to run; at worst the entire operating system could crash. The JVM has to perform at least as well as other systems in these circumstances and preferably better.

For all of the above reasons, an extra stage of checking is required before executing Java code and this is where the class file verifier comes in.

After loading an untrusted class via a ClassLoader instance, the class file is handed over to the class file verifier which attempts to ensure that the class is fit to be run. The class file verifier is itself a part of the Java Virtual Machine and as such cannot be removed or overridden without replacing the JVM itself.

5.3.1 The Duties of the Class File Verifier

Before we discuss what the class file actually does we look at the possible ways in which a class file could be "unsafe." By understanding the threat, we can see better how the Java architecture goes about countering it and expose any holes in the security provided by the class file verifier.

The following are some of the things that a class file could do which could compromise the integrity of the JVM:

- **Forge illegal pointers**. If a Java class can obtain a reference to an object of one type and treat it as an object of a different type then it effectively circumvents the access modifiers (private, protected or whatever) on the fields of that object. This type of attack is known as a class confusion attack since it relies on confusing the JVM about the class of an object.
- **Contain illegal bytecode instructions**. The JVM's execution engine is responsible for running the bytecode of a program in the same way as a conventional processor runs machine code.

  When a conventional processor encounters an illegal instruction in a program, there is nothing that it can do other than stop execution. You may have seen this in Windows programs where the operating system can at least identify that an illegal instruction has been found and display a message.

  Similarly, if the execution engine finds a bytecode instruction that it cannot execute, it is forced to stop executing. In a well written execution engine this would not be good but in a poorly written version it is possible that the entire JVM, or the Web browser in which it is embedded or even the underlying operating system might be halted. This is obviously unacceptable.
- **Contain illegal parameters for bytecode instructions**. Passing too many or too few parameters to a bytecode instruction, or passing parameters of the wrong type, can lead to class confusion or errors in executing the instruction.
- **Overflow or underflow the program stack**. If a class file could underflow the stack (by attempting to pop more values from it than it had placed on it) or overflow the stack (by placing values on it that it did not remove) then it could at best cause the JVM to execute an instruction with illegal parameters or at worst crash the JVM by exhausting its memory.

- **Perform illegal casting operations**. Attempting to convert from one data type to another – for example, from an integer to a floating point or from a String to an Object – is known as casting. Some types of casting can result in a loss of precision (such as converting a floating point number to an integer) or are simply illegal (such as converting a String to a DataInputStream).

  The legality of other types of casts is less clear, for example, all Strings are Objects (since the String class is derived from the Object class) but not all Objects are Strings. Trying to cast from an Object to a String is legal only if the Object is originally a String or a String derivative. Allowing illegal casts to be performed will result in class confusion and thus must be prevented.

- **Attempt to access classes, fields or methods illegally**. As discussed above, a class file may attempt to access a nonexistent class. Even if the class does exists, it may attempt to make reference to methods or fields within the class which either do not exist or to which it has no access rights. This may be part of a deliberate hacking attempt or as a result of a break in release-to-release binary compatibility.

By tagging each object with its type, the JVM could check for illegal casts. By checking the size of the stack before and after each method call, stack overflows and underflows can be caught. The JVM could also test the stack before each bytecode was executed and thus avoid illegal or wrongly numbered parameters.

In fact, all of these tests could be made at runtime but the performance impact would be significant. Any work that the class file verifier can do in advance of runtime to reduce the performance burden is welcome. With some idea of the magnitude of the task before the class file verifier, we now look at how it meets this challenge.

5.3.2 The Four Passes of the Class File Verifier

Before we go into any detail on how the class file verifier works it is important to note that the Java specification requires the JVM to behave in a particular way when it encounters certain problems with class files, which is usually to throw an error and refuse to use the class.

The precise implementation varies from one vendor to the next and is not specified. Thus some vendors may make all checks prior to making a class file available; others may defer some or all checks until runtime. The process described below is the way in which Sun's HotJava Web browser works; it has been adopted by most JVM writers, not least because it saves the effort of reinventing a complex process.

The class file verifier makes four passes over the newly loaded class file, each pass examining it in closer detail. Should any of the passes find fault with the code then the class file is rejected. For reasons which we explain below, not all of these tests are performed prior to executing the code. The first three passes are performed prior to execution and only if the code passes the tests here will it be made available for use.

The fourth pass, really a series of ad hoc tests, is performed at execution time, once the code has already started to run.

5.3.2.1 Pass 1 - File Integrity Check

The first and simplest pass checks the structure of the class file. It ensures that the file has the appropriate signature (first four bytes are 0xCAFEBABE) and that each of the structures within the file is of the appropriate length. It checks that the class file itself is neither too long nor too short and that the constant pool contains only valid entries. Of course class files may have varying lengths but each of the structures (such as the constant pool) has its length included as part of the file specification.

If a file is too long or too short, the class file verifier throws an error and refuses to make the class available for use.

5.3.2.2 Pass 2 - Class Integrity Check

The second pass performs all other checking which is possible without examining the actual bytecode instructions themselves. Specifically, it ensures that:

- The class has a superclass (unless this class is Object).
- The superclass is not a final class and that this class does not attempt to override a final method in its superclass.
- Constant pool entries are well formed, and that all method and field references have legal names and signatures.

Note that in this pass, no check is made as to whether fields, methods or classes actually exist, merely that their names and signatures are legal according to the language specification.

5.3.2.3 Pass 3 - Bytecode Integrity Check

This is the pass in which the bytecode verifier runs and is the most complex pass of the class file verifier. The individual bytecodes are examined to determine how the code will actually behave at runtime. This includes data-flow analysis, stack checking and static type checking for method arguments and bytecode operands.

It is the bytecode verifier which is responsible for checking that the bytecodes have the correct number and type of operands, that datatypes are not accessed illegally, that the stack is not over or underflowed and that methods are called with the appropriate parameter types.

The precise details of how the bytecode verifier operates may be found in Appendix C, "The Bytecode Verifier in Detail" on page 219. For now, it is important to state two points:

First, the bytecode verifier analyzes the code in a class file *statically.* It attempts to reconstruct the behavior of the code at runtime, but does not actually run the code.

Secondly, some very important work has been done in the past and more recently by one of the authors of this book which demonstrates that it is *impossible* for static analysis of code to identify all of the problems which may occur at runtime. We include this proof in Chapter 6, "An Incompleteness Theorem for Bytecode Verifiers" on page 95.

To restate this in simple terms, any class file falls into one of three categories:

- Runtime behavior is demonstrably safe.
- Runtime behavior is demonstrably unsafe.
- Runtime behavior is neither demonstrably safe nor demonstrably unsafe.

Clearly the bytecode verifier should accept those class files in the first category and reject those in the second category. The problem arises with class files in the third category.

These class files *may or may not* contain code which will cause a problem at runtime, but it is impossible from static analysis of the code alone to determine which is the case.

The more complex the bytecode verifier becomes, the more it can reduce the number of cases which fall into the third category but no matter how complex the verifier, it can never completely eliminate the third category and for this reason there will always be bytecode programs which pass verification, but which may contain illegal code.

This means that simply having the bytecode verifier is not enough to prevent runtime errors in the JVM and that the JVM must perform some runtime checking of the executable code.

Lest you be panicking at this stage you should comfort yourself with the thought that the level of verification performed by the JVM prior to executing bytecode is significantly higher than that performed by traditional runtime environments for native code (that is, none at all).

5.3.2.4 Pass 4 - Runtime Integrity Check

As we have hinted, the JVM must make a tradeoff between security and efficiency. For that reason, the bytecode verifier does not exhaustively check for the existence of fields and classes in pass 3. If it did, then the JVM would need to load all classes required by an applet or application prior to running it. This would result in a very heavy overhead which is not strictly required.

We'll examine the following case with three classes, MyClass, MyOtherClass and MySubclass, which is derived from MyClass. MyOtherClass has two public methods

- methodReturningMyClass() which returns an instance of MyClass (huzzah! for meaningful method names!) and
- methodReturningSubclassOfMyClass( ) which returns an instance of SubclassOfMyClass.

Against this background, consider the following code snippet.

```
MyOtherClass x = new MyOtherClass( );
MyClass y = x.methodReturningMyClass( );
```

In pass 3, the class file verifier has ascertained that the method methodReturningMyClass( ) is listed in the constant pool as a method of MyOtherClass which is public (and therefore reachable from this code).

It also checks that the return type of methodReturningMyOtherClass( ) is MyClass. Having made this check and assuming that the classes and methods in question *do* exist, the assignment statement in the second line of code is perfectly legal. The bytecode verifier does not in fact need to load and check class MyOtherClass at this point.

Now consider this similar code:

```
MyOtherClass x = new MyOtherClass( );
MyClass y = x.methodReturningSubclassOfMyClass( );
```

In this case, the return type of the method call does not return an object of the same class as y, but the assignment is still legal since the method returns a subclass of MyClass. This is not, however, obvious from the code alone: the verifier would need to load the class file for the return type SubclassOfMyClass and check that it is indeed a subclass of MyClass.

Loading this class involves a possible network access and running the class file verifier for the class and it may well be that these lines of code are never executed in the normal course of the program's execution in which case loading and checking the subclass would be a waste of time.

For that reason, class files are only loaded when they are required, that is when a method call is executed or a field in an object of that class is modified. This is determined at runtime and so that is when the fourth pass of the verifier is executed.

5.4 Summary

You have now seen the types of checking which take place before a class file from an untrusted source can be loaded and run inside the JVM. While not perfect, this is significantly more checking than is performed on any conventional operating system (that is, none at all).

Once it is running, code from untrusted sources is subject to further checking at the hands of the *security manager* which we have mentioned briefly here. Chapter 7, "Playing in the Sandbox" on page 97 describes how the security manager works and looks at ways in which it is possible to reduce the burden placed on the class loader and class file verifier by extending the range of classes which the JVM regards as trusted.

Chapter 6. An Incompleteness Theorem for Bytecode Verifiers

> *Über den Unentscheidbarsatz für den Bytecode Verifier*
>
> This is an allusion to the most famous Unentscheidbarsatz, or incompleteness theorem, proved by Kurt Gödel and published in 1931 in *Über formal unentscheidbare Sätze der Principia Mathematica und verwandter Systeme*

The bytecode verifier is a key component of Java security. Practical bytecode verifiers divide bytecode programs into three classes: those that will not cause problems when they run, those that will cause problems when they run, and those where the verifier is not certain. You can improve a bytecode verifier by reducing its area of uncertainty. Can you eliminate uncertainty completely? Can you build a complete bytecode verifier that determines whether a program is safe or not before it runs?

The answer is no, you cannot. It is mathematically impossible. This short chapter shows why.[1]

To demonstrate this, we focus on one aspect of bytecode verification, stack-underflow checking. This involves determining whether a bytecode program will underflow the stack, by removing more items from it than were ever placed on it. Then we use the argument known as *reductio ad absurdum*. We assume that there is a complete stack-underflow checker and show that this assumption leads to a contradiction. This means that the assumption must have been false – a complete stack-underflow checker is impossible. Since a complete bytecode verifier must contain a complete stack-underflow checker, a complete bytecode verifier is impossible too.

Suppose then that there is such a thing as a complete stack-underflow checker. We write a method in standard Java bytecode which takes as its argument the name of a class file and returns the value *true* if the specified class file does not underflow the stack, and *false* if it does.[2] We call this method doesNotUnderflow( ).

[1] The problem has been deliberately stated in terms that mathematicians may recognize as being similar to the halting problem. The proof, a diagonalization argument, follows the flow of Christopher Strachey's halting-problem proof (Computer Journal 1967).

[2] We have here used Church's Thesis, which states that a programming language (such as the Java bytecode language) which can code a Turing machine can code *any* computable function.

We now consider the bytecode program Snarl, whose main method contains:

```
if doesNotUnderflow( classFile )
   while true pop( );            // thus underflowing Snarl's stack
else
    { }                          // exiting gracefully
```

pop( ) – which removes the top element from the stack – may not be pure Java, but can certainly be written in bytecode. The bytecode program Snarl is compiled into the class file Snarl.class.[3]

What happens if we give Snarl itself as a parameter? The first thing it does is to invoke the method doesNotUnderflow on Snarl.class:

- If doesNotUnderflow(Snarl.class) is *true*, then Snarl immediately underflows the stack.
- If doesNotUnderflow(Snarl.class) is *false*, then Snarl exits safely, without underflowing the stack.

This contradiction means that there could never have been a method doesNotUnderflow which worked for all class files. The quest for a way of determining statically that a class would behave itself at run time was doomed. Complete checking for stack underflow **must** be done at runtime if it is to be done at all.

This result can be generalized and applied to any aspect of bytecode verification where you try to determine statically something that happens at runtime. So all bytecode verifiers are incomplete. This does not, of course, mean that they are not useful – they contribute significantly to Java security – nor that they cannot be improved. It does mean, however, that some checking has to be left until runtime.

[3] Snarl is a pretty nasty piece of programming, and most practical bytecode verifiers would reject it out of hand. The reason for this is that while true pop ( ); is disastrous if executed and has no practical purpose; a good rule of thumb is to leave it out. But there's nothing invalid about Snarl – if we really have finite bytecode for the method doesNotUnderflow( ), then we can readily construct the bytecode for Snarl – and doesNotUnderflow( ), being complete, has no need for rules of thumb.

Chapter 7. Playing in the Sandbox

> *"Open the pod bay doors, Hal"*
> *"I'm sorry, Dave, I'm afraid I can't do that" - 2001, A Space Odyssey*
>
> (Stanley Kubrick and Arthur C. Clarke)

As we say in "Java as a Threat to Security" on page 9, we can imagine four levels of attack to which a Java applet can be subjected:

1. System Modification, in which the applet makes some change to the browser system (read/write access).
2. Privacy Invasion, in which the applet can steal restricted information from your system (read-only access).
3. Denial of service, in which the applet uses system resources without being invited.
4. Impersonation, in which the applet masquerades as the real user of the system.

The browser security manager implements the sandbox restrictions that are designed to prevent the first two of these. In this chapter we look at what the security manager does, how it does it, and then look at some of the loopholes (now closed) in which it has been circumvented. Finally we briefly consider the tricks that an applet can use to perform the "nuisance" attacks – denial of service and impersonation.

7.1 What the Security Manager Does

SecurityManager is an abstract class that any application developer can extend to implement a set of controls. SecurityManager contains a set of methods with names starting *check*, for example checkWrite() or checkConnect(). These methods answer the question "is the applet allowed to do this?" either by quietly returning to the caller (an implicit "yes") or by throwing a security exception (an emphatic "no").

Although the class itself is abstract, the methods within it are not, which means that if a subclass of SecurityManager does not implement a particular method, a default behavior will result. The default, in every case, is to deny the check by throwing an exception.

The security manager installed in most browsers overrides some of the default methods, but is still very restrictive, so that it prevents the applet from doing anything that would compromise the system. Table 7 summarizes the checks and the normal browser implementation.

Table 7. Security Manager Controls

Area of control	Check method	"Is the applet allowed to..."	Allowed in an applet?
Network connections	checkAccept	accept a socket connection?	No
	checkConnect	request a socket connection?	Restricted. Can only request a connection to the same server from which the applet was originally loaded
	checkListen	listen for connection?	No
	checkMulticast	use multicast?	No
Threads	checkAccess	modify thread arguments?	Restricted to threads within the same thread group (that is, threads that are descended from a single parent thread).
File system	checkDelete	delete a specified file?	No
	checkRead	read from a specified file?	No
	checkWrite	write to a specified file?	No
Operating system access	checkExec	execute a system command?	No
	checkPrintJobAccess	create a print job?	No
	checkSystemClipboardAccess	access the system clipboard?	No
	checkLink	link to a system library?	No

Area of control	Check method	"Is the applet allowed to..."	Allowed in an applet?
Java Virtual Machine control	checkExit	kill the JVM?	No
	checkPropertyAccess checkPropertiesAccess	access specified system properties?	Restricted to a small list of uninteresting items. Cannot get a list of available property names.
	checkAwtEventQueueAccess	access the AWT event queue?	Yes
	checkCreateClassLoader	create a new class loader?	No
Packages and classes	checkPackageAccess checkPackageDefinition	access a specified Java class package?	Yes
Security extensions		use a specified security package feature?	Yes

7.2 Operation of the Security Manager

Although any Java program, applet or application, can extend SecurityManager, the JVM will allow only one security manager to be active at a time. To make a security manager active you have to call a static system method: java.System.setSecurityManager(). This can be done only *once* in an application environment; any subsequent call results in an exception. In the case of an applet, the web browser has already installed a security manager as part of the JVM initialization. This means, assuming that the trusted classes are not subverted, that an applet has no choice but to live within the limitations of the security manager provided by the browser.

The installed security manager is only really active on request: it does not check anything unless it is called by other system functions. Figure 17 illustrates the flow for a specific restricted operation, establishing a network connection. The calling code creates a new Socket class, using one of the constructor methods it provides. This method invokes the checkConnect method of the local SecurityManager subclass instance.

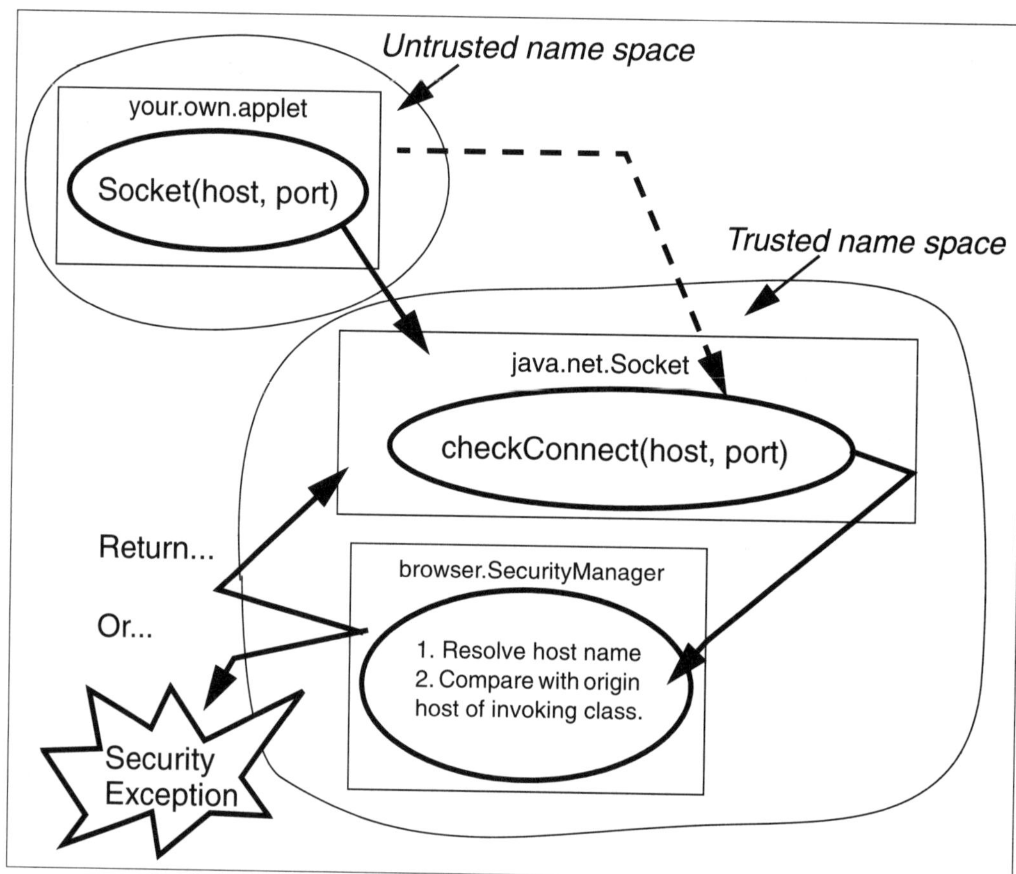

Figure 17. Security Manager Operation

In this case the security manager has a number of things to consider:

- It needs to know whether the top level class (in this case your.own.applet) is trusted or not. That is, was it loaded by a class loader over the network or by a local class loader, or was it installed locally, from the trusted class path? We have seen in "How Class Loaders Are Implemented" on page 81 that each of the active class loaders maintains a unique name space. Whether the classes within a name space are trusted depends on the type of class loader that created it.
- As an extension of the first point, if the security manager is checking a file access or network connection request (as here) it

not only needs to know if the applet is trusted, but also if it was loaded from the network or from a local file. This is because there are variations in the level of access allowed for these functions.

Refer to the JavaSoft security FAQ page for more information about this.

- It may have to run some further check specific to the type of access requested. In this case, for example, it has to check whether the host to which the socket connection is being attempted is the same host from which the calling class was loaded.

If all of these checks are successful, the security manager can permit the connection to go ahead.

7.2.1 Class Loader/Security Manager Interdependence

Although the three elements of JVM security – class loader, class file verifier and security manager – each have unique functions, this example illustrates their interdependence. The security manager relies on the class loader to keep untrusted classes and local classes in separate name spaces and to prevent the local trusted classes from being overwritten (for example, by a Socket class that failed to invoke checkConnect).

Conversely, the class loader relies on the security manager to prevent an applet from loading its own class loader, which could flag untrusted code as trusted. And everything relies on the class file verifier to make sure that class confusion is avoided and that class protection directives are honored.

The bottom line is this: if an attacker can breach one of the three defenses, the security of the whole system is usually compromised.

7.3 Attacking the Sandbox

We have now seen how the different parts of the Java defense act together to create a secure environment in which applets can run. If everything is working correctly, you should be safe from applets that try to attack your browser system or use it to mount attacks on other systems. In theory...

In practice, a number of holes have been found in the implementation of the Java defense, and a variety of attack applets have been demonstrated that exploit them. We do not go into the details of these applets here, partly because all of the publicized holes have already been closed by the main browser vendors, but mainly because most of them have already been described in detail in *Java Security: Hostile Applets, Holes and Antidotes*, by Gary McGraw and Ed Felten. Dr. Felten is the leader of the Princeton Secure Internet Programming team, which has, more than any other group, subjected the JVM environment to scrutiny and attack in its lab.

Attack techniques do not stand still, so you should also regularly monitor the sources listed in Appendix A, "Sources of Information about Java Security" on page 211.

It is not surprising that holes have been found in the Java defenses. The JVM is a large piece of code and, inevitably, there are bugs in it. Some of the attacks have exploited bugs, but most of them rely on finding ambiguities: using JVM facilities in a way that the original writers did not envision. If one were to redesign Java from scratch, with the benefit of hindsight, it would be possible to reduce the areas in which there is scope for ambiguity. However, we should not let this detract from the fact that, in general, the Java defenses have proven very strong and effective.

7.3.1 Types of Attack

Although we do not describe any attacks in detail, it is worth summarizing some of the techniques that have been successfully used:

- **Infiltrating local classes**. You will have realized from the descriptions of the class loader and security manager functions that they depend completely on the integrity of Java classes on the local browser disk. This applies not only to "system" classes – the java.* classes of the JVM – but to any class installed in the browser system (in the browser home directory or in the CLASSPATH). This is because these classes operate outside the controls of the sandbox.

  There was a bug (discovered by David Hopwood) that allowed an applet to load a class from *any* directory on the browser system. This has been fixed, but opportunities still exist for the opportunist cracker. Downloading code packages from the Internet has become a part of everyday life for many people. Any of those packages could have been modified to plant a Trojan horse class file along with their legitimate payload. Of course, this is not just a Java problem, but more like a new form of computer virus. One solution lies in signed content, so that you know that the package you download has not been tampered with. JDK 1.2 also promises some additional protection by applying restrictions to locally-loaded classes, as described in "Protection Domains" on page 129.

- **Type confusion**. Java goes to great lengths to ensure that objects of a particular type are dealt with consistently, whenever they are referenced. We see this both in the compiler and later in the third pass of the class file verifier (see "Pass 3 - Bytecode Integrity Check" on page 91). It is crucial to the operation of the sandbox that the class of an object and level of access it allows (as specified by the `private`, `protected` or `public` keywords) is preserved. In the JVM, objects are referenced by entries in the constant pool. As the example in "The Constant Pool" on page 62 showed, each entry includes the type of the referenced object.

  If, somehow, an attacker can create an object reference that is *not* of the type it claims to be, there is a possibility of breaking down the sandbox protection. Several exploits have shown ways to achieve type confusion, by taking advantage of a various flaws, such as:

  - A bug that allowed a class loader to be created but avoided calling the ClassLoader constructor that normally invokes checkCreateClassLoader() (see Table 7 on page 98).
  - Flaws in JVM access checking which allowed a method or object defined as private in one class to be accessed by another class as public.
  - A bug in the JVM that failed to distinguish between two classes with the same name but loaded by different class loaders.

- **Network loopholes**. The first JVM flaw to get worldwide attention was a failure to check the source IP address of an applet rigorously enough. This was exploited by abusing the domain name service (DNS, a network service responsible for resolving names to addresses and vice versa) to fool the security manager into allowing the applet to connect to a host that would normally have been invisible to the server from which the applet was loaded. In this way the attacker could access a system that would normally be safe behind a firewall.

- **JavaScript back doors**. There was a series of JavaScript exploits that allowed a script to persist after the Web page it was invoked from had been exited. This was used to track the user's Web accesses. The flaw was fixed, but then reappeared when Netscape introduced LiveConnect, which allows a JavaScript script to create

Java objects and invoke Java methods. Both languages have strict limitations on what they are allowed to do, but the limitations are *different* limitations. By combining them you effectively get a union of the two protection schemes.

Looking at this catalog of flaws, you may feel gloomy about the whole question of making Java secure. However, the encouraging thing about these examples is that they have all been identified by researchers in the field and fixed rapidly by Sun and the browser vendors.

7.3.2 Malicious Applets

So much for finding holes in the JVM protection scheme. What about the last two categories of exposure – the things that *are* allowed by the framework but which can still be annoying or damaging?

Setting the rules for the client environment is always a question of striking a balance. The browser needs to give the applet some system and network resources; otherwise, it will not be useful at all. On the other hand, it must not allow an attacker to have free reign over the browser system.

We have said that there are two types of malicious applets, denial of service and impersonation. There is also another type of malice that is not Java-specific. This is based on deception, that is, to try to trick the user into entering information that they would not normally give away. This sort of thing is not specific to Java, in fact there are much easier ways to do the same thing using scripting languages or simple HTML forms, so we won't consider them further here.

7.3.2.1 Cycle Stealing

Denial of service attacks have, for a long time, been a scourge of the Internet. Normally you think of them taking down a server or even a whole site. A denial of service applet is unusual in that it normally only affects a single system or user.

"Denial of service" implies that the user can no longer use the system, but we refer here to "cycle stealing" to mean any applet that consumes resources, whether computer or human, without the user's permission. The most extreme form of these *are* denial of service applets, but the most insidious ones may not be detected by their victim at all.

There are obvious denial of service attacks. For example an applet could try to create an infinite number of windows, or it could sit in a tight loop, using up CPU cycles. These are very annoying and they can have a real impact, if the user has to reboot the machine to recover, for example. However, if they are tied to a particular web page the user will quite quickly realize where the problem is coming from and simply not go there. To be effective takes something that is not so easily traced back to its source.

The key to this kind of applet lies in persistent, background, threads. Every implementation of the Java virtual machine supports threads, and the language makes it very easy to use them. In fact there are two ways to implement a thread, either by creating a subclass of Thread, or by implementing the Runnable interface. The danger of threads lies in the fact that they are not tied to a particular Web page. When you leave the page containing an applet, that applet and all of the threads it has started will normally be terminated. This job is handled by the stop() method, which is a *final* method in Thread (that is, it cannot be overridden by the programmer). However, if you implement Runnable, you can design the stop() method to do anything you like, including nothing at all. Figure 18 shows an example of this technique.

```
public class Annoy extends Applet implements Runnable {
    Thread fred ;
    URL fortuneURL ;
    public void init() {
         try { fortuneURL = new URL(this.getCodeBase() + "cgi-bin/getFortuneCookie"); }
         catch ( MalformedURLException e) {
              System.err.println("Bad URL: " + fortuneURL);
         }
         if (fred == null) {
              fred = new Thread(this) ;
              fred.start() ;
         }
     }
```

init method for applet just sets up a URL object, starts a new thread ("fred") running and then ends.

Figure 18. Never Ending Fortune Cookie Applet (Part 1 of 2)

```
public void run() {
     String line;
     URLConnection conn;
     DataInputStream data ;
     while ( true ) {
          StringBuffer buf = new StringBuffer();
          try { Thread.sleep(300000) ; }
          catch ( InterruptedException e) {} ;
               try {
                    conn = fortuneURL.openConnection();
                    conn.connect();
                    data = new DataInputStream(new BufferedInputStream(conn.getInputStream()));
                    while ((line = data.readLine()) != null) {
                         buf.append(line + "\n");
                    }
                    FortuneWindow fw = new FortuneWindow(buf.toString()) ;
               }
               catch (IOException e) {
                    System.err.println("IO Error:" + e.getMessage());
                    System.err.println("Trying to get " + fortuneURL) ;
               }
          }
     }

public void stop() {
}
```

run() method of new thread wakes up every 5 minutes, reads a URL and displays the result in a window.

Null stop() method allows the thread to keep running, even after the parent applet has gone.

Figure 19. Never Ending Fortune Cookie Applet (Part 2 of 2)

In this case the applet is just mildly annoying, popping up a new window containing a fortune cookie every five minutes (well, OK, after the first dozen times the annoyance could be more than mild). The subtle thing about it is that it seems to appear from nowhere; there is no sign of it on the Web page from which it loads and it does not appear until some time after you have left the page and surfed happily onward. The only way to get rid of it is to quit the browser completely.

This applet is fairly benign, and at least it is visible, so you know that something strange has happened. Really, what has happened here is that the attacker has got free use of machine cycles on your system. What sort of thing might he or she want to do with them? One example would be to do *brute force* cipher cracking. A feature of any good symmetric key encryption algorithm is a uniform key space. That is, if you want to crack the code there is no mathematical shortcut to finding the key, you just have to try all possible keys until you find one that works. Several recent encryption challenges have been solved by using spare cycles on a large number of computers working as a loosely-coupled complex, each being delegated a range of keys to try, under the direction of a central coordinator.

This sort of effort depends on the cooperation and goodwill of a lot of people who donate machine time and access. But, if we replaced the getFortuneCookie URL in the above example with, for example, getNextKeyRange, it would be possible to do the same thing without having to ask anybody. A number of other applets along the same lines have been demonstrated, such as applets that kill the threads of other applets executing concurrently.

7.3.2.2 Impersonation

Internet e-mail is based on the Simple Mail Transfer Protocol (SMTP). Mail messages are passed from one SMTP gateway to another using sessions on TCP/IP port 25. Abusing these connections to send bogus e-mail is an old-established nuisance of the Internet. A hacker can create mail messages that appear to come from someone else, which can be used to embarrass or annoy the receiver of the mail and the apparent sender.

Mail that has been forged in this way is not impossible to tell from the real thing, however. The SMTP gateways keep track of the original IP address, so you can trace the message back, if not to a person, at least to a machine (unless the originator was also using a spoofed IP address).

A Java applet allows this kind of errant behavior to go one stage further. There is nothing to prevent an applet from connecting to port 25 and appearing to be a mail client. However, the only system it can connect to is the one that it was originally loaded from, because of the sandbox restrictions. So now, if an attacker has control over a web page, he or she can cause an applet to be sent to a client machine, which connects back to the server and sends e-mail to the target of the attack. When the recipient checks the IP address, it belongs to a complete stranger, who has no idea that anything has happened.

7.4 Summary

The applet security manager enforces a well-defined, secure environment in which to run an applet. In doing so, it places some severe restrictions on what the applet can do, which may impede the development of effective network applications. We show in Chapter 9,

“Java Gets Out of Its Box” on page 119 how signed applets can break out of these restrictions.

There are some types of undesirable behavior that the sandbox does *not* prevent. These are generally a nuisance, rather than a serious threat, and at present you have to view them as one of the risks of the Internet. As the concept of protection domains in Java develops, we expect to see more granular controls that will prevent this behavior from the general hacker, while offering a wider range of function to the trusted host.

Chapter 8. Cryptography in Java

> *"I am fairly familiar with all forms of secret writings, and am myself the author of a trifling monograph upon the subject, in which I analyze one hundred and sixty separate ciphers, but I confess that this is entirely new to me." - Sherlock Holmes, The Adventure of the Dancing Men*
>
> (A.Conan Doyle)

From JDK 1.1 onwards, Java provides general purpose APIs for cryptographic functions, collectively known as the Java Cryptography Architecture (JCA) and Java Cryptography Extensions (JCE). Signed applets, which we will discuss in the next chapter, are one specialized use of the JCA capabilities.

In this chapter we describe the sort of problems for which cryptography can provide solutions and then look in more detail at JCA and JCE.

8.1 Security Questions, Cryptographic Answers

We want to create secure applications, but "secure" means different things depending on what the application does and the environment in which it operates. In each case we need to understand what the requirements are, based on the following categories:

Authentication How sure does the client need to be that the server really is who it claims to be? And does the server need to identify the client, or can he or she remain anonymous? Normally, authentication is based on either *something you know* (such as a password), or *something you have* (such as an encryption key or card). A developing form of authentication is based on *something you are*, including biometric measurements such as retinal scans or voice recognition.

Access control Having found out who is at the other end of the session, the next step is to decide whether they are allowed to do what they want to do.

Data integrity You want to be sure that data has not been altered between what was sent and what was received.

This is especially true if the application crosses an insecure network, such as the Internet, where a man-in-the-middle attack may be easily mounted.

Confidentiality If any of the data that you are sending is sensitive, you do not want an attacker to be able to read it in transit. To prevent this it needs to be encrypted.

Non-repudiation In a business application you often have to be able to prove that a particular transaction took place.

If we measure applet sandbox security against these requirements we find that the only one it helps us with is access control. The control is very strict: the security manager says "I can't authenticate the server that delivered this applet, so I will allow it to only do safe things."

As we mentioned in "Cryptographic Tools in Brief" on page 31, we have a trio of tools to answer the questions that these requirements pose, namely: symmetric key encryption, public key encryption and hashing/digital signatures.

Symmetric key, or bulk, encryption provides confidentiality, by making sure that a message can be read only if the recipient has the same key as the sender. But how to share the key in a secure manner? A common answer is to use public key encryption. This is too inefficient for general encryption of the whole data stream, but it is ideal for encrypting a small item, such as a bulk encryption key. The sender uses the receiver's public key to encrypt it, knowing that only the owner of the private half of the key pair, that is to say the receiver, will be able to decrypt it. Having secretly shared the bulk encryption key in this way, they can then use it to encrypt the real data that they want to keep private.

Digital signatures also use public key encryption, but the other way around. Figure 20 illustrates how they work.

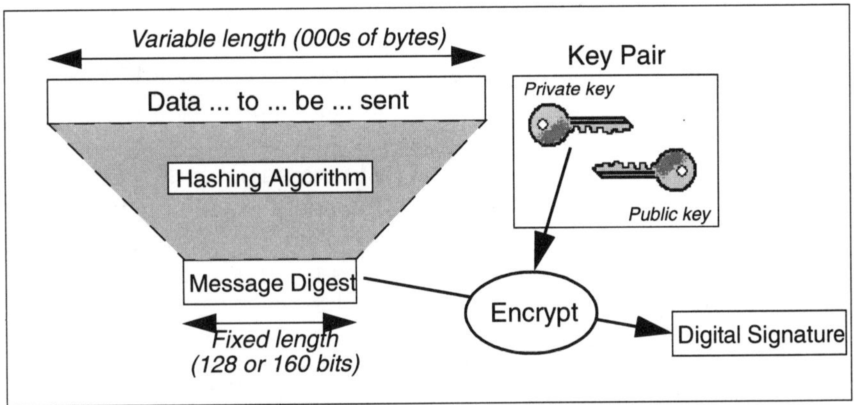

Figure 20. Creating a Digital Signature

The sender generates a digest from the data and then encrypts it with its private key. It then sends the result, together with the public key, along with the data. The receiver uses the public key to decrypt the signature and then performs the same hashing function on the data. If the digest obtained matches the result of the decryption, the receiver knows:

1. That the data has not been changed in transit (data integrity)
2. That it really was sent by the owner of the key pair (authentication)

8.1.1 Public Key Certificates

Whenever public key encryption is used, the owner of the key pair has to make the public key available to the session partner. But how can the session partner be sure of where the key really came from? The answer lies in *public key certificates*. Instead of sending a naked key, the owner sends a certificate, which is a message containing:

- The public key
- Detailed information about the owner of it (This is known as the *distinguished name*. It is a formatted string that contains the name, address, network information, etc. about the person or organization that owns the key pair.)
- The expiry date of the certificate
- Optionally, additional application-specific data

The whole message is digitally signed by a *trusted third party*, that is, an organization that is trusted by both sender and receiver (usually known as a Certificate Authority, or CA). The resulting certificate electronically ties the real identity of the user to the public key.

The international standard for public key certificates is called X.509. This has evolved over time and the latest version is V3. The most significant enhancement in X.509 V3 is the ability to add other, arbitrary, data in addition to the basic identity fields of the distinguished name. This is useful when constructing certificates for specific purposes (for example, a certificate could include a bank account number, or credit card information).

8.1.1.1 Certificate Hierarchies

A public key certificate can also embody a chain of trust. Consider the situation shown in Figure 21. A system has received a request containing a chain of certificates, each of which is signed by the next higher CA in the chain. The system also has a collection of root certificates from CAs that it views as trusted. It can match the top of the chain in the request with one of these root certificates ("Ham"). If the chain of signatures is intact, the receiver can infer that Nimrod is trustworthy and that it inherits its trustworthiness from Ham.

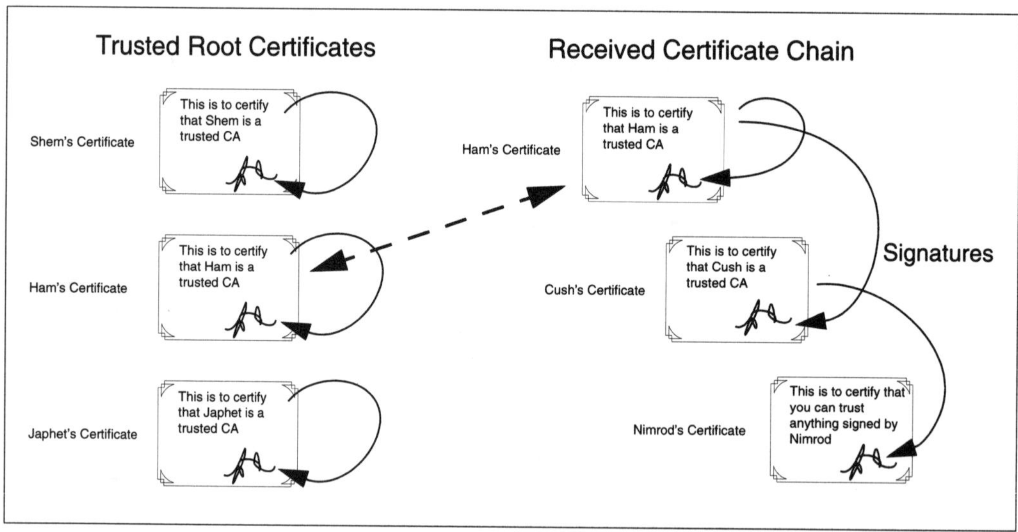

Figure 21. Certificate Hierarchy

Note that one of the implications of a certificate chain is that the certificate at the top of the chain is *self-signed*.

8.2 Introducing JCA: the Provider Concept

From the brief discussion above you can see that to use cryptographic solutions you may require a whole collection of tools and functions, not only the encryption algorithms themselves, but functions for message digests, certificate management and key generation. And of course, life would be too simple if there were only one way to do each of the functions. So, for example, there are two different message digest algorithms in common use, the MD5 algorithm from RSA and the US Government SHA standard.

The provider architecture of JCA aims to allow algorithm independence, by representing all functions of a given type by a generic *engine class*. This masks the idiosyncrasies of the algorithm behind standardized Java class behavior. Vendor independence is supported in the same way, by allowing any number of vendors to register their own implementations of the algorithms. Figure 22 illustrates how the provider architecture works in practice.

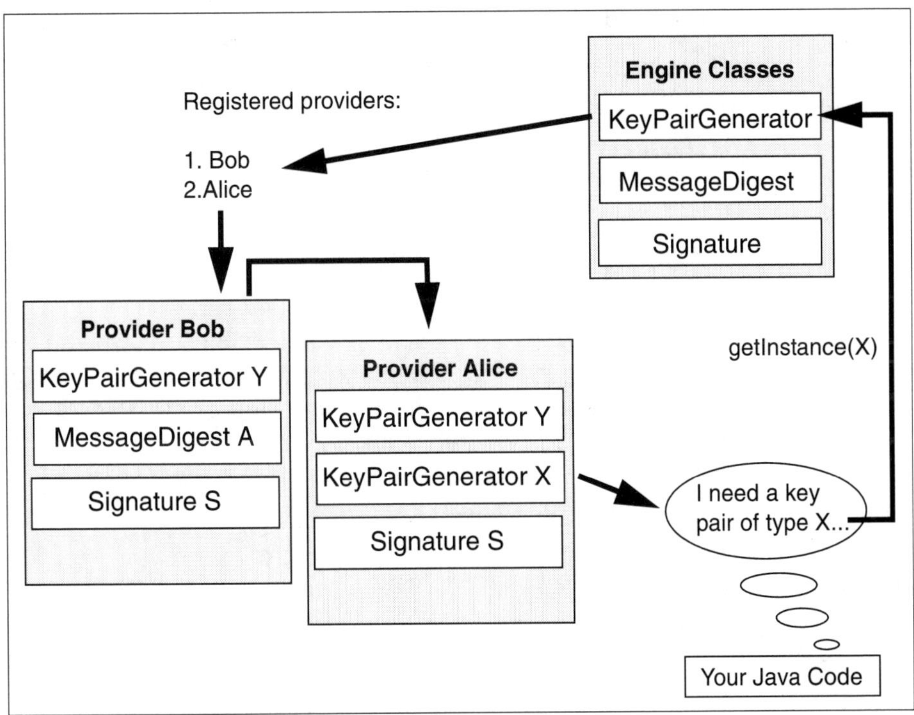

Figure 22. Vendor and Algorithm Independence

The figure shows two providers of cryptographic algorithms, Bob and Alice. These are in fact subclasses of the java.security.provider class. The acceptable algorithms are defined in *engine classes*. In JCA the only engine classes are related to digital signatures: creating the keys and digests needed for signing and then performing the signature itself. Bob and Alice both implement a number of algorithms that fall into these classes.

Now, let's assume that in your Java code you want to generate a key pair. You invoke the getInstance() method of the KeyPairGenerator engine class, passing it the specific type of key pair as an argument. The engine class reads the provider registration information from the java.security configuration file. This identifies the provider package names and assigns each one a preference order. In this case, the "Bob" provider package comes before "Alice" in the preference order. The engine class then searches through the providers until it finds an implementation of the algorithm required.

JDK1.1 offers one built-in provider package as standard, named *SUN*. This includes:

- An implementation of the Digital Signature Algorithm (NIST FIPS 186)
- An implementation of the MD5 (RFC 1321) and SHA-1 (NIST FIPS 180-1) message digest algorithms

It is worth noting here what is *not* contained in this package. The main omission is a facility for managing user IDs (more properly called *principals* in crypto-speak) and public key certificates. This makes the practical uses of the 1.1 package rather limited, as we show in an example using the SUN provider functions in "The Security Classes in Practice" on page 115. JDK1.1 *does* include a set of tools for manipulating signed applets and these do provide management of principals, keys and certificates. We explore them in "JavaSoft Signed JAR Example" on page 122.

8.2.1 JCE and Export Considerations

As we discussed in "US Export Rules for Encryption" on page 33, JCA only provides for the digital signature part of the cryptographic spectrum. This allows us to perform reliable authentication which, in turn, can be used as a basis for implementing access controls that relax the sandbox restrictions. However, it does not provide the general purpose encryption needed to send confidential data.

The Java Cryptography Extension (JCE) package uses the same structure as JCA, being composed of engine classes that expose the algorithms in a generic way. The exact specification of the API is not openly published. This is because it is not only the JCE package itself that falls under the US export restrictions, but also the documentation for it.

What can be said about JCE is that it provides engine classes for bulk (symmetric key) encryption algorithms and for generating and manipulating the secret keys that such algorithms require.

8.3 The Security Classes in Practice

In this section we describe an example of the kind of application that JCA could be used for. We will illustrate it using snippets of code that use the APIs. In this way we aim to show, not only the useful features of JCA, but also the areas in which, at the JDK 1.1 level, it is lacking.

8.3.1 The Scenario

Imagine a home banking application, in which the customer, sitting in front of a browser in the comfort of his or her home, wishes to make a payment. Two things, at least, are required here:

1. The server (the bank) wants to authenticate the user, to make sure that it is not an imposter.
2. The customer will want to be sure that the bank is really who it claims to be.

We assume that the user will be authenticated by normal means: a PIN number or pass-phrase. Both client and server side are written in Java.

8.3.1.1 Step 1: Generate Keys and Certificates

Before the transaction can start, the bank must have generated a key pair and requested a certificate for it. The first part is simple:

```
try {
   KeyPairGenerator kg = KeyPairGenerator.getInstance("DSA");
   kg.initialize(1024, new SecureRandom()) ;
   // Now generate a key pair
   keypair = kg.generateKeyPair();
}
catch (NoSuchAlgorithmException e) {
   System.err.println("No implementation of DSA keypair generator");
```

```
    System.exit(1) ;
}
```

This instantiates the provider class for a DSA key pair and then generates it. Now it gets tricky. The server needs to use the same key pair each time it restarts, which means that it has to somehow save it securely in a file. There is no built-in facility for this, so the programmer would need to create a method to do it. Secondly, the server needs to generate an X.509 certificate request. JCA 1.1 defines an interface named Certificate, but there is no implementation of it in the SUN provider package.

8.3.1.2 Step 2: Challenge the Server

The client applet starts off the transaction by establishing a socket connection to the server using the Socket class from java.net (alternatively, it could use RMI). There may be some firewall considerations here, as discussed in Chapter 11, "Firewalls: In and Out of the Net" on page 169, but we assume the connection can get through.

Next, the browser generates a random array of bytes and sends it to the server. There are two types of algorithm for generating random numbers, *true* and *pseudo*. Pseudo random number generators are based on a seed, which means that they become predictable if you can predict the seed value. The standard JDK Random class is seeded from the system clock, so it is theoretically predictable, but in our case the predictability of the random data does not matter, so we can use it.

When the server receives the data, it signs it using the private key from the key pair generated earlier:

```
try {
    siggi = Signature.getInstance("SHA/DSA");
    siggi.initSign( keypair.getPrivate() );
    // Pipe the string into a stream and sign it
    StringReader sr = new StringReader(line) ;
    byte b ;
    while (( b = (byte) sr.read()) != -1) {
        try {
            siggi.update(b);
        }
        catch (SignatureException e) {
            failmsg((Exception) e, "Problem performing the signature") ;
        }
```

```
}
```

It then sends the signature, plus the certificate, to the client. It also generates and sends another piece of random data, this time challenging the client.

8.3.1.3 Client Accepts the Challenge

The client receives the data from the server and verifies the signature. The verification uses a standard method of the Signature class, but, as before, there is no way to handle the certificate using JDK 1.1 functions. Even if there was a way to handle a certificate, the browser sandbox would pose some problems, because the applet would need to check the signature against a trusted root CA, which implies reading the CA certificate from disk.

Finally, the client needs to prove his or her identity. The way to do this is to take the random data provided by the server, combine it with the PIN or pass-phrase, encrypt it using the public key from the server certificate and send it to the server. This, too, is not possible with JDK 1.1, because JCE has no general purpose public key encryption function.

8.3.2 What Do We Learn from This?

The scenario described above has shown that the facilities provided by JCA and JCE in JDK 1.1 are very limited. Future versions of the development kit will fill in the gaps.

The scenario also prompts another, more fundamental, question: challenge-based authentication is a common requirement; *should there not be a common solution that implements it*? In other words, an application developer should be able to plug in code that performs the whole process, instead of designing the protocol from scratch and building it from basic components. This becomes more obvious when you start to consider the legal, contractual and practical implications of writing cryptographic code, for example:

- The question of US export controls. Even if the final result of the development uses lower-strength encryption and is therefore exportable, the toolkit used to create it still falls under export control. In addition, other countries, such as France, impose further restrictions which the developer must conform to.
- The question of licensed code. You have to pay a fee to use the RSA public key system in your code. Furthermore, other methods,

such as the Diffie-Hellman key exchange algorithm, are subject to license issues in some parts of the world.

- Questions of the management of multiple keys. For example, public key pairs are mainly used for digital signatures, but those signatures may have different meanings. Imagine an online banking scheme in which you have to prove your identity by digitally signing a challenge. The same application may also use digital signatures for authorization purposes ("transfer amount X to account Y"). A well-designed application should use different keys for each function. Otherwise an imposter could trick the user into signing a transfer request by presenting it as an identification challenge.

Buying a package that implements a complete protocol does not remove these obligations, of course, but it does mean that they have already been considered and resolved.

8.3.3 IBM Packages for Cryptographic Protocols

IBM Research in Zurich has developed a complete cryptographic framework in Java, which handles most application requirements. For example, it includes classes for bulk-key and public-key encryption and for X.509v3 certificate management. This is compatible with JDK 1.1, but it uses its own provider framework (because it was built before JDK 1.1 became available).

IBM Zurich has built implementations of Secure Sockets Layer (SSL) as Java classes, based on this framework. SSL is a protocol that provides bulk data encryption with server and client authentication. We discuss it further in Chapter 12, “Java and SSL” on page 195. The Java crypto-framework has also been used by IBM Development in Hursley, UK, to create a package that is optimized for consumer transactions such as home banking, insurance and financial services.

The Consumer Transaction Framework (CTF) is a set of Java classes which are used by the sample programs. CTF provides a number of services such as menuing, user validation and a secure interface to the server so that the application developer need not be concerned with the infrastructure, but may concentrate on the end-user function. Furthermore the CTF package uses cryptography for specific, well-defined purposes, which means that IBM has been able to obtain an export license for the use of full strength (128-bit) encryption.

Chapter 9. Java Gets Out of Its Box

> *"My suspicions were all confirmed by his peculiar action in typewriting his signature, which, of course, inferred that his handwriting was so familiar to her that she would recognize even the smallest sample of it." -Sherlock Holmes, A Case of Identity*
>
> (A. Conan Doyle)

We have seen in previous chapters that the applet sandbox is (at least in theory) a very safe place to run a program. However, one persons's "safe" is another person's "boring". To create effective client/server applications using Java often requires us to give the applet some freedom from the security of the sandbox.

The Java security model is built around the concept of a *protection domain*. The applet sandbox is a protection domain with very tight controls. By contrast the Java application environment is a protection domain with no controls at all, other than those imposed by the underlying operating system. What we are looking for is a protection domain that lies somewhere between the two.

As we have discussed, JDK 1.1 offers *signed applets* as a way to escape from the sandbox restrictions. Signed applets provide the mechanism for the protection domain we describe above.

9.1 JAR Files and Applet Signing

One characteristic of the dynamic loading of class files is that a typical applet may involve a number of small network transfers. It may also involve the retrieval of other files, graphic images for example. Given the indifferent performance of many World Wide Web connections, this can be a serious performance hit. JDK 1.1 provides relief for this by introducing the *JAR* (Java Archive) format for packing everything into a single file. JAR also allows for compression, which can further improve performance.

JDK 1.1 provides the `jar` command line tool for creating and managing JAR files. If you know the UNIX `tar` command, `jar` will be very familiar. As an example, the following command will create an archive for the PointlessButton applet:

```
jar -cvf pbutton.jar PointlessButton.jar JamJar\examples\Button.jar
```

Figure 23 shows the format of the pbutton.jar file that this creates

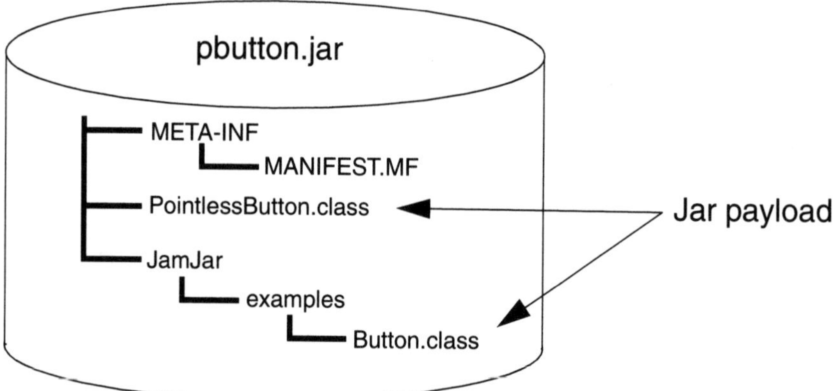

Figure 23. The pbutton Archive

The files that make up the payload of the JAR are packed into a copy of the original directory structure. The MANIFEST.MF file contains details of the "payload" of the JAR. This is what the manifest looks like in this case:

```
Manifest-Version: 1.0
Name: PointlessButton.class
Digest-Algorithms: SHA MD5
SHA-Digest: Sj15dptWhrZhiIFRNU27WRY1brc=
MD5-Digest: vB0/XzCeLLiykR///CBfUQ==
Name: JamJar/Examples/Button.class
Digest-Algorithms: SHA MD5
SHA-Digest: Fo6pYkn6ZR17eessxEiN7fK5xpE=
MD5-Digest: Hzs6oj85/blmcTW1fNQm4Q==
```

The digest values recorded in the manifest are calculated from the contents of the payload files they refer to. They are used to validate the payload files when they are unpacked.

Jar signing allows you to generate digital signatures for any of the files in the archive. In fact, files can be signed by more than one signer. So, for example, an applet could be signed by the developer who created it and then also signed by the IT department of the company who use it. When the user loads the applet, he or she not only knows that the applet comes from a trustworthy source, but also knows that it has been approved for corporate use.

When you sign the files in a JAR, two new files are added to the META-INF directory:

Signer file This is very like the manifest file shown above, except that the digests in it are calculated from the manifest file entries, not from the actual contents of the payload files. The signer file may contain fewer entries than in the manifest file, because a signer does not have to sign every file in the archive. The file name is <signer ID>.SF, where <signer ID> is an arbitrary name for the creator of the signature. If the JAR has been signed by more than one signer, each will have a separate .SF file.

Digital signature file This is a binary file, containing the digital signature in PKCS7 format.[1] The signature file name depends on the type of signature algorithm used. For example, a DSA signature would be in a file named <signer ID>.DSA (other possibilities are .RSA, for a signature using an MD5 digest and RSA encryption and .PGP for a Pretty Good Privacy signature).

9.1.1 Current Implementations

The JAR format is quite new and at the time of writing there are some discrepancies between the way that different vendors have interpreted the signature part of the standard. There are also different philosophies in the way that signed JARs are used to elicit extra permissions from the client. In the Sun case, the browser is configured in advance to allow a signed applet to do certain things that are normally forbidden by the security manager. In the Netscape case the applet has to ask for the specific permissions it wants, using a special API. Microsoft has taken yet another approach, not using JARs at all.

Let's look at some examples of the different implementations.

[1] Public Key Cryptography Standards, PKCS, is a set of rules for encoding various cryptographic structures. PKCS7 defines a general-purpose signature format, including the signed digest, the certificate of the signer and the CA certificates that support it.

9.2 JavaSoft Signed JAR Example

JDK 1.1 provides the `javakey` and `jar` commands for managing databases of public keys and for creating, signing and manipulating JAR archives. In this section we show how to use the commands to create three key databases:

1. A certificate authority database
2. A database for a Web server
3. A database for a Web client

We then use these keys to sign a JAR file containing an applet that attempts to read a file on the browser system.

In the following sections we show the command dialog as it appears on a Windows NT system, using bold type for commands and normal type for the system and command responses, like this:

```
C:\directory\path>command
system response...
```

9.2.1 Creating the Certificate Authority Key Database

The certificate authority is a principal in its own key database, with a self-signed certificate. We create it as follows:

1. The first thing to do is to create a new key database. The key database is created implicitly when you add the first principal to it:

   ```
   D:\work\sun_signed_jar>javakey -cs "JamJar CA" true
   Created identity [Signer]JamJar CA[identitydb.obj][trusted]
   ```

   This creates key database itentitydb.obj in your home directory.

2. Next, generate a key pair for the CA principal. We choose to use a 1024 bit key:

   ```
   D:\work\sun_signed_jar>javakey -gk "JamJar CA" DSA 1024
   Generated DSA keys for JamJar CA (strength: 1024).
   ```

   This can take a while to do. We ran it on a 75 MHz 486 machine and the command ran for 2 min 40 sec (the time is related to the key size). You can use the list option of javakey to check the results so far:

   ```
   D:\work\sun_signed_jar>javakey -ld
   Scope: sun.security.IdentityDatabase, source file:
   C:\users\default\identitydb.obj
   [Signer]JamJar CA[identitydb.obj][trusted]
   ```

```
public and private keys initialized
certificates:
No further information available.
```

3. The key pair allows the CA to sign certificates, but we also need to generate a certificate for the CA itself, so that others can accept the CA's signatures. The first thing to do is to create a certificate information file, containing the distinguished name information for the CA and the certificate issuer. In this case, the certificate is self-signed, so the issuer and the subject are the same:

```
issuer.name=JamJar CA
subject.name=JamJar CA
subject.real.name=Project JamJar Certificate Authority
subject.org.unit=ISL
subject.org=IBM
subject.country=UK
start.date=12 Sep 1997
end.date=12 Sep 1998
serial.number=1
out.file=cert.jamjar
```

   We save this file as certinfo.jamjar.

4. Finally we can sign the CA's certificate:

```
D:\work\sun_signed_jar>javakey -gc certinfo.jamjar
Generated certificate from directive file certinfo.jamjar.
D:\work\sun_signed_jar>javakey -ld
Scope: sun.security.IdentityDatabase, source file:
C:\users\default\identitydb.o
bj
[Signer]JamJar CA[identitydb.obj][trusted]
        public and private keys initialized
        certificates:
        certificate 1   for  : CN=Project JamJar Certificate
Authority, OU=ISL,O=IBM, C=UK
                        from : CN=Project JamJar Certificate
Authority, OU=ISL,O=IBM, C=UK
        No further information available.
```

9.2.2 Creating the Server Key Database

Now we want to create a key database for our server:

1. If we go ahead and use javakey to create the principal for the server, it will add it to the CA database. So first we must choose to use a different key database, by setting the identity.database directive in the main security properties file.

(<JDK_root>\lib\security\java.security, where <JDK_root> is the directory where JDK 1.1 was installed). We added the following line:

```
identity.database=D:/work/sun_signed_jar/serverdb.obj
```

2. The server has to know about the CA that signed its own certificate, so first we add the CA principal to the key database and import the CA certificate:

```
D:\work\sun_signed_jar>javakey -cs "JamJar CA" true
Created identity [Signer]JamJar
CA[D:/work/sun_signed_jar/serverdb.obj][trusted]
D:\work\sun_signed_jar>javakey -ic "JamJar CA" cert.jamjar
Imported certificate from cert.jamjar for JamJar CA.
D:\work\sun_signed_jar>javakey -ld
Scope: sun.security.IdentityDatabase, source file:
D:/work/sun_signed_jar/server
db.obj
[Signer]JamJar CA[D:/work/sun_signed_jar/serverdb.obj][trusted]
        no keys
        certificates:
        certificate 1    for  : CN=Project JamJar Certificate
Authority, OU=ISL,O=IBM, C=UK
                         from : CN=Project JamJar Certificate
Authority, OU=ISL,O=IBM, C=UK
```

   Notice that in this case the list command shows a key database with no keys in it, just a public key certificate (this is slightly misleading, because the certificate contains the public key; the display should really say that there are no key pairs).

3. We create the principal and generate a key pair for our server:

```
D:\work\sun_signed_jar>javakey -cs "Robusta"
Created identity
[Signer]Robusta[D:/work/sun_signed_jar/serverdb.obj][not trusted]
D:\work\sun_signed_jar>javakey -gk "Robusta" DSA 512
Generated DSA keys for Robusta (strength: 512).
```

4. Next we want to use the CA key pair to sign the server's public key. First we export the public key to a file:

```
D:\work\sun_signed_jar>javakey -ek Robusta pubkey.robusta
Public key exported to pubkey.robusta.
```

5. We need to import this key into the CA's key database. To do this we comment out the identity.database entry that we added to java.security (above), create the server's principal in the CA database and import the public key:

```
D:\work\sun_signed_jar>javakey -cs "Robusta"
Created identity
[Signer]Robusta[D:/work/sun_signed_jar/serverdb.obj][not trusted]
D:\work\sun_signed_jar>javakey -ik Robusta pubkey.robusta
Set public key from pubkey.robusta for Robusta.
```

6. Now we can sign the server's certificate. The process is the same as for the CA certificate. First we create the certificate information file:

```
issuer.name=JamJar CA
issuer.cert=1
subject.name=Robusta
subject.real.name=All Java is secure but signed Java is Robusta
subject.org.unit=ISL
subject.org=IBM
subject.country=UK
start.date=12 Sep 1997
end.date=12 Sep 1998
serial.number=2
out.file=cert.robusta
```

   Then we sign the certificate:

```
D:\work\sun_signed_jar>javakey -gc certinfo.robusta
Generated certificate from directive file certinfo.robusta.
```

7. To use the certificate, we have to import it into the server's key database, which means that we first have to find out the number assigned to the certificate in the CA database and export the certificate to a file:

```
D:\work\sun_signed_jar>javakey -li Robusta
Identity: Robusta
[Signer]Robusta[identitydb.obj][not trusted]
        no keys
        certificates:
        certificate 1   for  : CN=All Java is secure but signed
Java is Robusta
OU=ISL, O=IBM, C=UK
                        from : CN=Project JamJar Certificate
Authority, OU=ISL,O=IBM, C=UK
D:\work\sun_signed_jar>javakey -ec Robusta 1 cert.robusta
Certificate 1 exported to cert.robusta.
```

8. Finally, we switch the active key database back to the server (by restoring the identity.database entry in java.security) and then import the certificate:

```
D:\work\sun_signed_jar>javakey -ic Robusta cert.robusta
```

```
Imported certificate from cert.robusta for Robusta.
D:\work\sun_signed_jar>javakey -ld

Scope: sun.security.IdentityDatabase, source file:
D:/work/sun_signed_jar/serverdb.obj
[Signer]JamJar CA[D:/work/sun_signed_jar/serverdb.obj][trusted]
        no keys
        certificates:
        certificate 1    for  : CN=Project JamJar Certificate
Authority, OU=ISL,O=IBM, C=UK
                         from : CN=Project JamJar Certificate
Authority, OU=ISL,O=IBM, C=UK
        No further information available.
[Signer]Robusta[D:/work/sun_signed_jar/serverdb.obj][not trusted]
        public and private keys initialized
        certificates:
        certificate 1    for  : CN=All Java is secure but signed
Java is Robusta OU=ISL, O=IBM, C=UK
                         from : CN=Project JamJar Certificate
Authority, OU=ISL,O=IBM, C=UK
```

9.2.3 Creating and Signing a JAR File

To illustrate the use of the key databases we have a simple Java applet that attempts to perform an action normally prohibited by the sandbox; it reads a local file and displays the contents on screen. We need to package this in a JAR archive and then sign it.

1. We create the jar file and display its contents using the `jar` command:

   ```
   D:\work\sun_signed_jar>jar -cvf jam.jar GetFile.class
   adding: GetFile.class (in=2239) (out=1201) (deflated 46%)
   D:\work\sun_signed_jar>jar -tf jam.jar
   META-INF/MANIFEST.MF
   GetFile.class
   ```

2. We have to tell javakey which key pair to use for the signature (in fact, the key database only has one key pair in it, but javakey does not know that). To do this we create a signature directive file, as follows:

   ```
   signer=Robusta
   cert=1
   chain=0
   signature.file=ROBUSTA
   ```

   The signature.file directive does not define a real file, but the file name part of the signer and signature files that are placed in the

META-INF directory of the JAR (see "JAR Files and Applet Signing" on page 119).

3. Now we can sign the JAR:

```
D:\work\sun_signed_jar>javakey -gs sign_directive.robusta
jam.jar
Adding entry: META-INF/MANIFEST.MF
Creating entry: META-INF\ROBUSTA.SF
Creating entry: META-INF\ROBUSTA.DSA
Adding entry: GetFile.class
Signed JAR file jam.jar using directive file
sign_directive.robusta.
```

Notice the conflicting use of forward slash (/) and back slash (\) in the metadata files. In theory a JAR should use forward slashes only, but this mixed use does not seem to cause a problem.

4. The result of performing the signature is a file named jam.jar.sig. Now we can put that on the Web server and reference it in a web page using the <APPLET> tag:

```
<APPLET CODE=GetFile.class archive=jam.jar.sig WIDTH=600
HEIGHT=600>
<PARAM NAME=FileToTry VALUE="c:\thingy">
</APPLET>
```

5. Finally we can try to load the page into a Web browser (or, for testing purposes, the JDK 1.1 applet viewer). However, when we do so we get the same error as if it was a normal applet running under the sandbox restrictions:

```
sun.applet.AppletSecurityException: checkread
at sun.applet.AppletSecurity.checkRead(AppletSecurity.java:384)
at sun.applet.AppletSecurity.checkRead(AppletSecurity.java:346)
at java.io.FileInputStream.<init>(FileInputStream.java:58)
at GetFile.init(GetFile.java:15)
at sun.applet.AppletPanel.run(AppletPanel.java:287)
at java.lang.Thread.run(Thread.java:474)
```

You can see that the checkRead method of the security manager is throwing an exception. Why is this? The reason is that the client does not have the certificate that it needs to decrypt the JAR's signature, and hence establish trust in the signer.

According to the signature hierarchy the client should only need the JamJar CA certificate to authenticate the server (because JamJar CA signed the server's certificate). However, at the time of writing this did not work as expected for JDK 1.1. We found we had to add the server certificate to the client's key database, as follows:

1. We set the key database to a new one for the client, by changing the identity.database directive in java.security:

```
identity.database=d:\work\sun_signed_jar\clientdb.obj
```

2. Then we create the entry for the server and import the certificate:

```
D:\work\sun_signed_jar>javakey -cs "Robusta" true
Created identity
[Signer]Robusta[D:/work/sun_signed_jar/clientdb.obj][trusted]
D:\work\sun_signed_jar>javakey -ic "Robusta" cert.robusta
Imported certificate from cert.robusta for Robusta.
```

3. Now, at last, the applet runs as we want it to:

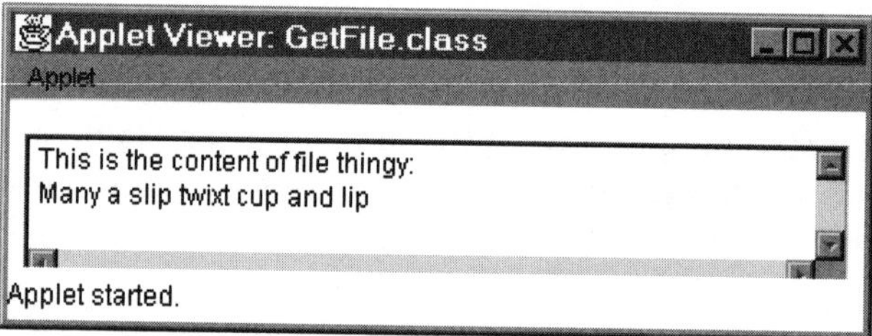

Figure 24. Running the Signed Applet

The applet viewer gives full access to any signed applet, which is acceptable because it is a test tool. A real browser needs to provide more control over access. HotJava, for example, allows you to set a range of different trust levels:

Untrusted This is like the normal sandbox environment, except that it is even more restricted because the applet cannot make any network connections.

High Security This is similar to the sandbox, with the addition of the ability for an applet to listen on network ports above 1024.

Medium Security Prompts the user whenever the applet tries to do something that is normally not allowed, so that the user can permit or deny it.

Low Security Allows the applet to do anything, without prompting the user.

9.3 Coming Next from JavaSoft: JDK 1.2

From the example in the previous section, you can see that applet signing, as implemented in JDK 1.1, really only implements half of the process – it provides a mechanism for creating signed JAR files but it does not provide a real implementation of access control.

At the time of writing, JDK 1.2 is still under development and only limited information about its security model is publicly available. What *is* known is that Sun will develop the sandbox model with the following objectives in mind:

- **To provide fine-grained access control**. Under the present scheme you have to write customized SecurityManager and ClassLoader classes to do this. The intention is that the JDK and Java Runtime Environment (JRE) will provide much of this programming by default.
- **To enable an easily configurable security policy**. When the HotJava browser was introduced it provided some limited capabilities for modifying the restrictions of the sandbox. However, in the face of press coverage, later Java-capable browsers removed all such controls, leaving the restrictive virtual machine of today. The runtime environment needs to be fitted with controls that allow a user or administrator to define their security policy.
- **To allow security checks to be extended to other Java programs**. Under the present scheme, local code is always treated as being trusted, whereas applet code is not. The new model will apply consistently to local code as well, whether classes permanently installed on a browser that interact with applets or part of Java applications. This does *not* eliminate the concept of system code. There must always be a layer of trusted code that applet and local classes invoke when they need access to protected resources. What it does mean is that applets and applications can be subjected to the same set of controls.

9.3.1 Protection Domains

The JDK 1.2 security model will extend the concept of *protection domains*. These are logical boundaries within which a given security policy applies. A protection domain is defined by a set of permissions, which act as a set of filters to tie together:

- The *code source,* made up of an *origin* (where a piece of code comes from) and a *principal* (who the code is signed by).

- *Resources* (protected system or network elements)

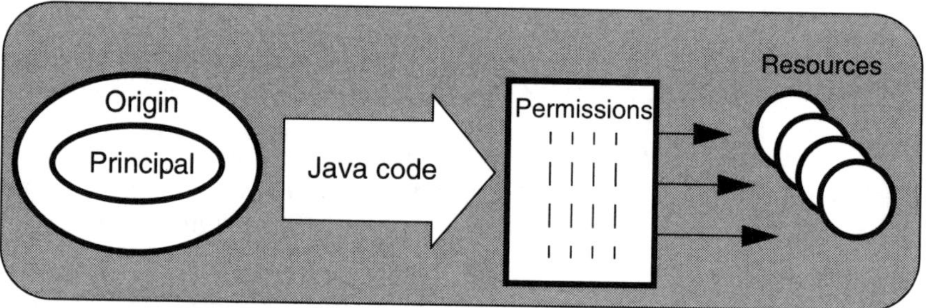

Figure 25. A Protection Domain

The way the permissions are applied will mirror the current SecurityManager function. That is, every attempt to access a protected resource will be routed to the access control function, which will examine the permissions of its protection domain and either return quietly or throw an exception (in fact it will have to trace back the execution thread to check all of the protection domains, so that unauthorized code cannot beat the system by calling an authorized function).

The elements for the protection domain will initially be controlled by a policy configuration file. So, for example, you could specify an entry in the file that would grant applet code from a specific site, signed by a named trusted signer, read-only permission to a specific file.

Each of the elements of the protection domain can be defined as tightly or as loosely as required. This means that at one extreme it will be possible to define a protection domain that re-creates the operation of the sandbox by specifying an origin of "any URL" and a principal of "unsigned."

9.4 Netscape Signed JAR Example

While Javasoft has been working on developing the security model for JDK 1.2, the major browser manufacturers have also been wrestling with ways to relax the access control applied to signed applets.

Netscape have embraced the JAR format and the opportunities that signing offers. In fact, they are using the format for other types of Web content, such as JavaScript programs, plug-ins and Web pages. However, at the time of writing you could not simply use a Netscape

However, at the time of writing you could not simply use a Netscape browser to access a JAR signed using the javakey command as described in "JavaSoft Signed JAR Example" on page 122. There are two reasons for this:

1. Netscape browsers require that the CA that signs a JAR file be predefined as a trusted root. The self-signed certificates used by javakey cannot be loaded into the browser.
2. The trust model implemented by HotJava works on an exception basis: the applet tries to do something that is forbidden, which causes a prompt to ask the user if it is acceptable. Netscape have implemented a more sophisticated model, in which the applet code requests the permissions it needs and in which it can control the period for which each permission is active.

In other words, the programmer decides in advance what permissions are needed, instead of trying to use the permissions and relying on the browser to handle the exception. Although this may seem like a small distinction, it does allow a more natural style of application. For example, if an applet attempts several privileged actions, the user can be prompted to allow access to all of them at once, instead of being repeatedly interrupted each time one of them is encountered in the code.

The ability to turn permissions on and off within the code is also important, because it reduces the exposure to an attack where another applet invokes the trusted applet's methods, thereby using the JAR signature illicitly.

The Netscape access control request mechanism is implemented as a Java class package named *netscape.security*. We illustrate the security model with an example of an applet that requests permission to read system properties and also to read a file on the browser disk. There are three parts to the setup: writing the applet to use the netscape.security extensions, installing and configuring the key pairs and certificates and then signing the JAR and running the applet.

9.4.1 Using the netscape.security Package

The netscape.security mechanism is based on *privilege targets*. These are definitions of operations that the applet may want to perform. Control over whether they should, or should not be permitted lies with a new security function, the *privilege manager*. This places indicators on the JVM stack to show what privileges the applet has been allowed.

The Netscape version of the security manager then refers to the indicators when performing its authorization checking.

The package includes a large number of predefined privilege targets and also allows the programmer to register new targets. The applet shown in Figure 26 requests access to two of the standard targets: access to system properties and read access to a local file.

```
import java.awt.*;
import java.io.*;
import netscape.security.* ;
public class GetFileNS extends java.applet.Applet implements Runnable {
     String filename ;
     Thread t ;
     TextArea ta = new TextArea("",10,50);
     public boolean granted = false ;
     PrivilegeManager privMgr ;
     protected Principal lil0lMe ;
     public void init() {
          filename = getParameter("FileToTry"
          add(ta);
          // Find out what operating system we are on
          try {
               PrivilegeManager.enablePrivilege("UniversalPropertyRead");
               String osName = System.getProperty("os.name");
               a.appendText("\nI see you are running " + osName);
               PrivilegeManager.revertPrivilege("UniversalPropertyRead") ;
          }
          catch (netscape.security.ForbiddenTargetException e) {
               ta.appendText("\nPermission to read system properties denied by user.");
          }

          / Request permission to read a specific file
          lil0lMe = PrivilegeManager.getMyPrincipals()[0] ;
          privMgr = PrivilegeManager.getPrivilegeManager() ;
          try {
               Target freadTgt = Target.findTarget("FileRead") ;
               privMgr.enablePrivilege(freadTgt , lil0lMe, (Object) filename) ;
               granted = true ;
          }
          catch(ForbiddenTargetException e) {
               ta.appendText("\nUser won't let me read " + filename) ;
          }
```

Here we request permission to read system properties. The enablePrivilege() method causes a dialog box to pop up asking for permission. If the user refuses, it throws an exception. Otherwise the applet goes on to read the property (the type of operating system that the browser is running on)

Note that we revert the privilege immediately. This minimizes the time for which the applet is open to abuse.

The second example is more complex. In this case the privilege is not universal ("view any system property") but specific ("read file X"). We therefore cannot just refer to the privilege target by name, but have to pass a netscape.security.Target object to enablePrivilege. This could be a target that we created ourselves, or, as in this case, a target provided by the package. The file name is passed to enablePrivilege(). This version of the method also requires details of the applet signer, contained in a Principal object.

Figure 26. GetFileNS.java (Part 1 of 2)

Now you are probably wondering why we requested access to read the local file but then did not do so. In fact we are going to need the file access later in the applet, in another thread. Figure 27 shows the second half of the applet, in which the FileRead privilege is used. This illustrates an oddity of the mechanism: the privilege manager grants privileges for the life of the applet, but the indicators are placed on the program stack, which is unique to each method and the methods it invokes. This means that you have to re-issue the enablePrivilege() request from the method where the privilege is actually exercised. However, as the privilege manager has kept track of what permissions have been granted, it will not ask the user again.

```
    public void run() {
        // Did we get the permission we wanted?
        if ( granted == true ) {
            try {
                Target freadTgt = Target.findTarget("FileRead") ;
                privMgr.enablePrivilege(freadTgt , lilOlMe, (Object) filename) ;
                ta.appendText("\nThis is the content of file " + filename + ":\n" +
readTheFile(filename).toString());;
            }
            catch(ForbiddenTargetException e) {
                ta.appendText("\nShould never reach here...") ;
            }
        }
    }
    private StringBuffer readTheFile(String filename) {
        DataInputStream dis;
        String line;
        StringBuffer buf = new StringBuffer();
        FileInputStream theFile;
        try { theFile = new FileInputStream(filename);
            try {
                dis = new DataInputStream(new BufferedIn
                while ((line = dis.readLine()) != null)
                    buf.append(line + "\n");
                }
            }
            catch (IOException e) {
                System.out.println("IO Error:" + e.getMe
            }
        }
        catch ( FileNotFoundException e) {
            System.out.println("File not found: " + filen
        }
            return(buf) ;
    }
```

Here we request the FileRead privilege again and, this time, we actually read the file.

This method reads the data. It is a general purpose function, so we do not request privileges within it. If we did, an attack applet could invoke it using inter-applet communication and get privileges without a signature. It is also private, which protects the run() method from a similar attack.

Figure 27. GetFileNS.java (part 2 of 2)

When you start to ease the restrictions in your browser you have to be aware that you may be opening yourself to attack. The applet itself is signed by someone you trust, based on the signature in the certificate, so it should not do anything dangerous directly. However, as we alluded to in the example above, another applet could get a free ride on the signature by using inter-applet communications to invoke methods that have had privileges granted to them. You will recall that such an attack can only be launched from an applet within the same context (that is, contained within the same document). This highlights an important point about signed applets: *the signature implies a trustworthy programmer, not a trustworthy site.*

For the Applet Developer

Using Privileges with Care

The GetFileNS applet (above) illustrates a number of techniques for reducing the risk of a second applet abusing your privileges. In summary the techniques are:

1. Enable privileges for as short a time as possible.
2. Place privileged accesses within private or protected methods.
3. When creating general purpose methods (like readTheFile() in the example), enable privileges in the calling code, not the method itself.

http://developer.netscape.com/library/documentation/signedobj/capabilities has some more detailed guidelines on this issue.

9.4.2 Installing Keys and Certificates in Netscape

Now that we have written the code that will request and use special privileges, we need to install it in a signed JAR. But before we can generate a signature, we need a key pair and a certificate.

Public key signatures rely on a *web of trust*. That is, anyone receiving a signed message needs to have the certificates of certificate authorities that establish the trustworthiness of the signer. This does not only apply to signed Java, of course. One of the most widespread uses of digital signatures is in the Secure Sockets Layer (SSL), a general purpose protocol for encrypting Web data and authenticating the server and client.

To get around the problem of establishing the web of trust needed by SSL, the browser manufacturers provide key databases containing *trusted roots* (the certificates of a number of widely-accepted CAs) as part of the browser installation. This allows a browser to accept any signature that is supported by a certificate from one of the known CAs. But signed Java poses other problems:

1. If you are creating a signed JAR for general use you can purchase a certificate from one of the well-known CAs. But if you are creating a local, intranet, application with a limited web of trust, you need a way for the signer and the browser to install the local CA certificate as a trusted root.
2. As the signer of the code, you need the facility to generate a key pair and then acquire a certificate for your own public key and install it into your own key database.

Netscape has developed mechanisms to solve both of these problems. They are based on messages with special MIME types that trigger key management functions in the browser. The MIME types are:

- **application/x-x509-ca-cert**. This message delivers a new CA certificate. When it is received, the browser pops up a dialog in which the user can check the details of the certificate before installing it as a trusted root (see Figure 29).
- **application/x-x509-user-cert**. This message delivers a new personal certificate. This does not make sense unless the browser has previously generated a key pair and provided distinguished name information to place in the certificate. Netscape uses a special HTML tag: <KEYGEN>, which causes the browser to generate the key pair. Figure 28 shows how this works.

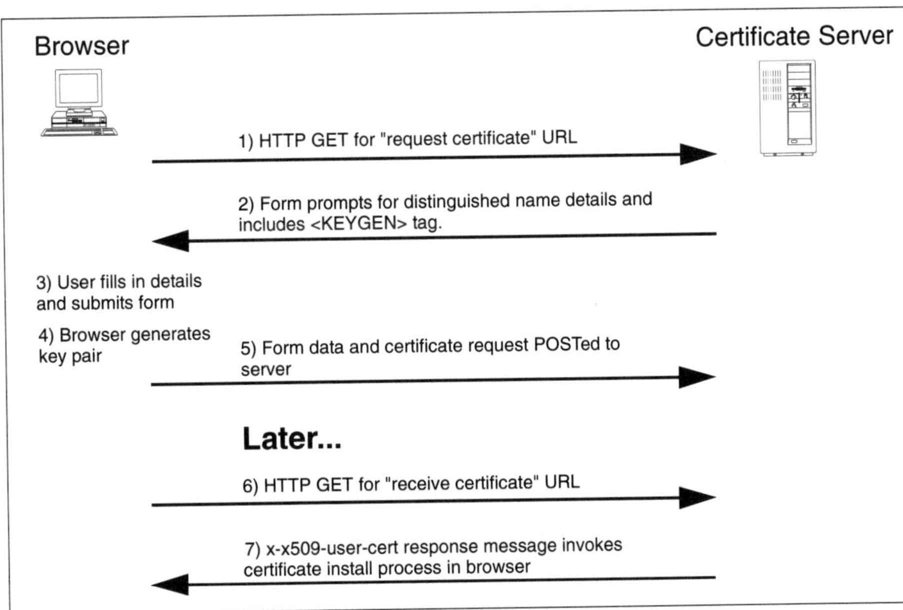
Browser
Certificate Server
1) HTTP GET for "request certificate" URL
2) Form prompts for distinguished name details and includes <KEYGEN> tag.
3) User fills in details and submits form
4) Browser generates key pair
5) Form data and certificate request POSTed to server
Later...
6) HTTP GET for "receive certificate" URL
7) x-x509-user-cert response message invokes certificate install process in browser

Figure 28. Requesting a Certificate: the KEYGEN Mechanism

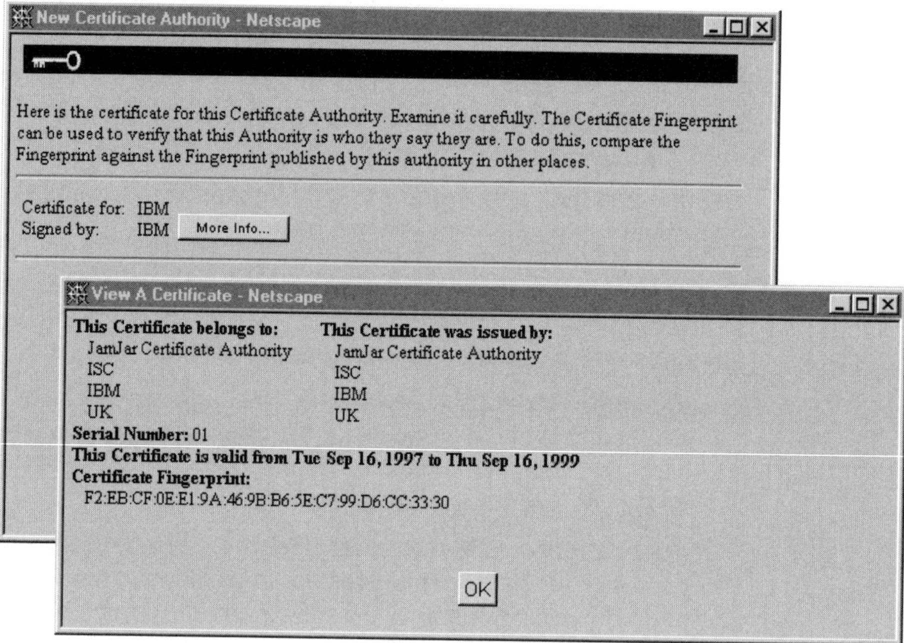

Figure 29. Receiving a New CA Certificate

In our example we used the Netscape Certificate Server product to generate and install a new CA key and a personal key for code signing. Any suitable key management software could be used, so long as it supports the special MIME types and KEYGEN tag. The IBM Registry product has this capability, for example, and it will also be available in a future release of the Lotus Go Web server.

In order to use the key pair for signing JAR files, it must be a X.509 v3 certificate with a special attribute set to indicate that it is suitable for code signing.

9.4.3 Signing JAR Files with Netscape JAR Packager

Now everything is in place to store the applet in a JAR and to sign it. Netscape provide a tool called the JAR Packager which makes this easy to do. At the time of writing the tool was available for download from the Netscape Developer Connection Web site.

We used the graphical version of the tool, which is a Java application invoked from Netscape Navigator (see Figure 30).

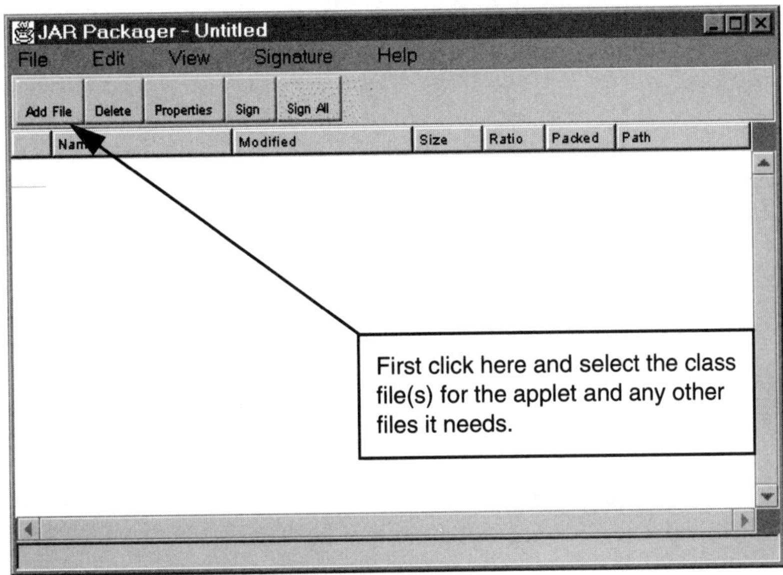

Figure 30. JAR Packager, Initial Screen

Once you have selected the file(s) that you want in the JAR, you can sign them all by clicking on the appropriate button (see Figure 31).

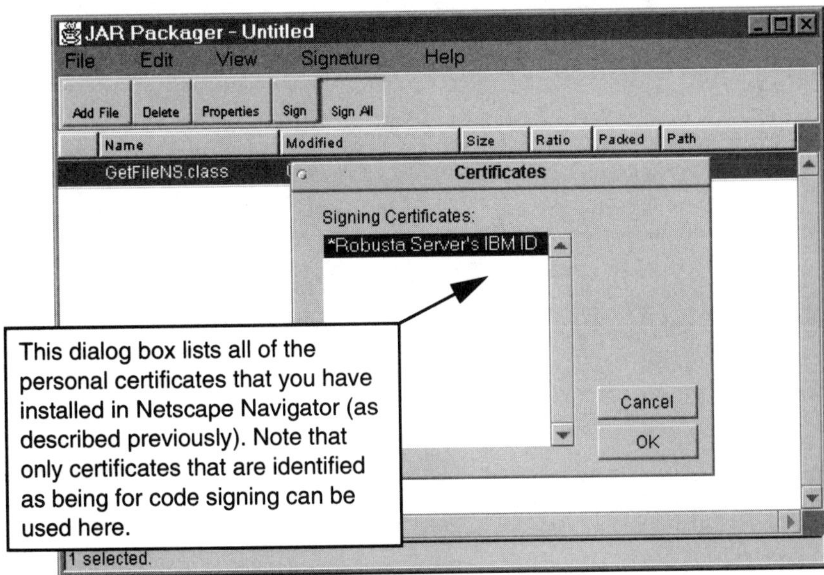

Figure 31. Signing the Files in a JAR

Now we can save the signed JAR file and quit the JAR Packager. If we look at the file with the `jar` command we see the expected structure of manifest, signer and signature files:

```
D:\work\ns_signed_jar>jar -tvf nsjam.jar
   249 Tue Sep 16 20:08:12 GMT+01:00 1997 META-INF/MANIFEST.MF
   250 Tue Sep 16 20:08:14 GMT+01:00 1997 META-INF/robusta.SF
  1518 Tue Sep 16 20:08:26 GMT+01:00 1997 META-INF/robusta.RSA
  3008 Tue Sep 16 20:08:26 GMT+01:00 1997 GetFileNS.class
```

To use the JAR, we must place it on the Web server and reference it in an <APPLET> tag as we did in the javakey/jar example. When we load the page in a Netscape browser, each of the enablePrivilege() method calls causes a dialog box to pop up on the user's screen, as shown in Figure 32.

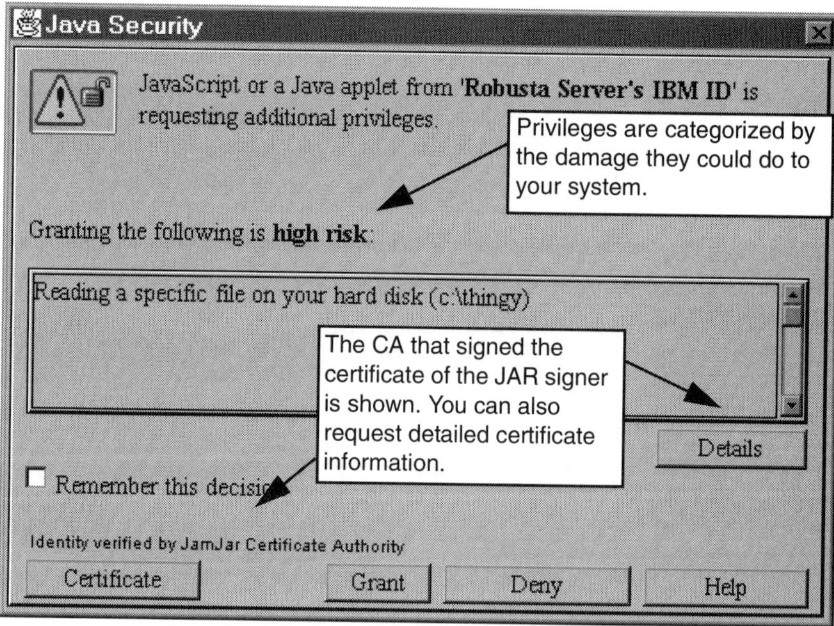

Figure 32. Applet Requests a Privilege

Figure 33 shows the applet running successfully, after we gave it the two permissions it needed.

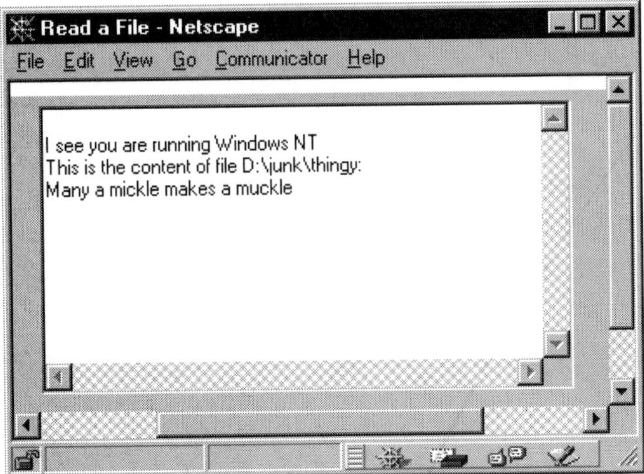

Figure 33. Signed Applet Running in Netscape

You can also review the permissions that you have given a particular signer, as shown in Figure 34 on page 140. Note that under this scheme there is no way to predefine permissions in this dialog; they only appear when a signed applet (or JavaScript script) requests privileges.

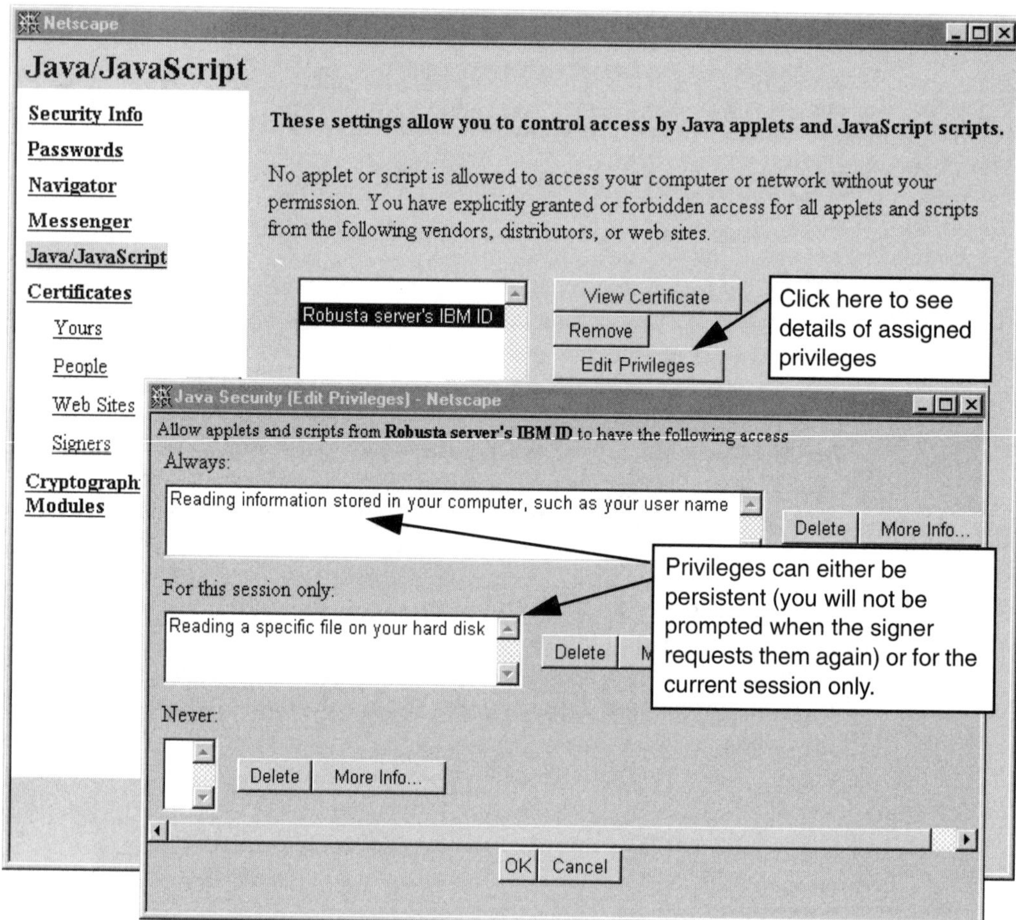

Figure 34. Displaying Privileges Given to a Signer

9.5 Microsoft and Signed Applets

At the time of writing, Sun Microsystems is locked in litigation with Microsoft over the way they have implemented Java in Internet Explorer 4.0. Part of that quarrel relates to the approach to signed applets. We will not discuss the rights and wrongs of that suit, but simply describe the way that Microsoft Internet Explorer works.

Externally, the most distinctive thing about the Microsoft approach is that it uses *Cabinets* (files with extension .cab, we will call them CABs for brevity) to contain the applets and other data, instead of JARs. This is not to say that Internet Explorer will not handle JAR archives, but it does not deal with signed JARs in any special way. CABs are also used for packaging the installation images of other Microsoft software. And, just as Netscape are using signed JARs to deliver many types of Web content, CABs are used by Microsoft to install ActiveX controls and other platform-specific code.

The Internet Explorer security model is built around *Security Zones*. These are groupings of applet sources, based on URLs. By default four zones are defined:

Intranet Web sites that are within the local, secure, network or are only accessed via secure (SSL) connections. Sites in this category may be defined by URL or by other attribute, for example, sites that are not reached through a proxy server.

Trusted sites A list of sites that are trustworthy, but which don't quite give the same level of reassurance that the intranet sites do.

Internet The great unwashed horde of Web sites.

Restricted sites Sites that you have reason to believe are actually dangerous.

Each of these zones has a *security level* associated with it of low, medium, high or custom. These apply for all sorts of Web elements, such as ActiveX controls, cookies, and user IDs as well as Java. The first three are related to a very specific set of permissions. The high security level is equivalent to the sandbox restrictions, the medium level adds the ability for an applet to use a scratchpad directory on the browser disk for storing and retrieving persistent data. The low level allows an applet unrestricted access. The custom level allows you (or an administrator) to set specific controls for different types of Web content.

Of course, a protection scheme based solely on URLs and IP addresses would be very risky. To be effective, the security model requires Java code to be delivered in signed CABs. Functionally, a signed CAB is like a signed JAR with one, important, exception: in addition to identifying the originator of the code, the signature on a CAB *also defines the permissions that the code is requesting*.

The best way to understand this is to illustrate it with an example.

9.5.1 Two Signed CAB Examples

Here are two examples of signed cabinets:

1. A simple example that uses the base signature function
2. A more complex example that uses the scratchpad facility of the Internet Explorer browser.

9.5.1.1 Simple Signed CAB Example

For the first example we create an applet that attempts to read a file on the browser disk. It uses basic Java I/O stream classes and will therefore normally fail with a security exception. There are three steps to placing this into a signed CAB.

Step 1: Create a Signing Certificate

The Microsoft Software Development Kit (SDK) for Java 2.0 provides a command-line tool, `makecert`, for generating a software developer certificate:

```
makecert -sk jamjarkey -n "CN=JamJar Software Co" JamJar.cert
```

This command generates a key pair called "jamjarkey" and places it in the Windows registry under HKEY_Current_User/Cryptography. It also creates a certificate request file, using the public key and the distinguished name information from the command.

Normally, the next step would be to send this to a CA for authentication and signing (Internet Explorer defines just one root CA, the Microsoft Authenticode Root CA, for software signing, but there is a technique to update the list, using ActiveX controls). However, in our case we are only signing the applet for test purposes, so we can use another tool from the SDK, `cert2spc`, to convert the certificate file into a valid certificate:

```
cert2spc JamJar.cert JamJar.cert
```

Step 2: Creating and Signing the CAB

Cabinet files are potentially much more complex than JARs, but for our purposes we can create a simple one using the `cabarc` tool:

```
cabarc N jamjar.cab GetFileMS.class
```

This creates a CAB file called jamjar.cab with just one file, our applet, in it. To sign this as a Java archive we use the `signcode` tool, again from SDK for Java. At this point we must decide what level of security the applet will ask for – low, medium or high. The rule is that if we ask for a lower level of security than the browser is configured to give us, the user will receive a prompt asking if the action should be allowed. So if we ask for a level of "medium" and the browser has the default configuration, the user will be prompted when our applet comes from an internet URL, but not when it comes from the intranet.

The command to perform the signature is:

```
signcode -j JavaSign.dll -jp medium -spc jamjar.cert -k jamjarkey
jamjar.cab
```

Step 3: Using the CAB in a Web Page

The format for coding an APPLET tag using a CAB archive is different from the JAR version. This is the tag for our example:

```
<APPLET CODE=GetFileMS.class  WIDTH=350 HEIGHT=200>
<PARAM NAME="cabbase" VALUE="jamjar.cab">
<PARAM NAME=FileToTry VALUE="C:\Temp\thingy">
</APPLET>
```

Now we can try the applet. When we first select the URL from Internet Explorer the popup dialog in Figure 36 on page 144 appears. The security level we requested matches the level of the zone, so why does this happen? The reason is that Internet Explorer is warning us that the JamJar Software Co may not be trustworthy, because it does not own a valid software developer's certificate. Throwing caution to the winds we click on **Yes** and the applet runs as intended (Figure 35).

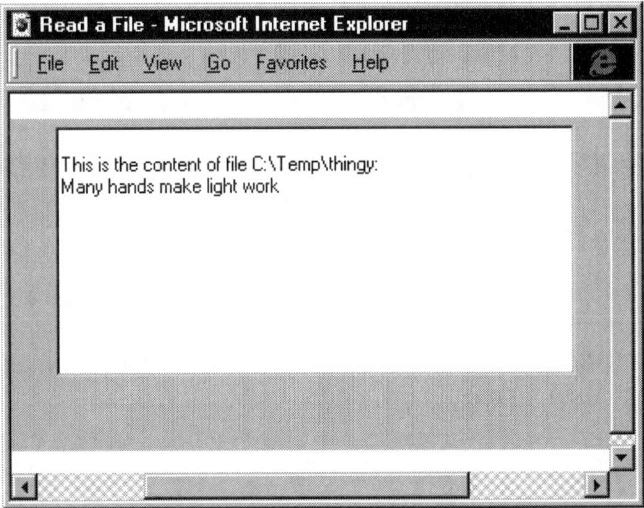

Figure 35. Our Signed Applet Can Read a File

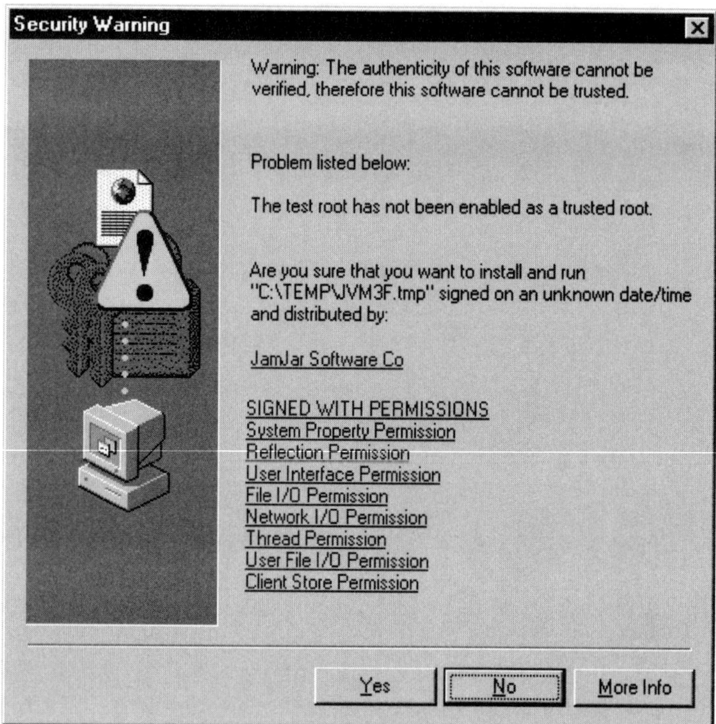

Figure 36. Warning from Internet Explorer

9.5.1.2 A More Complex Signed CAB Example

Not content with creating a method for delivering signed applets and requesting permissions, Microsoft has also produced classes that allow an applet to store and recover data from a limited disk cache on the browser. The rationale behind this is that for many developers the really irksome restriction imposed by the sandbox is the inability to store local configuration and state information.

The data caching function is in a class package called com.ms.io.clientstorage. The code snippet in Figure 37 is an example from an applet that uses the package to write information into a file and then reads it.

```
public void run() {
    String line ;
    ClientStore harrods ;

    try {
     harrods = ClientStorageManager.getStore() ;
        PrintWriter pw = new PrintWriter(harrods.openWritable("preserve.log",
ClientStore.OPEN_FL_APPEND)) ;
     pw.println("JamJar was here! " + new Date().toString()) ;
     pw.close() ;
    }
    catch (IOException e) { yikes(e, "Could not create or upda

    try {
        harrods = ClientStorageManager.getStore() ;
     BufferedReader br = new BufferedReader(new
InputStreamReader(harrods.openReadable("preserve.log"))) ;
     ta.appendText("This is the contents of client store file preserve.log:\n") ;
        while ((line = br.readLine()) != null) {
         ta.appendText(line + "\n");
        }
     br.close() ;
    }
    catch (IOException e) { yikes(e, "Could not read ou
}

public void yikes( Exception e, String msg) {
    ta.appendText(msg + ": " + e.toString()) ;
    System.exit(1) ;
}
```

First get access to the client store.

Open a "file" in the client store and update it.

The store is persistent, so we can read it later, but the maximum size of the store allocated to a given code signer is fixed, so the applet cannot fill the hard disk.

Figure 37. Section of Applet Using Client Storage Classes

We could place this applet in a signed CAB in the same way as the last example. However, when that applet loaded it told the user that we wanted a lot of permissions that, in fact, we did not (see Figure 36 on page 144). This is because we specified a security level of "medium" in the `signcode` command. It would be friendlier if we could just ask for the things we really need.

The way to do this is to create an .INI file specifying the requested permissions and then feed it to `signcode`. Figure 38 shows the file we used.

```
[com.ms.security.permissions.ClientStoragePermission]
; Limit is in bytes
Limit=100000
RoamingFiles=true
GlobalExempt=true
;
; ThreadPermission
;
[com.ms.security.permissions.ThreadPermission]
AllThreadGroups=true
AllThreads=true
```

Figure 38. JamJar.ini Requests Permission for Client Storage and Threads

The thread permissions are needed to run a multi-threaded applet.

The results of running this applet from a signed CAB are shown below.

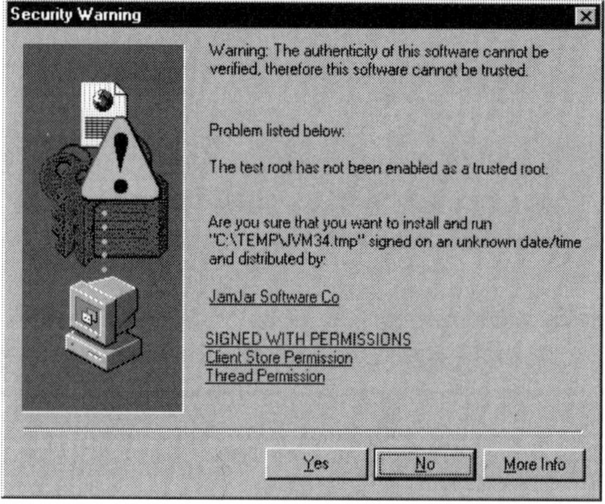

Figure 39. This Time the Warning Is More Reasonable

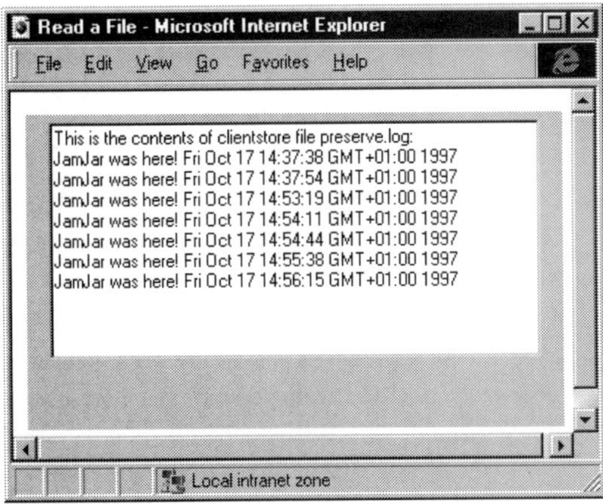

Figure 40. The Applet Keeps Persistent Data on the Browser Disk

9.6 Future Developments

In this chapter we have seen examples of four different approaches to the use of digital signatures for authenticating applet code and relaxing the constraints of the sandbox. The first, using the basic JDK 1.1 tools, is the first, unsophisticated foray into this area, but JDK 1.2 promises to fill in the missing function and set a standard for applet signing. The Netscape and Microsoft approaches are, as you would expect, strongly browser-centric. They both seek to reduce the impact of cryptography on the end user, not only for Java but also for other active Web content.

Table 8 summarizes the differences between the approaches.

Table 8. Comparison of JavaSoft, Netscape and Microsoft Signed Applet Support

Function	JDK	Netscape	Microsoft
Delivery mechanism	Signed JARs	Signed JARs	Signed CABs
Signing	Command-line tools shipped with JDK	Downloadable toolkit, both command-line and GUI versions	Downloadable toolkit, command-line tools.

Function	JDK	Netscape	Microsoft
Certificate handling	Facilities for self-signed root certificate. JDK 1.2 to provide more robust solution.	Uses the standard key and certificate management capabilities of Netscape Communicator. Well documented mechanism for installing trusted roots and personal keys.	Uses command-line tools for signer key creation and certificate requests. Standard key and certificate management capabilities of Internet Explorer for client side. Mechanism for updating trusted roots not openly documented.
Request for privileges	By exception. Applet attempts privileged action and an exception is thrown if it is not permitted.	Programmer defines the privileges required by calling PrivilegeManager methods.	Code signer defines the privileges required as part of CAB signature.
Configuration of permissions granted	Browser configuration file maps code origin (URL plus signer) to privileges.	User prompted the first time privileges are requested. Granted permissions can be perpetual or per session.	Basic security zone (low, medium, high) preset by user. More complex permission scheme can be defined by administrator.

Clearly, there are some basic incompatibilities between the different mechanisms. This is not to say that the development of competing extensions to the security framework is a bad thing; just that there should be a base level of function at which they should all interoperate.

It may be that by the time you read this book, the differences described above will have been resolved by the vendors and a common base will have emerged. We hope so. One thing that *is* clear from the discussion is that any solution cannot simply concentrate on the mechanics of code-signing and requests for privileges. The problems of the end user are equally important. Solutions must answer questions like: how to tell the user, in a clear way, the permissions an applet requires, and how to install and maintain certificates for signers and CAs.

Part 3. Beyond the Island of Java: Surfing into the Unknown

Chapter 10. Application Architectures

> *""The old world of architecture was simply self-expression. We have the task of making man a success."*
>
> R. Buckminster Fuller

The first two parts of this book have described the security issues in running Java programs on a single workstation, usually your PC. But that is only one application area for Java. Java can also be used on a Web server, or any other networked server, in a full-scale client/server approach. In the introduction we stated that security must be *holistic*, as attackers will concentrate on the weakest links. This applies even more forcefully when many computer systems are connected through a network, as there are more possible points to attack.

This chapter describes a number of different architectural approaches, illustrated with real examples that are in use today. We consider the security implications of these approaches.

Firewalls are often touted as a defense against network attacks. Chapter 11, "Firewalls: In and Out of the Net" on page 169 describes how firewalls work, and what the implications are, to both simple users of Web browsers and to Java application designers.

Cryptography is another valuable tool to provide integrity, confidentiality and authentication between distributed systems. We conclude by examining uses of cryptography to provide security to real-world applications.

10.1 Browser Add-on Applets

Perhaps the simplest use of a Java application is the browser add-on applet, to extend the facilities provided by a Web browser. This may be to enhance the user interface, by adding extra interactivity such as context-sensitive help or local search functions. Or it may be to handle additional data types such as compressed astronomical images or packed database records. These examples all depend directly upon the Java security architecture already described, where the security manager and sandbox prevent undesirable access. And because they read data only from the server, if at all, there are no wider security issues.

10.2 Networked Architectures

The next level of complexity is seen in network-aware applets, which perform more network operations than simply reading data. Terminal emulators fall into this category. These applets provide the functions of a "dumb terminal" or VDU (Visual Display Unit), connected via a LAN to a host system, where the applications are run. An example is IBM's Host On Demand, which emulates a 3270 mainframe display session, communicating with a mainframe over TCP/IP (see Figure 41).

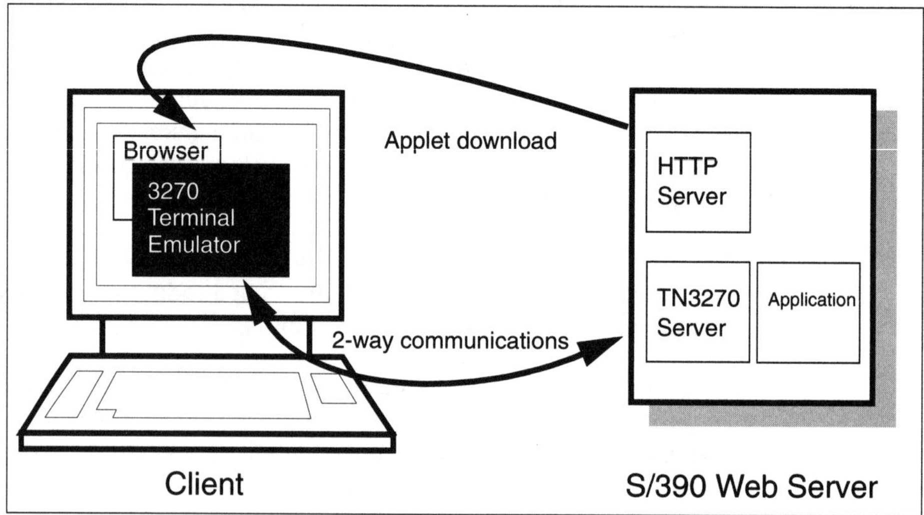

Figure 41. Host On Demand

When run as an applet, such programs are subject to the restrictions on the Java security manager; in particular, they may only open a network connection back to the system from which they were downloaded. However, terminal emulation programs usually wish to communicate with many different host systems, not just one. If the host is a large mainframe, crucial to business, its owners may be reluctant to install the TCP/IP software, preferring to remain with SNA (System Network Architecture) LANs. And even on other host systems, it might not be desirable to install, configure, run and maintain a Web server just to download the JAVA emulator applet, and this approach would still restrict access to that single host.

10.2.1 Two-Tier Architecture

One possibility would be to run the Java emulator as a stand-alone application, so relaxing the restrictions on which hosts the emulator may connect to. This is the classic "two-tier client/server" application architecture. The security issues are then very similar to running any other executable program, namely that it is wise to use trusted sources of supply only. Java has some safety and security advantages over other binary programs like .EXE files, and digitally-signed applets can provide a cryptographic guarantee that the code author is who they say they are. It would be possible to create a Java security manager that restricts the functions that the application is allowed to use, but this is not a solution of the non-programming user.

10.2.2 Three-Tier Architecture

The easiest solution is to run gateway software on the Web server which holds the Java applet. The applet will communicate over TCP/IP with the gateway software, which can then pass through the messages to the ultimate destination. In the case of 3270 terminal emulation, IBM's Communications Server (running on several operating systems) will provide the TCP/IP connection to the Java emulator, and can connect to hosts over both TCP/IP and SNA. This is then a "three-tier client/server" application.

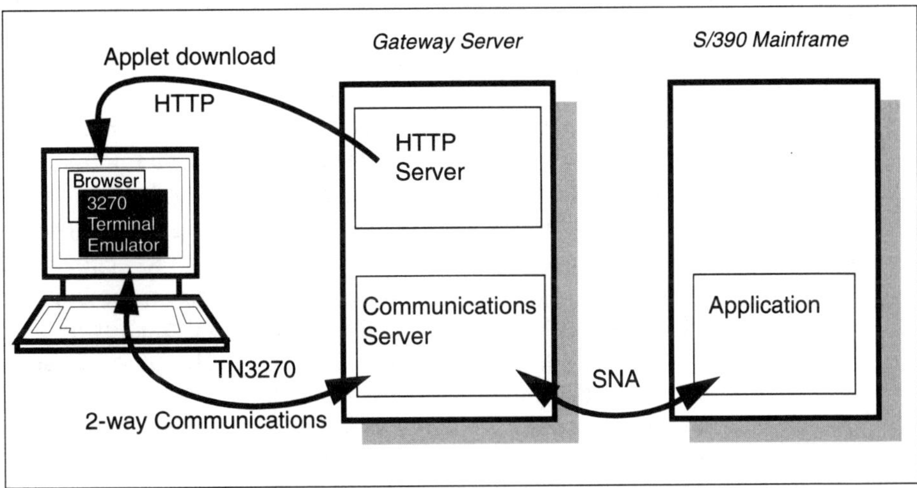

Figure 42. Three-Tier Example

Another approach is to use Web server Common Gateway Interface (CGI) programs to provide the middle tier. The IBM CICS Internet Gateway takes this approach. To the application server it emulates the functions of a 3270 terminal, but downstream it generates HTML code which is displayed in the Web browser window.

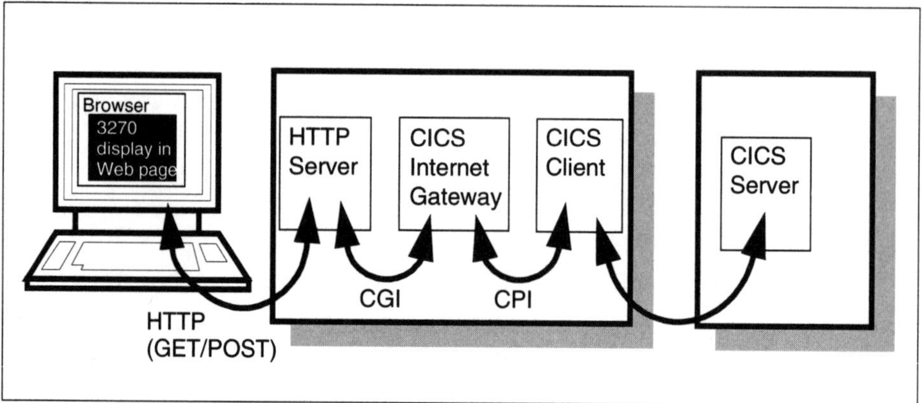

Figure 43. CICS Internet Gateway Example

This avoids using Java altogether in the client. It doesn't provide as much flexibility, as the display is restricted to what can be done in HTML. But it may be a simpler solution to the problem. Just because you happen to have a Java-shaped hammer doesn't mean that all solutions must be Java-shaped nails!

The gateway server approach can also be used to provide extended facilities to Java applets. The IBM CICS Gateway for Java is a good example of this; it allows a Java applet to access transaction processing capabilities of CICS servers running on a variety of server platforms. This provides a class library package to access CICS functions. The class library itself does not perform the bulk of the functions; instead, it transmits the request to the gateway server, and returns the server's response to the applet. The gateway server is a small program that receives the requests and calls the real CICS client library, which communicates with the CICS system itself. It would be common to run the CICS transaction processing engine on its own system, separate from the Web server (see Figure 44).

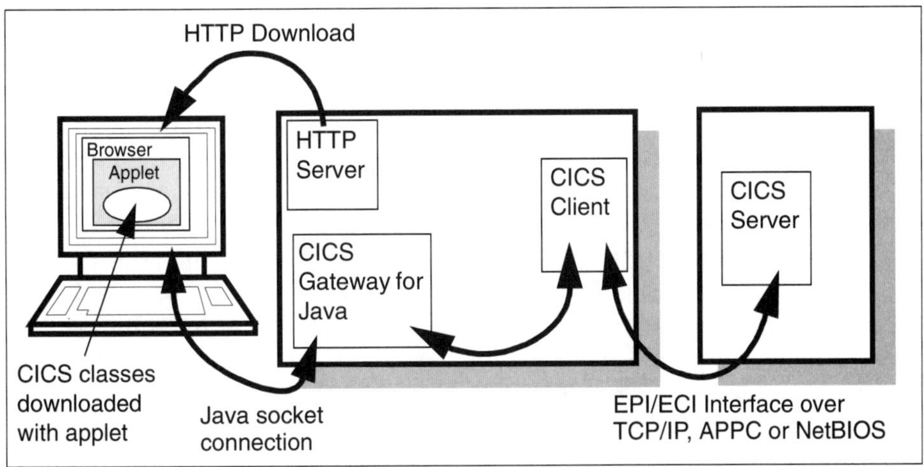

Figure 44. CICS Gateway for Java Example

The security analysis for this type of system is more complex. We wish to ensure the security of the gateway system as well as the systems with which it connects, especially if the server is on the public Internet, where any malicious hacker may attempt to access it. Intranet systems should already have some defenses in place to restrict access to company personnel, but security is still of concern, especially where sensitive data is at risk.

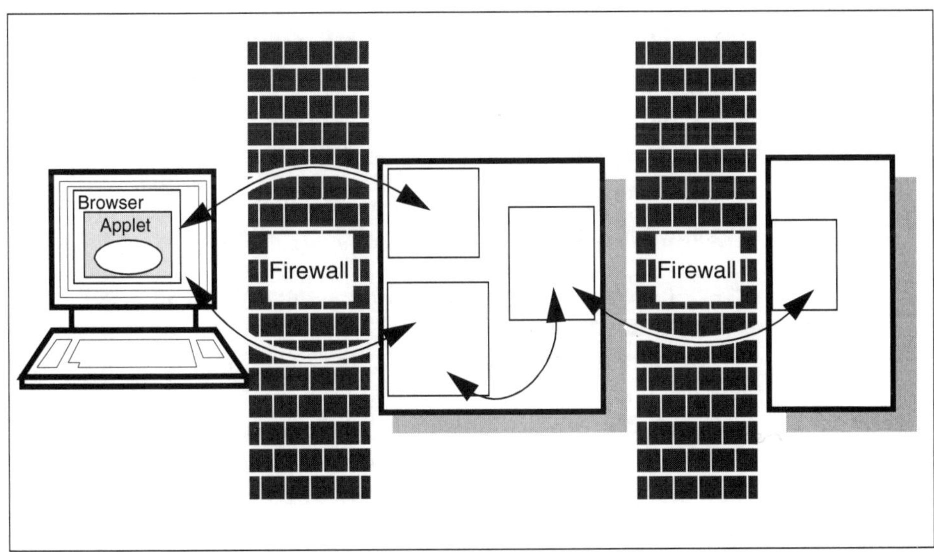

Figure 45. Adding Firewalls to the Mix

The normal approach is to provide a number of barriers which must be overcome before data access is granted. Often the first barrier is the company firewall system (see Chapter 11, "Firewalls: In and Out of the Net" on page 169 for more on firewalls). Firewalls can check that requests are coming from, and going to, apparently valid addresses; some firewalls will check the data content of selected protocols, but there are limits to what can be checked. There have been several embarrassingly public demonstrations of Web servers whose content has been replaced by derogatory pages, despite firewalls being in place. Often these hacks have succeeded because valid HTTP URL requests to the Web server allowed software to be run on the server which had an accidental "security hole" in it, such as allowing any data file to be read or written, or even executing arbitrary binary code supplied as part of the URL.

So it is necessary to secure the Web server against as many possible hazards as possible, and also to try to ensure that when (not if!) it is compromised, the attacker still does not have access to critical data.

Hardening Web servers against attack has been the subject of several books, such as *Practical Unix and Internet Security* by Simson Garfinkel and Gene Spafford, so only a brief checklist will be given here:

1. Disable all network services that do not need to be present; if possible only allow HTTP and the gateway protocol.
2. Check the Web server configuration files, to only allow access to the required set of pages.
3. Delete any cgi-bin and other executable programs that are not required; if they are not present, they cannot be run!
4. Restrict the privileges of the Web server program, if possible. UNIX allows it to be run as a normal user, with few access rights.

These guidelines also apply to *any* gateway software being run. Try to ensure it does not provide access to more facilities than needed. In particular, don't depend on the client to validate any requests, but assume that a hacker might have constructed a modified client which can generate *any* possible request. For example, for a 3270 gateway, don't assume that the client will only request connection to a limited set of hosts, but configure the gateway so that those are the only hosts that can be connected to, and that no other host names can be even made visible. For database access and transaction processing, make sure the gateway allows no more than the set of permitted requests.

10.2.3 Network Security

The classic three-tier architecture pictures can hide other attack routes. The diagram implies that there are separate connections between the client and the Web server/gateway, and the gateway and the end server. But maybe the real network is not configured that way. For simplicity or cost, there might be only a single network interface on the Web server, so that in reality the third tier server is on the same network, and can potentially be accessed directly from the firewall (Figure 46).

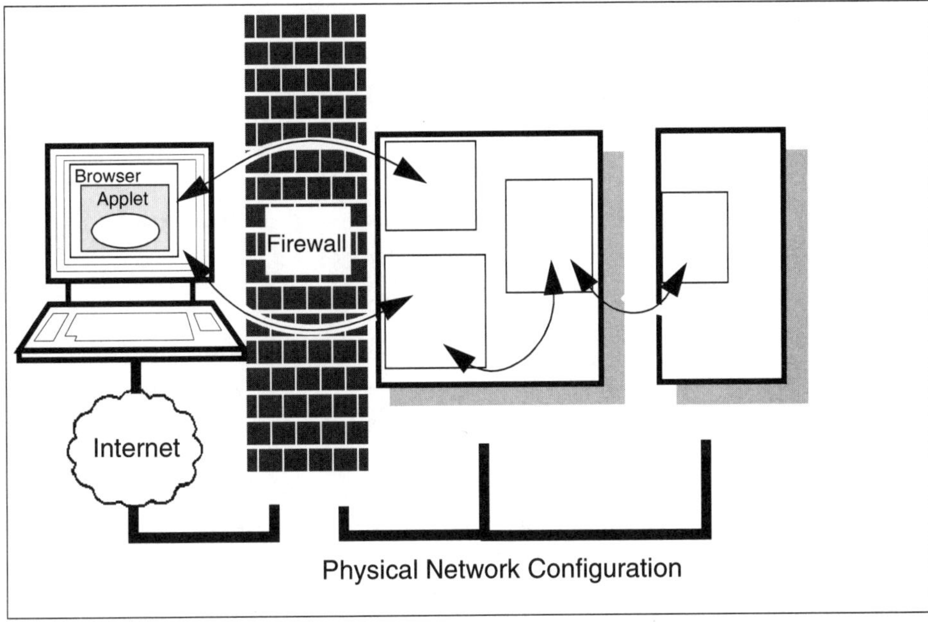

Figure 46. Web Server with One Network Interface

Now maybe the firewall *is* configured correctly, and will prevent direct access to the end server. But will this be true tomorrow, after additional services have been added? For very little extra cost, the networks can be physically separated by providing two network interfaces in the Web server.

(Make sure the cables are well labelled; we have heard of a firewall being bypassed when someone tripped over the cables, and plugged them back the wrong way round!)

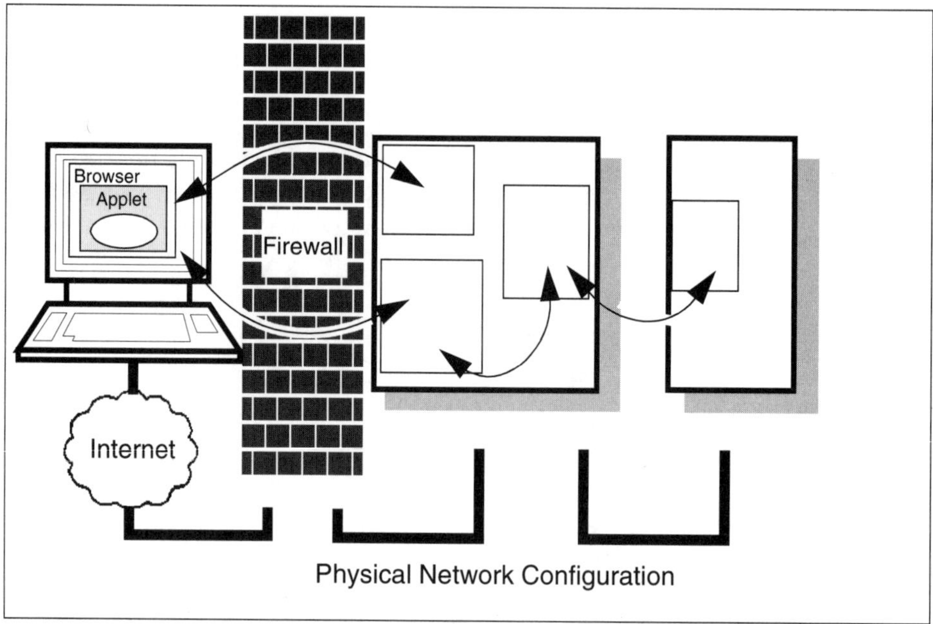

Figure 47. Separating the Third Tier

Or, a second firewall system can be used, which has the benefit that even if the Web server is compromised, the second firewall still restricts access to the rest of the network. It is more expensive to provide such a "De-militarized zone" (DMZ), though you may require such a configuration in any case, to provide safe Internet connection, in which case there is no extra cost. The cost of a second firewall is likely to be less than the value of the data it protects, so you need to do your own value calculations (this is the configuration shown in Figure 45 on page 155).

One additional security barrier to consider using is the type of network itself. You could link the gateway and end server using SNA protocols, or by a small custom-built program communicating over a dedicated serial link (Figure 48 on page 159). These effectively use the network connection as another firewall; if TCP/IP cannot travel over it, many possible hacking techniques are simply not possible. Don't forget, though, that if the Web server is totally compromised, the hacker has all your communications software at their disposal, if they can discover it, so you still should guard the third-tier server.

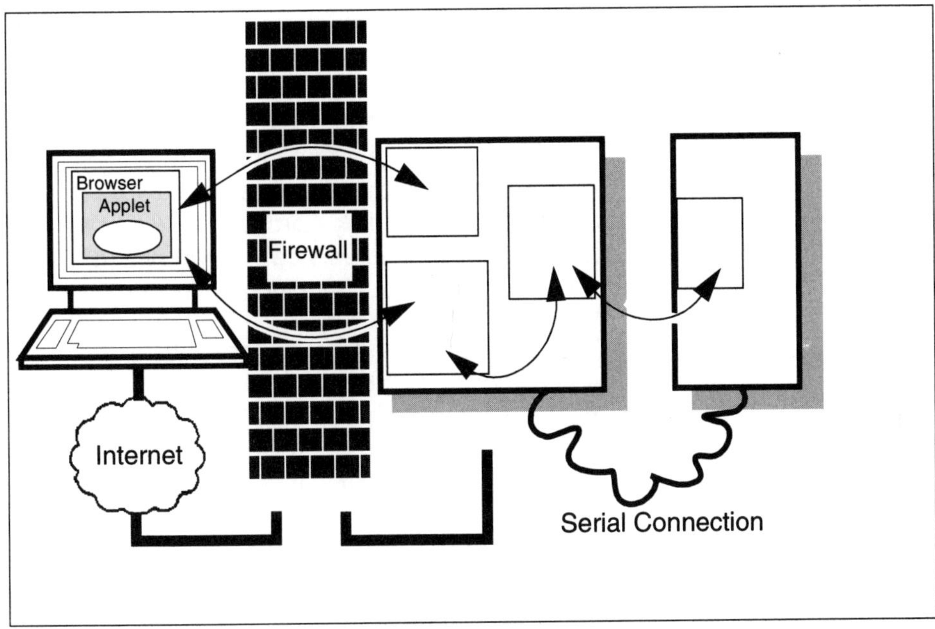

Figure 48. Protection Using Mixed Connection Protocols

10.3 Secure Clients and Network Computers

If you have great concern about what damage an applet may cause on your client, whether by malicious design or by programming accident, you may wish to consider the Network Computer approach. Many types of Network Computers (NCs) are now available on the market, with varying feature sets. Some are little different from ordinary Personal Computers, though they may have sealed cases to prevent expansion. Some may be intended for domestic use, and connect to a television set and a telephone line, for home Web browsing.

But the type we consider here are the diskless clients, such as the IBM Network Station. This is a small book-sized processor unit, without any local disk, which connects to a local area network (LAN). It has a display, keyboard and mouse. When switched on, it downloads its kernel software from a server on the LAN, and then downloads applications such as a Web browser and terminal emulator. These allow it to run applications on one or more remote servers. The IBM Network Station can also download and run Java programs locally, in fact Java is the only published API for running local programs.

In a secure environment, this has some advantages. There is no local disk storage at the Network Station, so there is little chance of permanent data corruption from malicious or misbehaving software. Although Java programs are not the only things that can run on the NS (it also supports terminal emulation, X-Windows and remote Windows access) there is no capability for integration between the different application types. This means that the Java security restrictions cannot be easily bypassed. All disk storage is held on the servers, allowing a fully managed backup service to be provided. Software updates are performed centrally, reducing administration workload.

For these reasons alone, Network Computers have a great potential in providing universal access to applications and data, with Java as a key technology. The main impetus behind the Network Computer is usually the potential for large cost savings. But in the appropriate application areas, the cost savings may be much less important than the other advantages listed above.

10.4 Server-Side Java

We've described the use of Java at the client in these distributed architectures, but what about using Java elsewhere? This can fulfill the goal of "write once, run anywhere" with a vengeance! It can greatly simplify the work of software developers, especially of distributed architectures. It might be possible to argue that the majority of client systems will be a PC running some flavor of Microsoft Windows, so that you can satisfy most people most of the time by only developing a Windows version of your code. But this is not true for servers; the majority of the world's crucial business data is kept on mainframe and UNIX servers. So if you develop the server side of your distributed application in Java, it will be capable of being run on almost any of these servers, whether they run MVS,VM, OS/390, Windows NT, OS/2, OS/400 or one of the many flavors of UNIX.

At the other end of the spectrum, the server-side Java might be running in an intelligent peripheral device, such as a printer, modem rack, photocopier or coffee vending machine. At the time of writing, these applications are just in the future, though Web browser interfaces for device configuration are becoming more common. But clearly there are immense opportunities to reduce development costs, providing there is agreement on common standards of Java classes. There are also clear security implications; imagine the effect of re-programming a rival company's vending machine if you managed to break the access codes!

In many ways, Java is an ideal environment for server applications. The multi-threaded environment is ideally suited for supporting simultaneous requests to a server. Even the standard classes are simplified, as many server programs are unlikely to need the java.awt windowing classes as well as several others, which is where most cross-platform problems have arisen to date (especially prior to JDK 1.1).

As an example, the gateway component of the CICS Java gateway could be written in Java, so it could be run on any Web server system without the need for extensive cross-platform porting and testing.

10.4.1 The Cost of Server-Side Java

But what is the cost of this portability? In the case of server-side Java, when Java is used as a program development language, the potential risk is reduced execution performance. This is not always a problem; the next section on Servlets shows how Java can sometimes *enhance* server performance.

Performance is more important for a server than a client, as the server needs to handle many simultaneous users. Just-in-time compilers may help somewhat, but the real solution is to use true Java compilers, at least until processors executing Java bytecode become commonplace. But doesn't this defeat the "write once run anywhere" approach? Not entirely, as vendors can still supply system-independent code, which gets compiled once during the installation process.

True compilers can take two different approaches. The first is to treat Java as just another programming language, and compile Java source into native object code for a given machine. This would imply that software would need to be supplied in source form, which would be less attractive to many developers, although it could be passed through an obfuscating program, to remove meaningful identifiers, etc.

The second approach, which is likely to be more promising, is to compile Java bytecode, rather than source code, into native object code. This allows the compiler to be run on all the wealth of Java bytecode that is available, not just that supplied by server developers. And since Java bytecode is closely related to source code under normal circumstances, some Java true compilers may provide both options and accept source or bytecode input.

10.4.2 Servlets

Java is not only used to develop stand-alone programs. In our Web-based world, many of the servers run an HTTP Web server. The traditional approach to add customized function to a Web server has been to write Common Gateway Interface (CGI) programs (often termed "cgi-bin" programs after the directory name where they are conventionally stored).

These CGI programs are stand-alone programs which are called by the HTTP server, when it receives requests for specific pages. Rather than return static HTML text, the HTTP server starts the CGI program, and passes it the user's request, together with many details about the server environment. The CGI program must handle the request, and return HTML text to the HTTP server, which in turn returns it to the user:

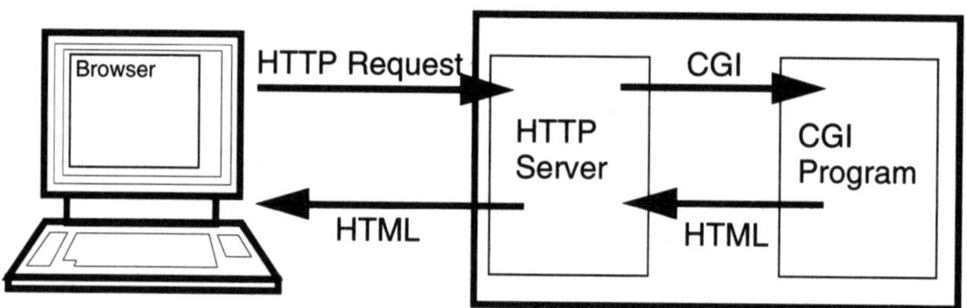

Starting execution of any program, not just a CGI program, can be a lengthy process. Memory needs to be allocated, the program code needs to be read from disk into memory, references to dynamic libraries need to be linked, standard input and output streams need to be created and connected, and finally the program needs to do the processing required.

In a very simple HTTP Web server, multi-threading may not be implemented, which means that no other HTTP requests could be served until the CGI program returns, possibly after many seconds. Most modern HTTP servers support multi-threading (on appropriate operating systems), so this is less of an issue. But there are still limits to the number of process threads that can be created, as the individual threads still need to wait for the CGI program to complete.

CGI programs are also the target of hackers; many of the successful attacks on Web servers have been through poorly tested CGI programs, which may fail to test the parameters passed to them, or may overflow input buffers when passed overlong data.

Other alternatives to CGI have been implemented, such as NSAPI from Netscape, MSAPI from Microsoft, or ICAPI from IBM. These permit native software routines to be directly called by the Web server, significantly reducing the startup overhead. But the add-on routines still need to be compiled for each platform, and the different programming interfaces may not be fully compatible, restricting the choice of Web server to a particular manufacturer (although ICAPI, for example, has been designed to include the NSAPI calls). Program testing is even more important, to prevent badly written software from corrupting the Web server itself.

Java can be employed to overcome these issues. A "servlet" is a small Java program called by the HTTP server. A JVM is started by the HTTP Web server, and when a request is received it is passed to the servlet object. The servlet must generate the HTML reply, and return it to the HTTP server.

Since the servlet is run from the server, there is no overhead in starting a new process, only that of creating a new Java thread. The built-in safety features of Java will prevent many types of attacks, such as buffer overruns, from taking place. And the Java servlet code is portable to other Web servers and systems. Performance of Java servlets is significantly greater than CGI programs, especially if the CGI programs are written in an interpreted language like Perl.

It is still necessary for servlets to perform some security checking; they need to check their input to ensure they cannot be tricked into returning more information than intended. As they are granted similar privileges to the HTTP server itself, it may be possible for a servlet to read from, or even write to, the HTTP server configuration or log files. Correct programming should prevent this. But deliberate corruption attacks which attempt to overwrite buffers or the program stack should not be possible, due to the built-in safety features of the Java language and the JVM.

10.5 Distributed Object Architectures - RMI

CGI uses a transaction model: the client issues a transaction request and then waits until the server returns the results. Distributed object architectures are a more elegant approach. Effectively, the "object space" that an applet or application is working with is extended to include objects on different systems. Client-side Java and server-side Java can be combined to create a full distributed architecture, where functions can be split between the client and server to optimize processing and network loads.

Apart from getting object-oriented purists excited, distributed object architectures have a number of advantages over more conventional transactional systems, including security advantages. For example, you can design systems in which mission-critical objects may be kept safe behind a firewall with access allowed only via method calls from clients. This is far safer than shipping data out of the organization to multiple clients who may simultaneously make changes.

Java JDK 1.1 has provided a tool kit to aid the creation of distributed architectures, the Remote Method Invocation (RMI). This extends the Java object model to the network, by allowing objects in one Java virtual machine to invoke methods seamlessly on objects in another, remote, virtual machine. The remote virtual machine can, in turn, invoke other remote objects.

With RMI, an object, B, residing on one machine (the server) may be manipulated by another object, A, on a remote machine (the client). Object B doesn't really exist on the client, rather an alternative object is used as a kind of "stunt-double." This stub- or proxy-object provides the same interface as the real object B, but under the covers it uses the RMI services to pass method requests over the network to the real object B. Object A therefore doesn't need to know whether object B is local or remote.

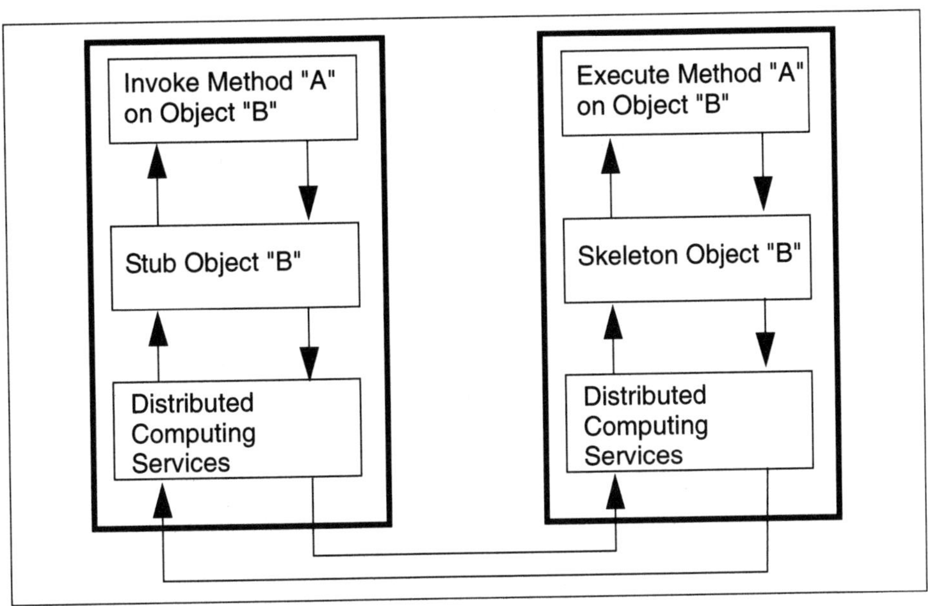

Figure 49. Invoking a Method with RMI

If another object, C, needs to be passed between the client and the server – for instance as a parameter for a method – RMI uses a technique called object serialization to "flatten" the object, turning it into a stream of bytes. These are sent to the RMI system on the remote machine, which rebuilds the object C and passes it into the method call. Return values from methods are handled in the same way.

A simple naming service, the RMI Registry, is provided to connect clients and servers together using a URL-style of names, such as rmi://host.port/name. A client asks for the remote objects, and the remote server returns the stub object to the client. Developers use the rmic compiler to generate the matching stub and skeleton classes for a remote object.

This means it becomes possible to write distributed applications, with little need to be aware of exactly where the software will be executed. A RemoteException may be thrown on error conditions, but apart from that, the program need not be aware that portions are executing remotely.

10.5.1 The Security of RMI

RMI appears to be a straightforward way of creating a distributed application. But there are a number of security issues:

- RMI has a simple approach to creating the connection between the client and server. Objects are serialized and transmitted over the network. They are not encrypted, so anyone on the network could read all the data being transferred.
- There is no authentication; a client just requests an object (stub), and the server supplies it. Subsequent communication is assumed to be from the same client. This negates one of the security advantages of distributed objects: the ability to hide the real object away and only allow client access through specific, well-defined methods. Key to this is that the clients are authenticated before being allowed to manipulate objects which is why the weak authentication services in RMI are dangerous.
- There is no access control to the objects.
- There are no security checks on the registry itself; it assumes any caller is allowed to make requests.
- Objects are not persistent; the references are only valid during the lifetime of the process which created the remote object.
- Stubs are assumed to be matched to skeletons; however, programs could be constructed to simulate the RMI network calls, while allowing any data to be placed in the requests.
- Network and server errors will generate exceptions, so applications must be prepared to handle these.
- There is no version control between stubs and skeletons; thus, it is possible that a client may use a down-level stub to access a more recent skeleton, breaking release-to-release binary compatibility.

The class loading mechanism also has to be extended to cater for RMI remote classes. When the RMIClassLoader is invoked, it attempts to load classes over the network. A security manager must be defined; otherwise, this would cause an exception. Programmers can write their own security manager, or can use the restrictive RMISecurityManager. This disables all functions except class definition and access. If used, it will also be invoked to subsequently load any local classes. If you require a different (more or less restrictive) security policy, you will need to create your own security manager instead.

If the client and server are connected through one or more firewalls, there are additional issues to be considered. These are covered in "Java Network Connections through the Firewall" on page 189.

Our conclusions are that you should only use RMI in pure intranet configurations, or for applications where it cannot usefully be attacked. An inter-company chat system may be a reasonable use of RMI, but designing remote objects to represent customer bank accounts would be asking for bankruptcy! Closely coupled internal systems might use RMI, if the appropriate access controls were put in place by network and firewall design. But the lack of authentication and access control in the raw RMI must limit the wider use in secure applications.

If you need to create a distributed secure application, you need to investigate alternatives to RMI. The CORBA (Common Object Request Broker Association) implementations available today provide heavier-weight remote execution methods, and other suppliers can provide alternatives to RMI. Plans are being made to extend JDK 1.2 to include some of these alternative remote execution systems.

Chapter 11. Firewalls: In and Out of the Net

"Moreover they that work in fine flax, and they that weave networks, shall be confounded."

Isaiah 19:9

In this chapter, we consider how Java security can be affected when firewall systems are used on the network.

11.1 What Is a Firewall?

By "firewall", we mean any computer system, network hardware or combination of them that links two or more networks, and enforces some access control policy between them. Thus one side of the network is protected from any dangers in the other part of the network, in an analogous way to the solid firewalls in buildings, which prevent a fire spreading from one part of the building to another.

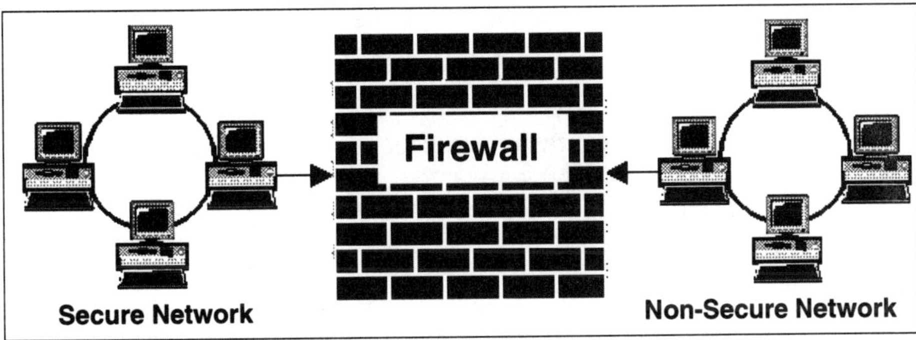

Figure 50. A Firewall

Until recent years, very few organizations thought seriously about the need for firewalls, despite the efforts of firewall vendors. Some well-publicized security breaches, when the content of several public web sites were vandalized, proved to be an ideal marketing opportunity. Almost any type of access control system was called a "firewall." The National Computer Security Association (NCSA) has subsequently created standard tests to enforce minimum standards for a firewall, but that has not stopped some vendors from using the term creatively.

To add to the complexity, sometimes a single hardware system is called a firewall, while other times a complex collection of multiple routers and servers implement the firewall function. But we only need to be concerned with the policies enforced by the firewall, and what the effect is on the data traffic.

11.2 What Does a Firewall Do?

Firewalls can have an effect on any type of network traffic, depending on their configuration. The areas we are especially concerned with are the loading of Java applets to a client from a server, and network accesses by Java applets to a server. Firewalls may be present at the client network, the server network, or both. In order to understand the implications, we shall need to understand the basic functions provided by a firewall.

If you have seen any literature on firewalls, you will be well aware that there are many buzzwords used by firewall specialists, to describe the different software techniques that can be used to create them. Current techniques include packet filtering, application gateways, proxy servers, dynamic filters, bastion hosts, demilitarized zones, and dual-homed gateways. Luckily, for the purpose of this book, we can ignore the details of the software technologies, and simply concentrate on what a firewall does with data packets flowing "through" it.

There are several other functions of firewalls which have no real affect on Java security; for example, logging, reporting and management functions will be required, and these may themselves be written in Java. As an example, the IBM Firewall has a graphical user interface using Java.

The basic security functions of any firewall are to examine data packets sent "through" the firewall, and to accept, reject or modify the packets according to the security policy requirements. Most of today's firewalls only work with TCP/IP data, so it is worth seeing what is inside a TCP/IP data packet, in order to understand the firewall's actions.

11.2.1 Inside a TCP/IP Packet

All network traffic exchange is performed by sending blocks of data between two connected systems. The blocks of data will be encapsulated within a data packet, by adding header fields to control what happens to the data block en route and when it reaches its final destination. Network architectures are constructed of layers of function, each built on the services of the layer beneath it. The most thorough layered architecture is the Open Systems Interconnection (OSI) model, whereas other architectures, such as TCP/IP use broader layer definitions. On the wire, these layers are translated into a series of headers prepended to the data being sent (see Figure 51).

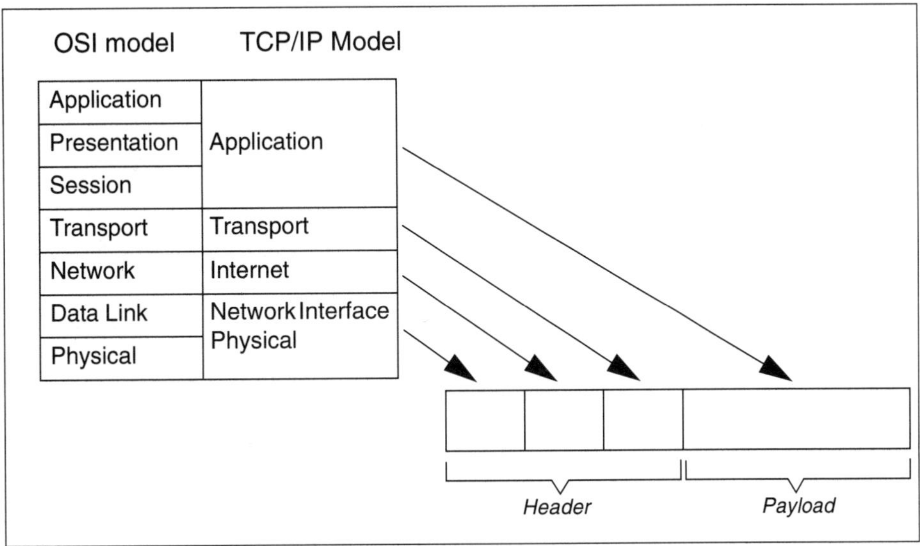

Figure 51. Mapping the Layered Network Model to Packet Headers

The first part of the header, the Data Link/Physical header, is determined by the type of network. Ethernet, token-ring, serial lines, FDDI, and so on, each have their own headers, containing synchronization, start-of-packet identifiers, access control, and physical (MAC) addresses as required by the network type. There may be fields to distinguish Internet Protocol (IP) packets from other types of packets, such as NetBIOS or SNA. We only need to consider IP packets here.

The next part of the header of IP packets is the standard Internet Protocol header, which specifies the originator (source) address and the intended recipient (destination) address, together with fields to control how the packet is forwarded through the Internet. There are two main types of IP headers: the common IPv4 standard, and the new IPv6 standard, which is intended to replace IPv4.

This is followed by the transport layer header, which controls what happens to the packet when it reaches its destination. Almost all the user-level protocols commonly referred to as "TCP/IP" use either a TCP (Transmission Control Protocol) or a UDP (User Datagram Protocol) header at the transport layer.

Finally, application protocol headers and data are contained in the payload portion of the packet, and are passed from the sending process to the receiving process.

Each of these packet headers contain a number of data fields, which may be examined by a firewall, and used to decide whether to accept or reject the data packet.

Each header has a number of data fields. For current purposes, the most important ones are:

Source IP address	a 32-bit address (IPv4) or a 128-bit address (IPv6)
Destination IP address	a 32-bit address (IPv4) or a 128-bit address (IPv6)
Source port number	a 16-bit value
Destination port number	a 16-bit value

The source and destination IP addresses identify the machines at each end of the connection, and are used by intermediate machines to route the packet through the network. Strictly speaking, an IP address identifies a physical or logical network interface on the machine, which allows a single machine to have several IP addresses.

The source and destination port numbers are used by the TCP/IP networking software at each end, to send the packets to the appropriate program running on the machines. Standard port numbers are defined for the common network services; for example, an FTP server expects to receive TCP requests addressed to port 21, and an HTTP Web server expects to receive TCP requests to port 80.

However, non-standard ports may be used. It is quite possible to put a Web server on port 21, and access it with an URL of http://server:21/. Because of this possibility, some firewall systems will examine the inside details of the protocol data, not just headers, to ensure that only valid data can flow through.

As an elementary security precaution, port numbers less than 1024 are "privileged" ports. On some systems, such as UNIX, programs are prevented from listening to these ports, unless they have the appropriate privileges. On less secure operating systems, a program can listen on any port, although it may require extra code to be written. HTTP Web servers, in particular, are often run on non-standard ports such as 8000 or 8080 to avoid using the privileged standard port 80.

The non-privileged ports of 1024 and above can be used by any program; when a connection is created, a free port number will be allocated to the program. For example, a Web browser opening a connection to a web server might be allocated port 1044 to communicate with server port 80. But what happens, you may ask, if a Web browser from another client also gets allocated port 1044? The two connections are distinguished by looking at all four values (source IP address, source port, destination IP address, destination port), as this group of values is guaranteed to be unique by the TCP standards.

11.2.2 How Can Programs Communicate through a Firewall?

Simple packet-filtering firewalls use the source and destination IP addresses and ports to determine whether packets may pass through the firewall. Packets going to a Web server on destination port 80, and the replies on source port 80, may be permitted, while packets to other port numbers might be rejected by the firewall. This may be allowed in one direction only and it may be further restricted by only allowing packets to and from a particular group of Web servers (see Figure 52).

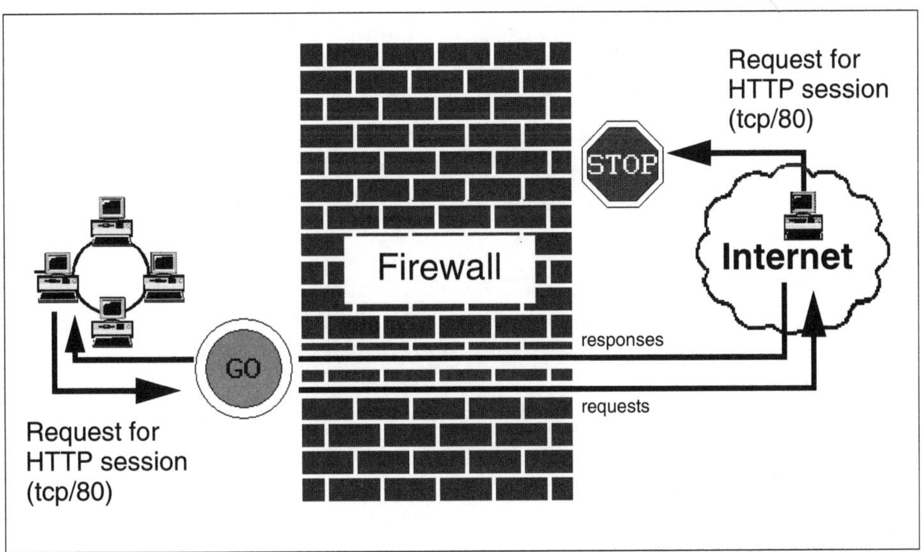

Figure 52. Asymmetric Firewall Behavior

There may be more than one firewall through which data needs to pass. Users in a corporate network will often have a firewall between them and the Internet, in order to protect the entire corporate network. And at the other end of the connection, the remote server will often have a firewall to protect it and its networks.

These firewalls may enforce different rules on what types of data are allowed to flow through, which can have consequences for Java (or any other) programs. It is not uncommon to find Java-enabled Web pages that work over a home Internet connection, simply fail to run on a corporate network.

There are two problem areas: can the Java program be downloaded from a remote server, and can it create the network connections that it requires?

The HTTP protocol is normally used for downloading. In order to understand the restrictions that firewalls put on HTTP, especially with regard to proxy servers and SOCKS servers (discussed in "Proxy Servers and SOCKS" on page 181), we describe this protocol in detail in the next section.

11.3 Detailed Example of TCP/IP Protocol

Let us consider the simple case of a browser requesting a Web page using HTTP. There are two steps to this: first the browser must translate a host name (for example, www.ibm.com) into its IP address (204.146.17.33 in this case). The normal way to do this in the Internet is to use the domain name service (DNS). The second step is when the browser sends the HTTP request and receives a page of HTML in response.

11.3.1 DNS Flow (UDP Example)

DNS uses the UDP protocol at the transport layer, sending application data to the Domain Name Service (udp/53) port of a nameserver. The packet header for UDP is shown in Figure 53)

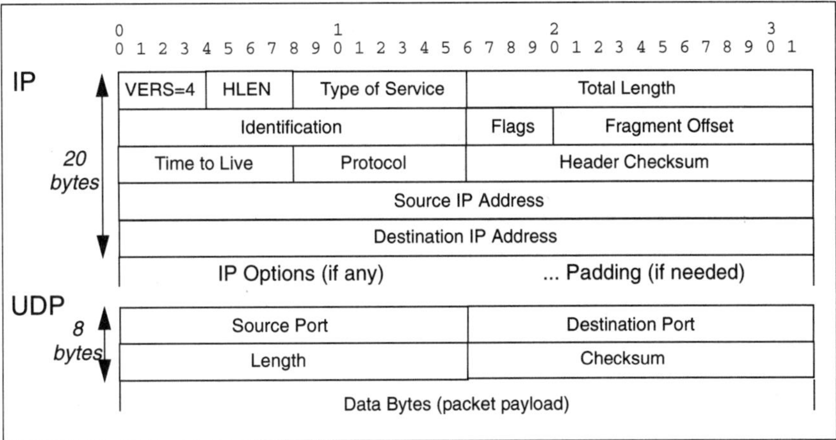

Figure 53. IP V4 and UDP Headers

If the newer IPv6 is used, the header is simpler, but with 128-bit long addresses, instead of 32-bit.

Now for the actual DNS request. It is a simple request and response sequence (see Figure 54 and Figure 55).

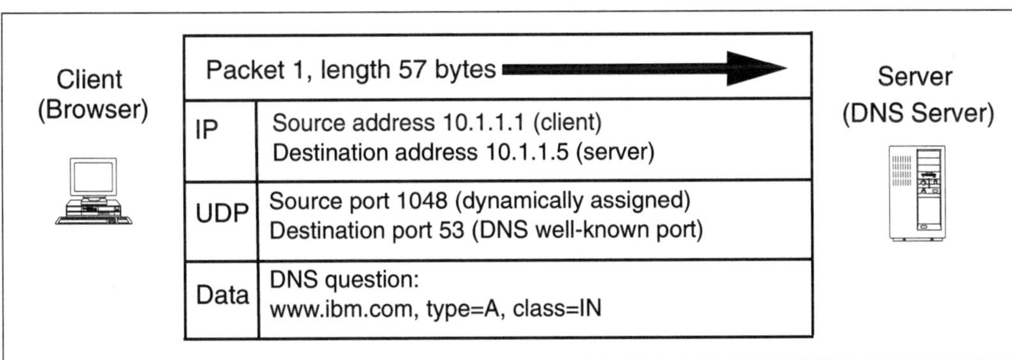

Figure 54. Client Requests Name Resolution

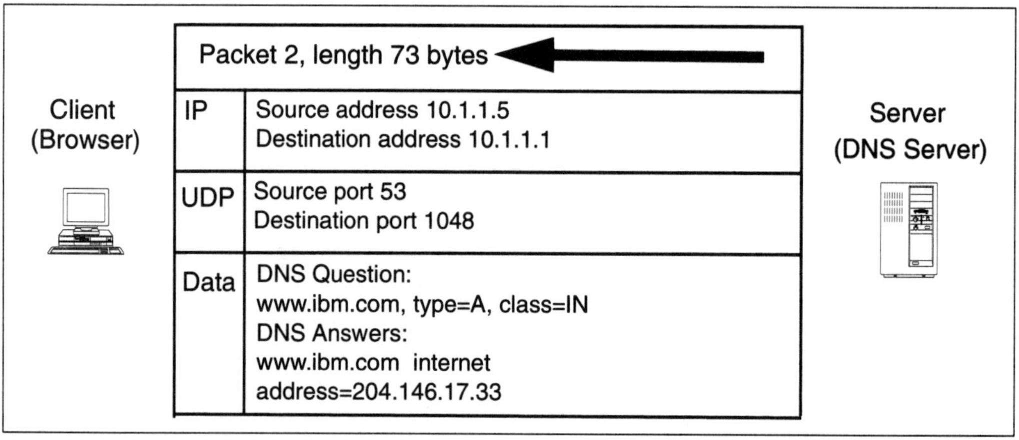

Figure 55. DNS Name Resolution Response

11.3.2 HTTP Flow (TCP Example)

Now the client can request the URL of http://www.ibm.com/example1.html, because it knows the real IP address of www.ibm.com (204.146.17.33). Requests such as this use TCP at the transport layer, to carry the HTTP application data. HTTP is a very simple protocol, where the client requests a particular item of data from the server, and the server returns the item, preceded by a short descriptive header.

TCP headers are similar to UDP, but have more control fields to provide a guaranteed[1] delivery service:

1. In this context, "guaranteed" means that the data will be delivered, or an error will be returned (eventually). With UDP, in comparison, data may be discarded without warning.

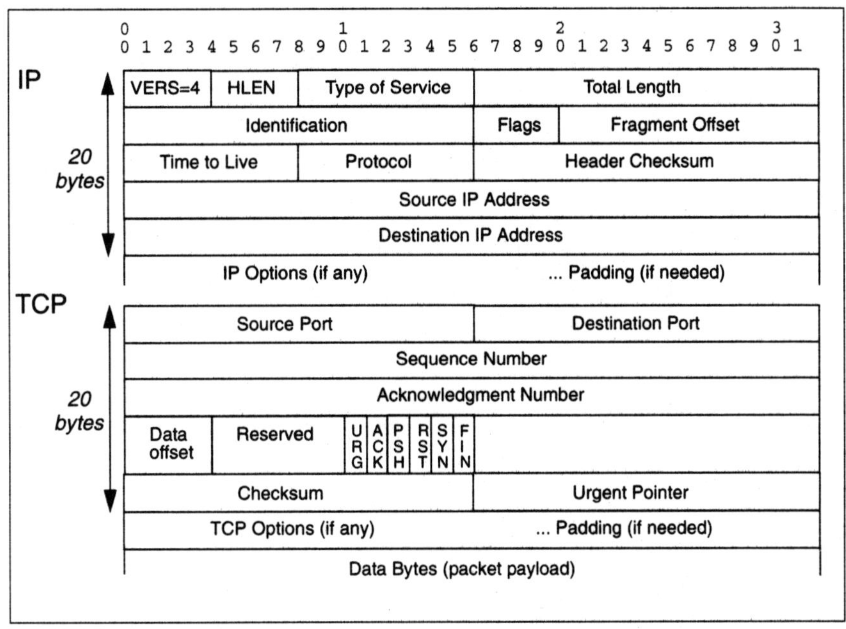

Figure 56. IP V4 and TCP Packet Headers

TCP using IPv6 is similar, with an IPv6 header followed by a TCP header.

The following data packets are sent:

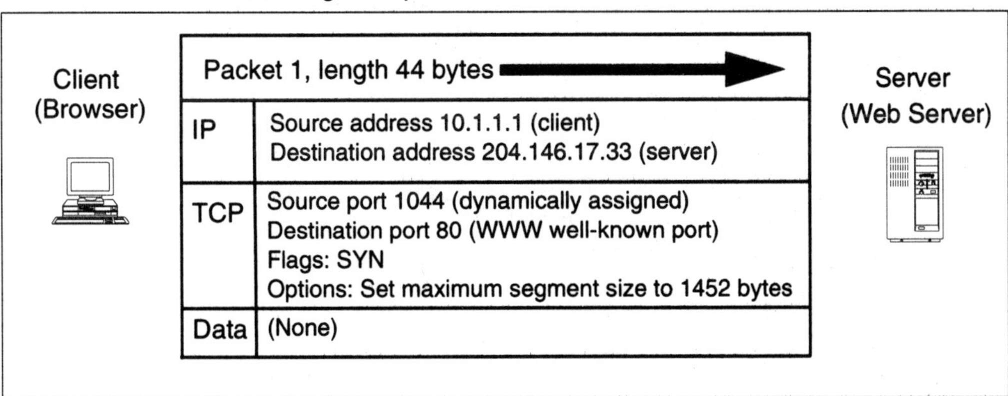

Figure 57. Web Page Request (1 of 4)

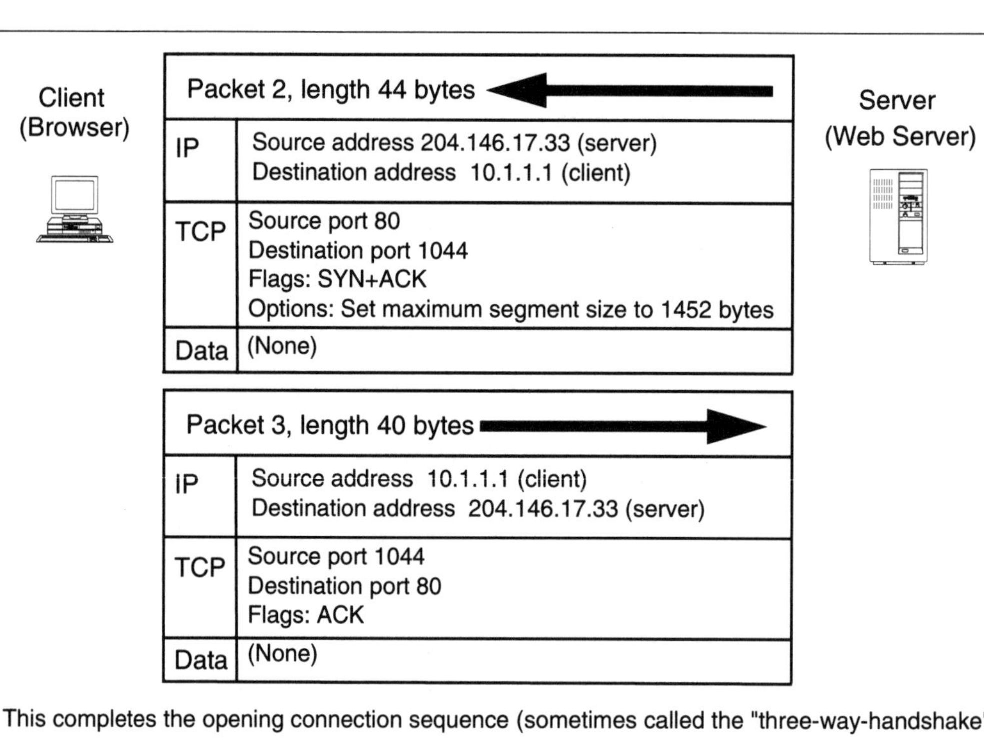

This completes the opening connection sequence (sometimes called the "three-way-handshake").

Packet 4, length 229 bytes	
IP	Source address 10.1.1.1 (client) Destination address 204.146.17.33 (server)
TCP	Source port 1044 Destination port 80 Flags: PUSH+ACK
Data	GET /example1.html HTTP/1.0 Connection: Keep-alive User-Agent: Mozilla/v3.01 (X11;I;AIX1) Host: www.ibm.com Accept: image/gif, image/x-xbitmap, image/jpeg, image/pipeg, */* <empty line>

Figure 58. Web Page Request (2 of 4)

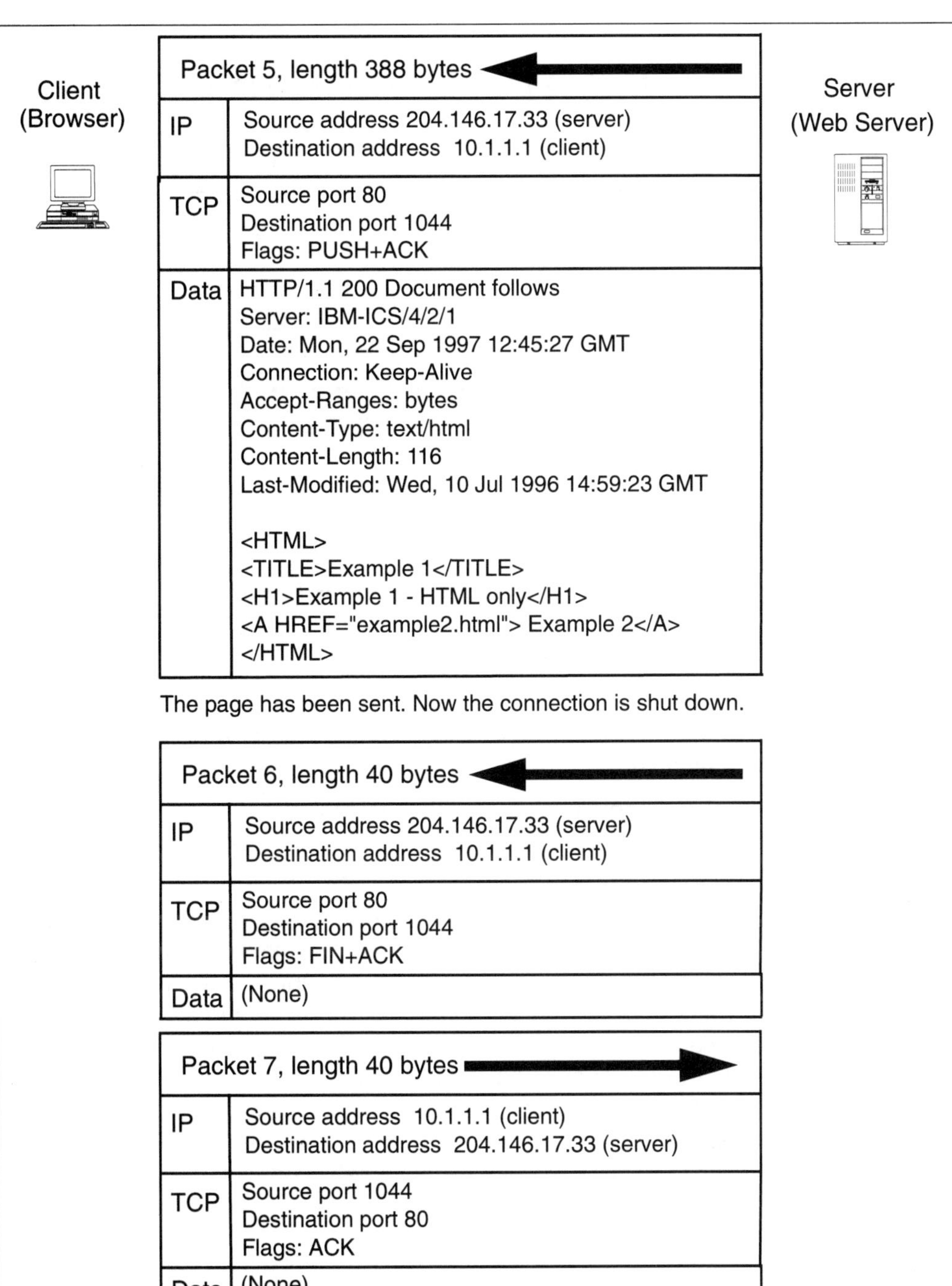

Client
(Browser)
Server
(Web Server)
Packet 5, length 388 bytes
IP
Source address 204.146.17.33 (server)
Destination address 10.1.1.1 (client)
TCP
Source port 80
Destination port 1044
Flags: PUSH+ACK
Data
HTTP/1.1 200 Document follows
Server: IBM-ICS/4/2/1
Date: Mon, 22 Sep 1997 12:45:27 GMT
Connection: Keep-Alive
Accept-Ranges: bytes
Content-Type: text/html
Content-Length: 116
Last-Modified: Wed, 10 Jul 1996 14:59:23 GMT
<HTML>
<TITLE>Example 1</TITLE>
<H1>Example 1 - HTML only</H1>
<A HREF="example2.html"> Example 2</A>
</HTML>
The page has been sent. Now the connection is shut down.
Packet 6, length 40 bytes
IP
Source address 204.146.17.33 (server)
Destination address 10.1.1.1 (client)
TCP
Source port 80
Destination port 1044
Flags: FIN+ACK
Data
(None)
Packet 7, length 40 bytes
IP
Source address 10.1.1.1 (client)
Destination address 204.146.17.33 (server)
TCP
Source port 1044
Destination port 80
Flags: ACK
Data
(None)

Figure 59. Web Page Request (3 of 4)

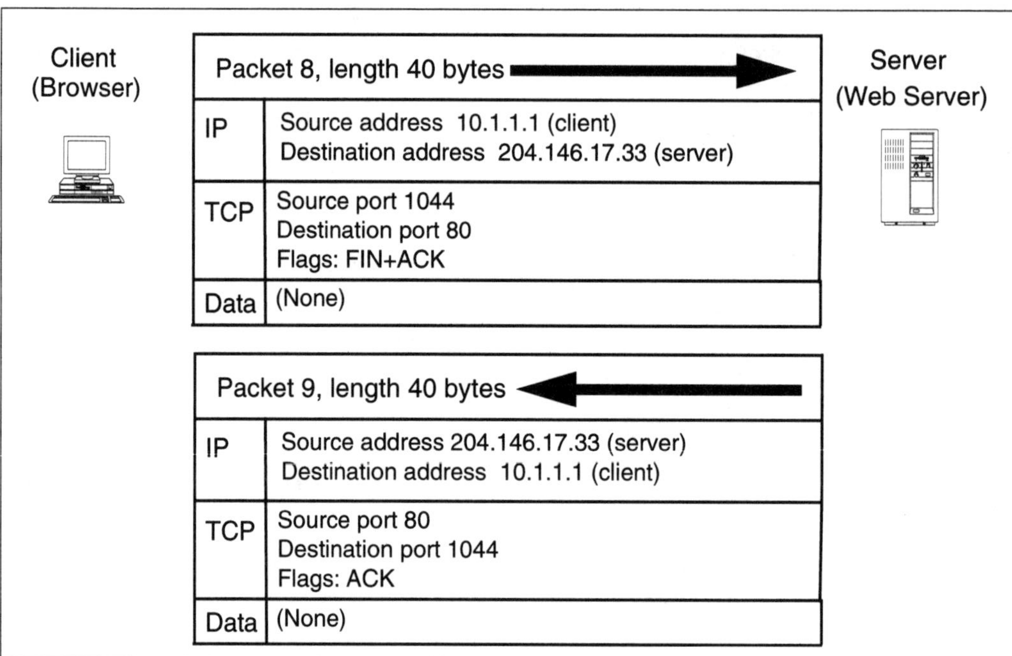

Figure 60. Web Page Request (4 of 4)

- Packets 1, 2 and 3 establish the TCP connection with a "three-way handshake."
- Packet 4 contains the HTTP request from the browser; you can see the GET request itself, together with other data being passed to the server.
- Packet 5 contains the reply from the server, with the page data preceded by page information. You can see this information using "view document source" and "view document info" from a Web browser. Larger replies would need to be sent in more than one packet, and the client would periodically send TCP acknowledgment packets back to the server. But only a single item of data is returned, so that the page data, images, applets and other components are returned separately. Using JAR files, several items can now be sent in a single TCP connection, which is more efficient.
- Packets 6 and 7 close the connection from the server end, and packets 8 and 9 close it from the client.

Although at first sight this seems quite complicated, on closer inspection it can be seen to be simply sending a request (in readable ASCII text) and receiving a reply, surrounded by packets to open and close the TCP connection.

11.4 Proxy Servers and SOCKS

Proxy Servers and SOCKS Gateways are two common approaches used to provide Internet access through corporate firewalls. The primary goal is to allow people within the company network the ability to access the world-wide Internet, but prevent people from outside from accessing the company internal networks.

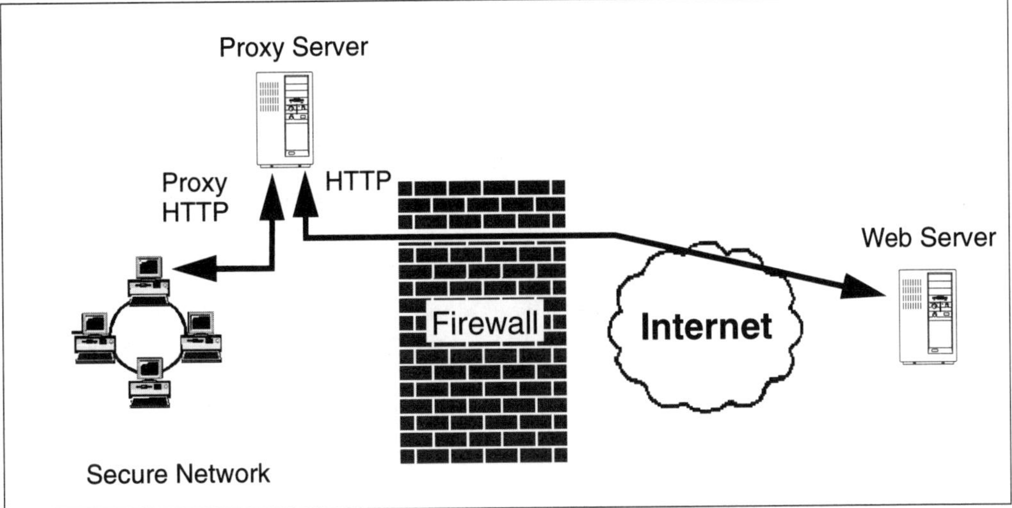

Figure 61. Where a Proxy Server Fits

11.4.1 Proxy Servers

A proxy server's function is to receive a request from a web browser, to perform that request (possibly after authorization checks), and return the results to the browser.

What actually happens is that, instead of sending a request directly to server www.company.com of:

```
GET /page.html
```

a browser will send a request to proxy.mycompany.com, asking:

```
GET http://www.company.com/page.html
```

proxy.mycompany.com will then contact www.company.com with the request

```
GET /page.html
```

There are several advantages to this indirect approach:

- All external web access can be forced to go through the proxy server, so creating a single control point. This is achieved by blocking all HTTP protocol data, except for that from the proxy server itself.
- All pages being transferred can be logged, together with the address of the requesting machine.
- Requests for certain sites can be restricted or banned.
- The IP addresses or names of the internal systems never appear on the Internet, just the address of the proxy server. So attackers cannot use the addresses to gain information about your internal system names and network structure.
- The proxy can be configured as a caching proxy server, and will save local copies of Web pages retrieved. Subsequent requests will return the cached copies, thus providing faster access and reducing the load on the connection to the Internet.
- Web proxy servers usually support several protocols, including HTTP, FTP, Gopher, HTTPS (HTTP with SSL), and WAIS.
- Proxy servers can themselves use the SOCKS protocol to provide additional security. This does not affect the browser configuration.

The disadvantages are that browser configuration is more complex, the added data transfers can add an extra delay to page access, and sometimes proxies impose additional restrictions such as a time-out on the length of a connection, preventing very large downloads.

11.4.2 What Is SOCKS?

The SOCKS protocol is mentioned several times in this section. It is a simple but elegant way of allowing users within a corporate firewall to access almost any TCP service outside the firewall, but without allowing outsiders to get back inside.

It works through a new TCP protocol, SOCKS, together with a SOCKS server program running in the firewall system. (SOCKS, incidentally, is a shortened version of "sockets," the term used for the data structures which describe a TCP connection.)

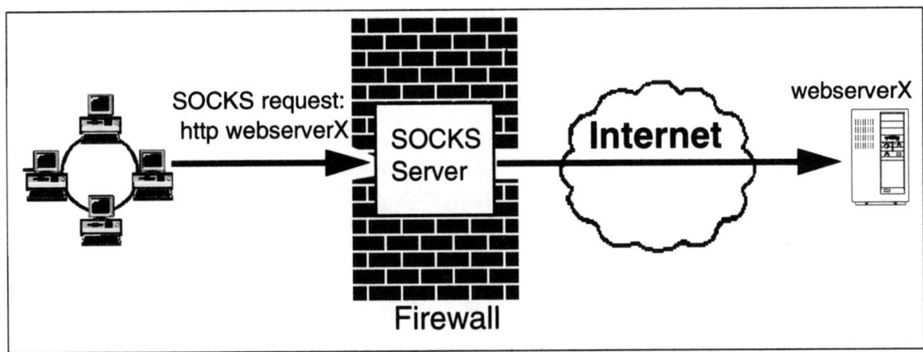

Figure 62. A SOCKS Connection

In basic terms, SOCKS is a means of encapsulating any TCP protocol within the SOCKS protocol. On the client system, within the corporate network, the data packets to be sent to or from an external system will be put inside a SOCKS packet and sent to a SOCKS server. For example, a request for http://server.company.com/page.html would, if sent directly, be contained in a packet with the following characteristics:

```
Destination address:   server.company.com
Destination port:      80 (HTTP)
Data:                  "GET /page.html"
```

If SOCKS were used, the packet sent would be (effectively):

```
Destination address:    socks_server.mycompany.com
Destination port:       TCP 1080 (SOCKS)
Data:                   Destination address = server.company.com,
                        Destination port = TCP 80 (HTTP),
                        Data = "GET /page.html"
```

When the SOCKS server receives this, it extracts the required destination address, port and data and sends this packet; naturally, the source IP address will be that of the SOCKS server itself. The firewall will have been configured to allow these packets from the SOCKS server program, so they won't be blocked. Returning packets will be sent to the SOCKS server, which will encapsulate them similarly, and pass on to the original client, which in turn strips off the SOCKS encapsulation, giving the required data.

(This description is simplified; in reality, requests between the client and the SOCKS server are in a socket API format, rather than the pure protocol data as shown above. Details!)

The advantage of all this is that the firewall can be very simply configured, to allow any TCP/IP connection on any port, from the SOCKS server to the non-secure Internet, trusting it to disallow any connections which are initiated from the Internet.

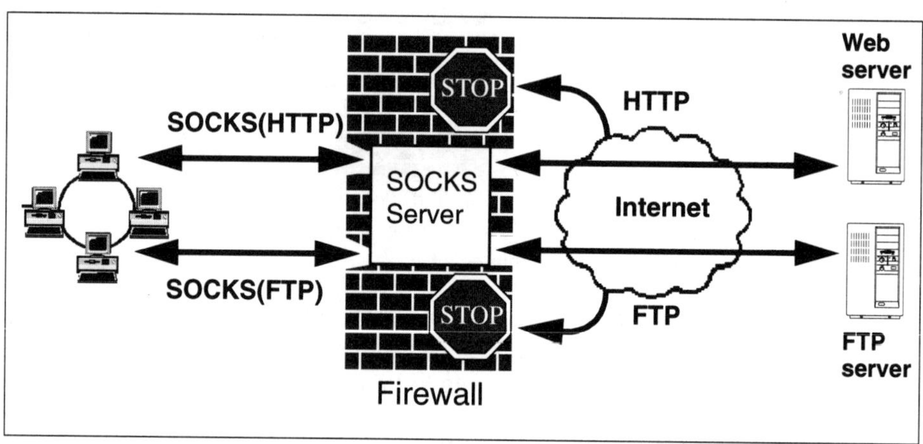

Figure 63. SOCKS Flexibility

The disadvantage is that the client software must be modified to use SOCKS. The original approach was to recompile the network client code with a new SOCKS header file, which translated TCP system calls (connect, getsockname, bind, accept, listen, select) into new names (Rconnect, Rgetsockname, Rbind, Raccept, Rlisten, Rselect). When linked with the libsocks library, these new names will access the SOCKS version, rather than the standard system version. This, therefore, creates a new "SOCKSified" version of the client software.

This approach is still used for clients running on UNIX. However, a new approach has become available for OS/2 and Windows operating systems, where the dynamically linked libraries which implement the TCP calls above are replaced by a SOCKSified version, usually termed a "SOCKSified TCP stack." This SOCKSified stack can then be used with any client code, without the need to modify the client. It just requires the SOCKS configuration to be specified, giving the address of the SOCKS server, and information on whether to use SOCKS protocol or to make a direct connection.

The SOCKSified stack comes as standard with OS/2 Warp Version 4 (add-on versions have been produced for OS/2 Warp Version 3), or can be purchased for Windows 95 or Windows NT.

11.4.3 Using Proxy Servers or SOCKS Gateways

We have described three options:

- Using a proxy server
- Using a SOCKS gateway with a "SOCKSified" client application
- Using a SOCKS gateway with a "SOCKSified" TCP/IP stack

Each of these options has its own advantages and disadvantages, for the company network security manager to evaluate for the company's particular environment. But what does the end user need to do to use these options?

Both Netscape Navigator and Microsoft Internet Explorer Web browsers have built-in support for both proxy servers and for the SOCKS protocol. Options are provided to select either a proxy server, or a SOCKS server (don't select both, or requests will be sent via the SOCKS server to the proxy server, causing unnecessary network traffic). But currently, support for SOCKS is limited to specifying the server name; all page requests will be passed to that server, whether or not direct access is possible (as in the case of internal Web servers).

The advantage in using the SOCKSified stack is that it provides better support for deciding whether to use SOCKS or not, rather than sending all requests to the SOCKS server (which may overload it), as well as supporting other clients. This is controlled by a configuration file, which specifies which range of addresses are internal and can be handled directly, and which must go through the SOCKS server. Of course, if you use a SOCKSified stack, you should not enable SOCKS in the browser configuration. Then again, a SOCKSified stack is not available for all platforms, so you may be forced to use the browser's SOCKS configuration.

The SOCKsified stack approach will also work with Java applets run from a Web browser, as the normal Java.net classes will use the underlying TCP protocol stack, so this provides a simple way of running Java applets through a SOCKS server through a firewall. But if a SOCKSified stack is not available, you will need to SOCKSify the library classes yourself, if you have source code, or look for a vendor who supports SOCKS.

11.5 The Effect of Firewalls on Java

We now consider the effect of firewalls on Java applets, first from the point of view of loading them, then on the network connections that the applets themselves may create.

11.5.1 Downloading an Applet Using HTTP

Java applets within a Web page are transferred using HTTP, when the browser fetches the class files referred to by the <APPLET> tag. So, if a Web page contains a tag of:

```
<APPLET code="Example.class" width=300 height=300>
<PARAM NAME=pname VALUE="example1">
</APPLET>
```

the browser would transfer the Web page itself first, then the file example.class, then any class files referred to in example.class. Each HTTP transfer would be performed separately (unless HTTP 1.1 is used).

JDK 1.1 allows a more efficient transfer, where all the classes are combined into a compressed Java Archive (JAR) file. In this case the Web page contains a tag of:

```
<APPLET archive="example.jar" code="Example.class" width=300
height=300>
</APPLET>
```

If there are problems finding example.jar, or if an older browser (Java 1.0) is used, the archive option is ignored, and the code option is used instead as in the previous example.

11.5.2 Stopping Java Downloads with a Firewall

But what effect do firewalls have on the downloading of Java class files? If the security policy is to allow HTTP traffic to flow through the firewall, then Java applets and JAR files will simply be treated like any other component of a Web page, and transferred. On the other hand, if HTTP is prohibited, then it is going to be very difficult to obtain the applet class files, unless there is another way of getting them, such as using FTP. Quite frequently, Web servers using non-standard TCP ports such as 81, 8000, 8080 may be blocked by the firewall, so if you are running a Web server, stick to the standard port 80 if you want as many people as possible to see your Web pages and applets.

Now since Java is transferred using HTTP, the IP and TCP headers are indistinguishable from any other element of a Web page. Simple packet filtering based on IP addresses and port numbers will therefore not be able to block just Java. If you require more selective filtering, you will need to go one step beyond basic packet filtering and examine the packet payload: the HTTP data itself. This can be done with a suitable Web proxy server or an HTTP gateway which scans the data transferred.

If a Web proxy server is used, a common arrangement is to force all clients to go through the proxy server (inside the firewall), by preventing all HTTP access through the firewall, unless it came from the proxy server itself. If you don't have an arrangement like this, a user could bypass the checking by connecting directly.

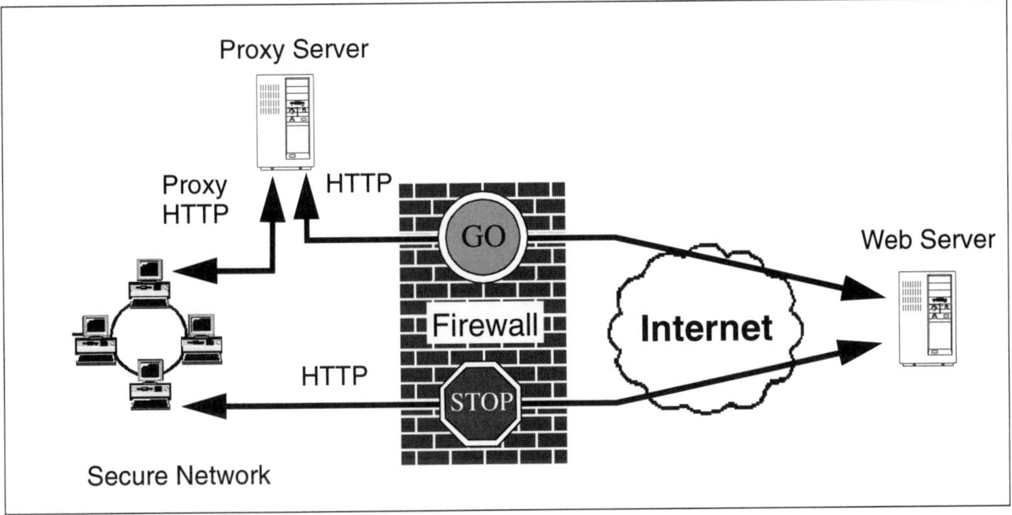

Figure 64. Forcing Connections through a Proxy

So what can we look for, inside the HTTP packet, to identify a Java class file? In an ideal world, there would be a standard MIME (Multipurpose Internet Mail Extensions) data type for Java classes, so that a Web browser might request:

```
Accept: application/java, application/jar
```

and firewalls could quite easily check for these requests and the Web server "Content-Type:" replies.

However, in practice servers respond with a variety of MIME types, such as:

```
application/octet-stream (for class files)
www/unknown
text/plain
multipart/x-zip (for JAR files)
application/zip
```

This means it is necessary to examine the actual data being transferred, to see if it might be Java bytecode or JAR files. Bytecode files must start with hexadecimal values "CAFEBABE" in the first four bytes (see “Java Bytecode” on page 69). This string will also be found in JAR files, but as a JAR file may be compressed, a scanner has to work harder to find the signature. Commercial products are available which can perform this inspection. They usually work as, or with, an HTTP proxy server, and check all HTTP requests passing through.

Searching for the class file signature in this way is an effective way to stop Java, but it indiscriminately chops out good code and bad. A more subtle scanner could extend the principle to other types of "signature". For example, it would theoretically be possible to filter out any applet that overrode the stop() method (see “Malicious Applets” on page 104), by analyzing the bytecode in detail.

Of course, in these restrictive environments, you would also want to filter out any other types of executable content which are less secure than Java, such as ActiveX, and maybe JavaScript, .EXE files, and so on. You would also have to consider other protocols such as FTP, HTTP or FTP encapsulated in SOCKS, HTTP encapsulated in SSL (which adds the problem of decoding the type of encrypted data).

We have been focussing on scanning for Java at a single point for the enterprise: the firewall or proxy server. Recent developments by the browser manufacturers and by systems management specialists, such as Tivoli Systems, point to an alternative strategy. They have developed mechanisms for installing and configuring browsers on multiple user systems from a single point. This certainly offers cost savings: a single administrator can be responsible for hundreds of workstations. However, as a security measure it can only work if it is backed up by controls and monitors that prevent individual users from overriding the "official" configuration.

The cleanest solution to the problem of selectively stopping Java is in the use of signed applets. As certificates become used more frequently, it will be possible to permit Java bytecode from sites where you trust the signer (maybe your own company sites), and disallow other sites.

For the Network Administrator

Should You Allow Java Through Your Firewall?

Leaving aside the question of *how* to block Java classes at the firewall. You may be faced with the decision of whether you *should* allow Java (or any other type of executable content) to travel through the firewall. If your site has public web servers, then you would expect that Java code is allowed to be sent to the Internet. But you might wish to make restrictions on Java code that can be received.

The most permissive policy is to allow Java to be received, and let users make their own defenses, or trust in the Java security model. More restrictive policies might only allow Java from trusted Web sites, or not at all. The question that you must ask is: what data is at risk if I allow this? We have shown that, compared with other types of executable content, Java applets are very safe, so if you choose to block applets you should also prevent other downloads. For example, macro viruses contained in word-processor files are a major problem, but few companies would prevent employees exchanging such files with customers and suppliers.

11.5.3 Java Network Connections through the Firewall

When a Java applet or application wishes to create its own network connections through a firewall, it faces all the difficulties above, and also, for applets, the default security manager restriction of only being able to contact the server it was downloaded from.

There are three approaches that an applet can take:

1. Use the URL classes from the java.net package to request data from a Web server using HTTP. JDK 1.1 adds a new class to this package – HttpURLConnection – as a specialization of the URLConnection class.
2. Use other classes from the java.net package to create socket connections to a dedicated server application.
3. Use remote object access mechanisms, such as RMI or CORBA.

The first of these is the easiest to implement (look at the never-ending fortune cookie applet in Figure 18 on page 105 for an example). It is also likely to be the most reliable, because the JVM passes the URL request to the normal browser connection routines to process. This means that, if a proxy is defined, the Java code will automatically use it. However, URL connections suffer from the fact that the server side of the connection has limited capability; it can only be a simple file retrieval or a CGI (or similar) program.

For the second approach – socket connection to the server – the applet will need to choose a port number to connect to, but many will not be allowed through firewall. Some types of applets have no real choice as to port number. For example IBM Host-on-Demand is a Java applet which is a 3270 terminal emulator, hence needs to use the tn3270 protocol to telnet port 23. It is quite likely that this standard port would be allowed through the firewall; otherwise, encapsulation of tn3270 inside the SOCKS protocol may be the only answer.

Other applets need to make a connection to the server, but don't need any special port. It may be that they can use a non-privileged server port of 1024 or greater, but often these, too, are blocked by simple packet filtering firewalls. A flexible approach is to let the applet be configurable to allow direct connections (if allowed), otherwise to use the SOCKS protocol to pass through the firewall.

For the Applet Developer

Different Kinds of Sockets

As we have described, SOCKS encapsulates the real data flow in its own TCP/IP connection. This means that the client code must call the SOCKS library functions instead of the functions provided by the normal TCP/IP APIs.

As far as we know, these library functions do not exist for Java, but the java.net package does provide a convenient technique for implementing such things, by using a specialized SocketFactory class.

Many HTTP proxy servers implement the *Connect Method*. This allows a client to send an HTTP request to the proxy which includes a header telling it to connect to a specific port on the real target system. The connect method was originally developed to allow SSL connections to be handled by a proxy server, but it has since been extended to other applications. For example, Lotus Notes servers can use it. The connect method operates in a very similar way to SOCKS and you can implement Java applet connections with it in much the same way as you would with SOCKS.

Another approach is to disguise the packets in another protocol, most likely HTTP, as this will have been allowed through the firewall. This will allow two-way transfer of data between applet and server, but will require a special type of Web server. The server will need to act as a normal Web server, to supply the Web pages and applets in the first place, but must be able to communicate with the applets to process their disguised network traffic.

11.5.4 RMI Remote Method Invocation

Java's RMI allows developers to distribute Java objects seamlessly across the Internet. But RMI needs to be able to cross firewalls too.

The normal approach that RMI uses, in the absence of firewalls, is that the client applet will attempt to open a direct network connection to the RMI port (default is port 1099) on the server. The client will send its request to the server, and receive its reply, over this network connection.

The designers of RMI have made provision for two firewall scenarios, both using RMI calls embedded in HTTP requests, under the reasonable assumption that HTTP will be allowed through the firewall (as the applet was delivered that way). The RMI server itself will accept either type of request, and format its reply accordingly. The client actually sends an HTTP POST request, with the RMI call data sent as the body of the POST request, and the server returns the result in the body of an HTTP response.

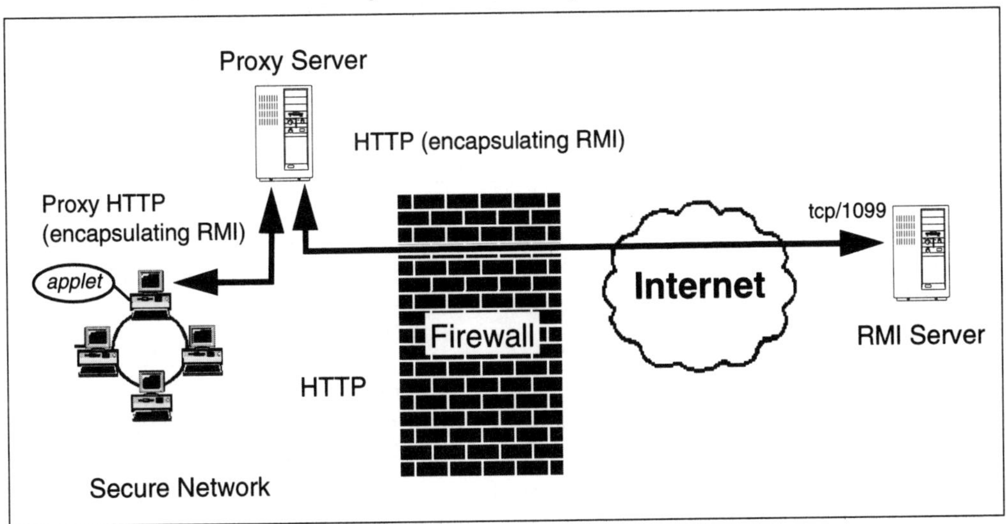

Figure 65. Proxy Configuration for RMI (1)

In the first scenario, we assume that the proxy server is permitted by the firewall to connect directly to the remote server's RMI port (1099). The client applet will make an HTTP POST request to http://rmi.server:1099/. This passes across the Internet to the remote server, where it is found to be an encapsulated RMI call. Therefore the reply is sent back as an HTML response. In theory this method could also be used with a SOCKS server, instead of a proxy server, if run by a SOCKS-enabled browser.

As well as assuming that the firewall on the client passes the RMI port, this assumes that the remote firewall also accepts incoming requests directly to the RMI port. But in some organizations, the firewall manager may be reluctant to permit traffic to additional ports such as the RMI port. So an alternative configuration is available, in case RMI data is blocked by either firewall.

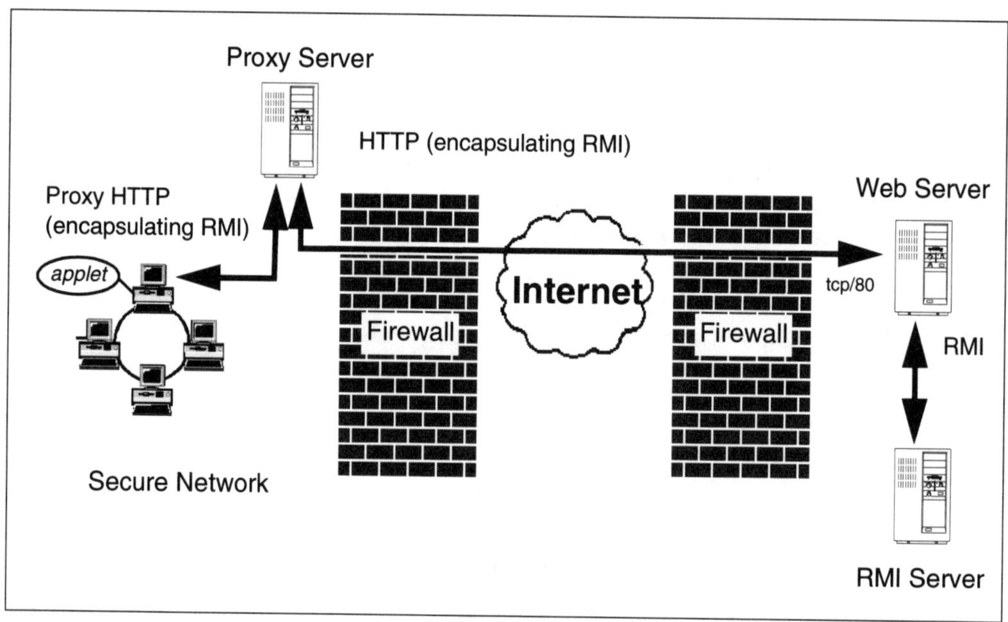

Figure 66. Proxy Configuration for RMI (2)

In the second scenario, the proxy server cannot use the RMI port directly, so the remote Web server (which supplied the applet) has a cgi-bin program configured, to forward HTTP on the normal port (80) into HTTP to the RMI server's port 1099. An example cgi-bin program is provided in the development kit, and needs to be installed on the Web server. This cgi-bin program invokes the Java interpreter on the server, to forward the request to the appropriate RMI server port. It also copies the standard CGI environment variables to Java properties.

So, the client code sends a POST request to http://rmi.server/cgi-bin/java-rmi.cgi?forward=1099. The cgi-bin program passes it on to the RMI port specified in the ?forward parameter. The reply will be passed back to the Web server, which adds the HTML header line, and returns the response to the client. In principle, this would allow the RMI server to reside on a different system than the remote Web server, in a three-tier model.

For the Network Administrator

What Is Allowed Through Your Firewall?

Do you allow your proxy servers access to any TCP/IP port on the Internet? If so, you may allow your internal users to access risky servers; if not, you may prevent them from accessing useful services. You can scan the proxy server log files for non-standard port accesses, to assess the balance of risk.

Fortunately, all the work above is performed automatically in the java.rmi package, so the software developer need not be concerned about the detailed mechanism. It is only necessary to configure the RMI server correctly, and to ensure the client uses the automatic mechanism for encapsulating RMI.

In the current version of RMI, the client stub code checks for the presence (not value) of system properties proxyHost or http.proxyHost, in order to decide whether to try using the HTTP encapsulation. If you are using a Web browser and encapsulated RMI does not seem to work, try explicitly setting these properties, as the browser may be using its own proxy HTTP, without setting proxyHost.

All this automatic encapsulation is not free, of course. Encapsulated RMI calls are at least an order of magnitude slower than direct requests, and proxy servers may add extra delays to the process as they receive and forward requests.

11.6 Summary

We've shown how firewalls provide added security to an organization's network, at the expense of some restrictions on what client users can do. Firewalls use a variety of techniques to provide this security, including packet filtering, proxy servers and SOCKS servers. We've described approaches which can be used with these techniques to allow secure access through the firewalls.

Chapter 12. Java and SSL

In Chapter 7, “Playing in the Sandbox” on page 97 we discussed the capabilities for invoking cryptographic functions from within Java code. We also stepped through a simple transaction, to show the ways that cryptography can be used in an application.

But, as we concluded at the time, most programmers and application designers would prefer ready-built cryptographic protocols, rather than having to create them from the basic elements of encryption and digital signatures. Secure Socket Layer (SSL) is the most widely used protocol for implementing cryptography in the Web. In this chapter we look at how it can be invoked from within Java.

12.1 What Is SSL?

SSL has two security aims:

1. To authenticate the server and (optionally) the client using public-key signatures.
2. To provide an encrypted connection for the client and server to exchange messages.

As the name suggests, SSL provides a secure alternative to the standard TCP/IP sockets protocol. In fact, SSL is not a drop-in replacement because the application has to specify additional cryptographic information. Nonetheless, it is not a large step for an application that uses regular sockets to be converted to SSL. Although the most common implementation of SSL is for HTTP, several other application protocols have also been adapted.

SSL is comprised of two protocols: the *record protocol* and the *handshake protocol.* The record protocol defines the way that messages passed between client and server are encapsulated. At any point in time it has a set of parameters, known as a *cipher suite,* associated with it, which define the cryptographic methods being used. There are a number of cipher suites defined by the SSL standard, with names that describe their content. For example, the cipher suite named SSL_RSA_EXPORT_WITH_RC4_40_MD5 uses:

- RSA public key encryption for key exchange, using an export-strength modulus (see “US Export Rules for Encryption” on page 33)

- RC4 cipher for bulk data encryption, using a 40-bit (export strength) key
- MD5 hashing to ensure data integrity

When the SSL record protocol session is first established it has a default cipher suite of SSL_NULL_WITH_NULL_NULL (no encryption at all). This is where the SSL handshake protocol comes in. It defines a series of messages in which the client and server negotiate the type of connection that they can support, perform authentication, and generate a bulk encryption key. At the end of the handshake they exchange ChangeCipherSpec messages, which switches the current cipher suite of the record protocol to the one that they negotiated (see Figure 67).

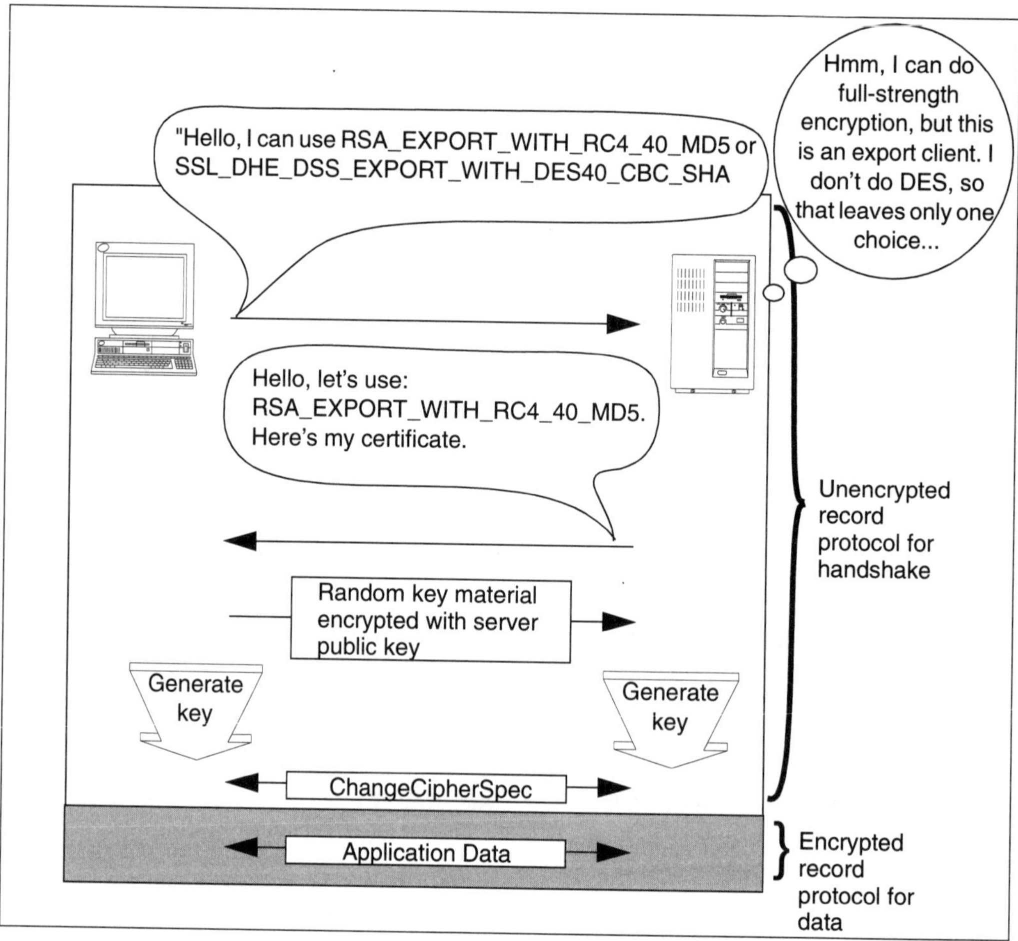

Figure 67. The SSL Handshake for Dummies

In the case shown in the diagram, only the server is authenticated, so the client does not need to provide a certificate. If client authentication was required, the handshake would be a little longer. The full specification is at http://home.netscape.com/newsref/std/SSL.html.

12.2 Using SSL from an Applet

The advantage of a protocol such as SSL is that it removes the need for the application developer to deal with the nuts and bolts of cryptography. There are two ways in which Java can exploit this function: by using the SSL support built into the browser, or by using an SSL class package.

12.2.1 Using SSL URLs with Java

When a Webmaster wants users of a site to enter an SSL connection, he or she simply codes a hypertext link with a prefix of "https:" in place of "http:". When the user clicks on the link, the browser automatically starts the SSL handshake, connecting to the default SSL port on the server (TCP port 443).

Any relative URL within an SSL page is also retrieved using SSL. For example, an <APPLET> tag could cause the applet bytecode to be encrypted as it passes across the network. More importantly, the user knows that the applet comes from a trustworthy site, because the authentication process in the SSL handshake will have checked the certificate of the server. You will recall that the signature on a JAR file only shows that the creator of the file can be trusted, not the site from which it came (discussed in Chapter 9, “Java Gets Out of Its Box” on page 119). By delivering a signed JAR file using SSL you can add the extra authentication without the Web site having to re-sign the file.

If an applet wants to read or write data to the server, it can use the URL classes from the java.net package. These allow the applet code to specify the URL of a Web page or CGI program and to receive the output from the URL in an I/O stream. We showed an example of doing this in the NeverEndingFortuneCookie applet in Figure 18 on page 105. If we changed the assignment of fortuneURL in that example to use an https: prefix, the browser would automatically retrieve the data using SSL.

12.2.2 SSL Class Packages

Fetching data using the URL technique (above) is a very simple approach, but it limits the applet because client/server communications can only exploit the capabilities offered by CGI (or another, similar, server interface). Even if this is adequate for the function, it imposes some performance overhead. A direct socket connection between client and server allows more sophisticated and responsive applets to be created.

One possibility is to use a package that provides SSL function in a Java class package. IBM Research in Zurich have created such a package, called SSLight, based on their comprehensive cryptographic toolkit for Java. Although this package is for internal IBM use (due in part to license and export restrictions), it can be used for joint projects with IBM customers. Alternatively, toolkits are available from other vendors.

In the SSLight package the context information for the current SSL connection (in other words, the cipher suite details) is maintained in a Java class named SSLContext. The package then provides a set of classes that mirror the java.net socket classes (including SSLSocket, SSLServerSocket and so on). These behave like their java.net equivalents, except that the constructor methods also require an SSLContext among their arguments. This means that it is a relatively simple matter to modify an application that communicates with sockets to use the package.

The tricky part is setting up the SSLContext class in the first place. It requires a *key ring* which is, conventionally, a file containing a database of keys and certificates. An SSL client always needs a key ring, even if client authentication is not in use, because it has to check the validity of the certificate presented by the server. To perform the check, the client needs the certificate for the CA that signed the server's certificate. The problem with reading a key ring from a file is that normally it is forbidden by the applet sandbox restrictions.

One solution to this lies in signed applets, but that can lead to further problems, due to the differences in implementation that we discussed in Chapter 9, "Java Gets Out of Its Box" on page 119. The SSLight package provides an innovative alternative, by defining an SSLightKeyRing interface. This means that a key ring can be sent imbedded in the Java class files of the applet, thus avoiding the need for disk I/O. How can the applet know that this key ring (and the CA certificates inside it) can be trusted? The answer is to send the *applet itself* in an SSL URL. The chain of trust from the point of view of the applet is then:

- This applet is from a host that is trusted, because the certificate it sent when downloaded in a URL was signed by an independent, trusted third party (a CA).
- Therefore the key ring that the applet includes can also be trusted.
- Therefore the CA key in the key ring can be trusted, and the applet can use it to validate the server certificate when the applet starts a connection with SSLight.

This is not a rigorous chain of trust, but even if the applet does not have strong authentication for the server, it can still establish an encrypted session. In other words, privacy of the data is guaranteed, even if authentication of the server is based on doubtful logic.

12.3 Summary

The history of the World Wide Web is based on pragmatism. For example, no one would argue that sending uncompressed ASCII text data on sessions that are set up and torn down for every single transaction is efficient in any way. However, this is what HTTP does, and it is very successful. The reason for its success is that it is simple enough to allow many different systems to interoperate without problems of differing syntax. The cost of simplicity is in network overhead and a limited transaction model.

Using cryptography in Java offers a similar dilemma. It is possible to write secure applications using a toolkit of basic functions. Such an application can be very sophisticated, but it will also be complex. Alternatively, using SSL URL connections offers a way to simplify the application, but at the cost of application function. SSL Java packages, such as SSLight, provide a middle way, retaining simplicity but allowing more flexible application design.

Chapter 13. Java and Cryptolopes

As we saw earlier, Java applets may be considered to be assets, pieces of intellectual property which need to be protected from prying eyes. We discussed the threat from decompilation attacks and how you might attempt to foil decompilers.

There is, however, another way in which applets may have value which must be protected.

Most Java applets you encounter on the Web are available to you free of charge. Usually the Web page owner uses them to make the page more attractive or to provide a function he or she wants you to use – such as an investment planning application intended to help sell you a mutual fund. Sometimes, however, it is you who want to use the applet: an applet might be a particularly good game, or a useful spreadsheet that you want to use. In this case the applet owner may wish to charge for the use of the applet.

If I am the applet owner, I have three main obstacles to overcome:

1. I would like to send my applet to you in a protected form, such that nobody – *including you* – can execute it. In addition, I would like to send you information about how much I intend to charge you for its use, what it does and other such information (technically known as *metadata*).
2. I must be able to accept some form of payment from you in order to allow you to use my applet. Ideally, you should be able to pay different amounts depending on how you wish to use it. For example, I might charge a single sum for unlimited use, a different sum for a single use and yet another sum to use the applet for a specified period of time.
3. I must be able to grant you the usage rights for which you have paid without allowing you any additional rights and particularly, without allowing you to give access to your friends (who haven't paid me for the privilege).

Of course, I could encrypt the applet code and sell you a key which would allow you to decrypt it and this would meet requirement 1 and some of requirement 2. It would fall short of requirement 3, however, since once you have decrypted the applet class files, you would be free to distribute them among your friends. In addition to this fundamental flaw, there is something deeply unsatisfying about the payment model. It lacks subtlety and flexibility: you either have the code and can use it as often as you please, or you don't.

In fact, the third requirement proves to be the most difficult to satisfy and it is this requirement which is addressed by IBM's *Cryptolope Live!* product, the latest evolution of Cryptolope technology.

13.1 Cryptolope History

Cryptolopes were first designed (at the IBM laboratory in Falls Church, Virginia) to address the general issue of charging for intellectual property on the Web, and on other networks. Like many other Internet security ideas, they have their roots in cryptography. If you access my Web page to download some chargeable material (which could be a magazine article or a detailed weather forecast just as easily as it could be an applet) and I send the material to you, I shall want to send a bill later. But how do I know whether you ever received it?

The Internet does not guarantee delivery, far from it, and if you say you never received it, how am I to know whether you are lying, let alone prove that you are lying. We can use SSL to authenticate both ends of the dialogue; that is, you can be sure that the Web page is really mine, and I can be sure that the browser is really yours. The use of public-key certificates ensures that. But it does not tell me that the delivery of the chargeable material happened without problems, and it does not give me anything that proves that you requested that particular chargeable material. Cryptolopes can give you both of these by the simple expedient of sending the material in encrypted form. When you request a decryption key, you confirm that you have received the material and that you are willing to pay for it.

Originally, Cryptolopes focused primarily on the delivery and payment mechanisms for content. Ultimately, whatever the asset, be it a font, some HTML, an audio or video file or even an entire application, it needed to be extracted from the protective shell of the Cryptolope and handed to an application which would render it. This exposed the asset to the risk of copying.

This sort of problem has affected copyright material for centuries, and people still manage to make money out of writing books and recording music. This is because honest citizens and respectable companies don't make a habit of massively infringing copyright – they want to have legal original copies. So does it matter? Well, yes, to some extent it does.

The difference between a book on paper and a book in HTML is that a photocopy of the paper book is much less usable than the original; a copy of an HTML book is identical to the original. A tape copy of a music CD is less clear than the original; a copy of a digital audio file isn't. Digital copies are perfect copies, and with the prevalence of Internet access, it is possible for a single unscrupulous vendor to create and sell many perfect copies of an original, all over the world and even from a server in a country with less restrictive copyright laws.

13.2 Today: Cryptolope Live!

Cryptolope Live! is a major evolution of the original Cryptolope concept. Whereas early Cryptolopes focused on content commerce, Cryptolope Live! emphasizes the process of presenting the content, installing the content, metering the content use and interacting with the end user. In short, it addresses requirement 3 above.

Cryptolope Live! deals in Cryptolope objects. These are a combination of content, scripts and extensions. The content (part) is the payload of a Cryptolope object and may be Java classes, digital audio or any type of digital content. A Cryptolope object may contain a number of parts all of which are held in a folder structure, similar to a filing system. The scripts are a small set of business rules associated with each part and folder which determine what the Cryptolope object will do in terms of rendering content, billing the user, metering usage or whatever. The extensions are pure Java classes which extend the capabilities of the scripting language when more complex functions are required (see Figure 68 on page 204).

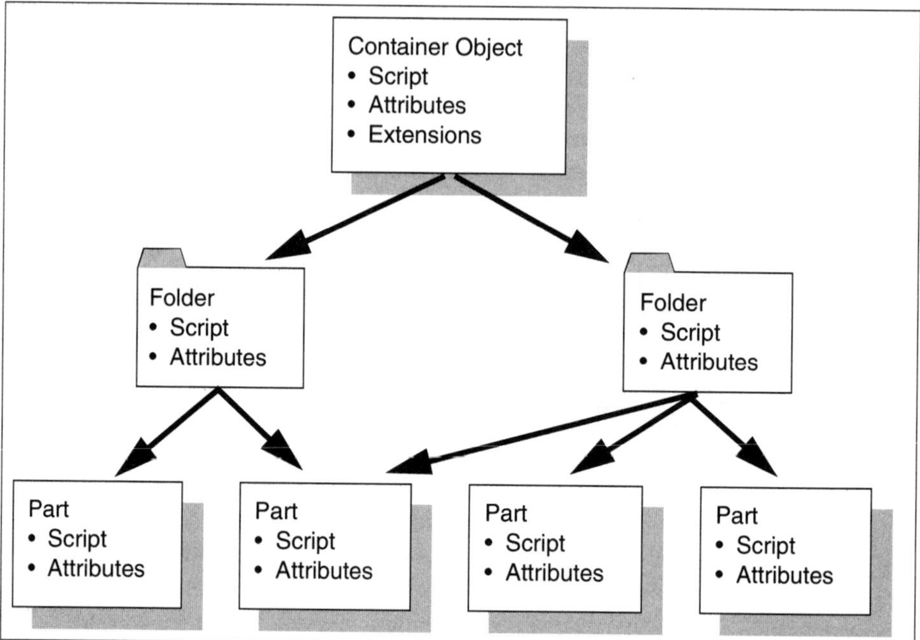

Figure 68. Cryptolope Live! Objects

Scripts are written using Cryptolope script, a simple yet powerful programming language based on ECMAScript, a standard scripting language defined by the European Computer Manufacturers' Association and based on JavaScript.

The main component of Cryptolope Live! is the Cryptolope Player. This is written in Java and runs the Cryptolope objects. There are several parts to the Cryptolope player as shown in Figure 69 on page 205.

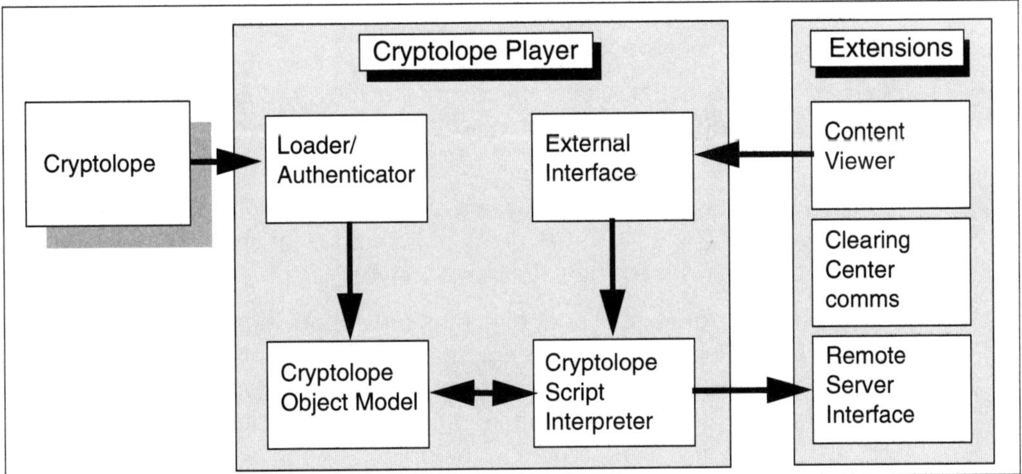

Figure 69. Components of the Cryptolope Live! Player

The Cryptolope player first loads the Cryptolope object and validates its structure. If the Cryptolope object has been digitally signed then the certificates are presented to the user who reviews this information and approves it. Finally, the Cryptolope object is authenticated and the main script is loaded and executed.

The Cryptolope Player implements a Sandbox and security manager, exactly like the JVM (indeed, it uses a Java security manager class). Thus, Cryptolope objects are prevented from accessing local storage, running native code and all of those restrictions which we saw earlier applied to unsigned applets. If this process seems familiar, then you should not be surprised. Any resemblance to the Java security architecture is purely intentional.

The script itself is responsible for implementing business rules which may require providing payment information for the content prior to making it available (decrypting the content) to the end user.

Another implementation may simply require authentication of the end user (for example, via a user ID and password) prior to rendering the information. The rules may only authorize the end user to view the content, or they may authorize saving it to a file, or printing it.

The Cryptolope Live! product is delivered with a set of scripts and extensions that let you write and customize your own information commerce system for the distribution of, and payment processing for, digital content. The provided scripts allow your enterprise to build a Cryptolope object and encrypt one or more documents within it. This system flow proceeds as follows:

- You specify if the content can be viewed, printed, or saved to file for specified prices, and whether the content within the Cryptolope object ever expires.
- When an end user receives a Cryptolope object (via the Internet as a Java applet or to be run as a Java application) the Cryptolope object is run by the Cryptolope Player.
- The Cryptolope Player executes the scripts located in the Cryptolope object and presents to the end user information about the documents they may select to purchase (for example, an abstract, authoring information, or a thumbnail diagram of a larger picture that is encrypted in the object), along with the information the end user requires to make a purchase decision.
- When the end user chooses to purchase the content, the script then presents a dialogue to request credit card payment information. This information is sent to a clearing center run by your enterprise or trusted third party. The clearing center works with the Cryptolope Cashier which can link to third-party payment systems.
- Upon completion of the credit card transaction, the clearing center sends the appropriate document key for decrypting the purchased document content back to the end user's Cryptolope Player. Then the application decrypts the document and renders the purchased content in the trusted viewer.
- After the content is displayed, the end user can elect to print or save the document if these options have been enabled.

When a Cryptolope object is loaded, the following actions occur:

- The Cryptolope object itself is evaluated for authenticity based on the digital signatures it may contain.
- If the Cryptolope object appears not to have been altered, then the loader creates the Cryptolope object model, representing the structure of the object and the elements comprising it.
- The object model calls the Cryptolope Script interpreter and starts running the script in the Cryptolope object.
- The scripts then control the actions of the Cryptolope object on the end user's system. The scripts can call extensions (Java class files either internal to the Cryptolope object or external on the user's

CLASSPATH) or can make available script functions that an extension can call directly.

Cryptolope Live! also includes the Cryptolope Builder. This is a simple mechanism for creating Cryptolope objects. In addition to the development tools, the IBM Cryptolope Live! system includes subsystems for security-rich content delivery and content commerce. They are:

1. The IBM Cryptolope Clearing Center, along with extensions for Cryptolope objects which allow them to connect to and communicate with the clearing center.
2. The IBM Cryptolope Cashier which is a gateway to a payment mechanism from the clearing center, allowing for the all important collection of money!

13.3 Example Applications

Imagine that you have developed the ultimate killer app. Perhaps it is a Java based streaming video viewer which tunes into an Internet news channel. You want to sell access to the channel on a pay-per-view basis.

First you embed your Java class files in a Cryptolope object. Then you write a simple script which charges the end user in blocks of five minutes, calls the clearing center, obtains a decryption key, decrypts the classes and executes them. When the time limit is up, viewing is interrupted by the script which prompts for more credit for the next five-minute period.

You now have a totally flexible, secure product which will run anywhere, either stand-alone or inside a browser. You can give it away to your customers who will be charged as they use it. If they give copies to their friends, this is fine since their friends will also be charged as they use it; thus, now your customers have become a distribution channel for your software and they even pay you for the privilege!

13.4 Tomorrow

This is only a first step. In the future, Cryptolope technology may be tightly integrated into the JVM rather than requiring the layer of indirection provided by Cryptolope Script. Then Java classes rather than whole applications or applets could be distributed on a pay-per-use basis.

Vendors of class libraries or software components will be able to distribute their code widely without charging developers who use it and without having to draw up complex licensing agreements. They will be able to rest easy, safe in the knowledge that they will be paid in full each time an end user uses their libraries, regardless of the product those libraries are embedded in.

Chapter 14. Epilogue

> *"The giant rat of Sumatra, a story for which the world is not yet prepared." - Sherlock Holmes, The Adventure of the Sussex Vampire*
>
> (A. Conan Doyle)

The authors believe that Java provides a powerful tool with which to create secure computer systems. This security does not depend on the underlying operating system; indeed, insecure PC operating systems will benefit, while secure operating systems like MVS and UNIX will have their security enhanced, using the same portable software as that on the PC. Java is sufficiently secure to allow other software to be run safely, even if it came from a dubious source.

This security depends on vigilance by the users, in ensuring that the software that they must trust does not contain any loopholes, and is correctly configured. Undoubtedly, Java flaws will continue to emerge and so continuing vigilance is needed.

The most publicized (and hence quickly fixed) flaws have appeared in the Java virtual machine. We believe that the next generation of flaws will appear in situations where Java is working together with other types of client executable content. For example, it is now very common to find Web pages that use a bewildering mixture of technologies – Java, JavaScript, ActiveX, Macromedia Shockwave and other plug-ins, dynamic HTML, and so on. Each of these works within its own zone of protection, which may overlap but are not identical. The wily cracker can take advantage of this fact to bypass the restrictions of one technology by exploiting another. Fixes for this type of exploit will probably not appear so quickly, because each component may be working correctly on its own terms.

Signed content (all types of content, not just Java) offers one solution to these problems, by guaranteeing the trustworthiness of its source. But there are dangers here also. Cryptography is not a simple subject and it is important to mask complexity from the end user. At the time of writing, the variety of different approaches to signed content reflects the difficulty of doing this. We hope that a consistent approach will soon emerge. One area that merits attention is the question of how to warn the user that some component of a Web page wants to perform some potentially dangerous function. The problem is that the user becomes "click-happy." When confronted by an endless sequence of dialog boxes warning of one thing or another, it is too easy to just keep clicking "OK." We need a method that makes it clear that, for example, a request by a Java applet to read environmental information is potentially an order of magnitude less dangerous than allowing an ActiveX control to run.

Java, because of its unique design, offers many safety and security advantages over alternative approaches. In this book we have illustrated this fact and, we hope, given you some insight into how to create secure Java applications, how to protect Java assets, and how to use Java securely.

Appendix A. Sources of Information about Java Security

This appendix contains information about Internet resources and interesting Java security sites. It is in two parts: the first covers companies involved in Java development, and the second contains sites which are maintained at educational establishments. This section also contains interesting sites which are maintained by individual experts within the educational establishments.

The purpose of this appendix is to give you an insight into where we have obtained some of our information and to give you the opportunity to look at other resource sites to obtain a view of Java security from different angles. This also gives you the opportunity to keep on top of new developments via the Web.

A.1 Companies

There are many companies which maintain Java Security sites; it would be an impossible task to list them all. For this reason we have decided to concentrate on the few companies who are at the cutting edge of the Java phenomenon.

A.1.1 JavaSoft

The main JavaSoft URL is:

http://www.javasoft.com

This is an excellent Web page and one to keep a regular check on, because it has many links to various topics related to Java. Many of these are not directly related to security, but have a bearing on it, for example, new versions of the JDK and standarization activity. There is also a page dedicated to security:

http://www.javasoft.com/security

This page contains lots of links to downloads and documentation for the latest JavaSoft Java security packages. These documents are very well constructed and easy to follow; however, they assume a high level of knowledge from the user. As an example of this, there are manual pages for UNIX commands which are not easy if you are not a UNIX user.

This page also contains links to specifications pages which, in general, describe various parts of Java specifications such as the Java cryptographic architecture. The core of this is in three guides linked from the page: Security API Overview, Java Cryptography Architecture API Specification and Reference, and How to Integrate Your Cryptography Algorithms into Java Security.

One especially interesting link is the JDK 1.1 Security Tutorial:

http://java.sun.com/docs/books/tutorial/security1.1/index.html

This tutorial claims, "You will learn the definitions of various cryptography terms, and see an overview of the Java Security API and its core classes. You will then learn how to produce "digital signatures" for data, and how to verify the authenticity of such signatures." The author of the tutorial is Mary Daegforde.

The JavaSoft Security page contains a lot besides the items already mentioned, such as links to FAQs, white papers and other articles.

Finally, you may wish to refer to the JavaSoft archives. These archives date back to November 96 and contain a massive amount of information about problems encountered in the development of the various Java tools since that time.

A.1.2 Sun

The Sun home page URL is:

http://www.sun.com

As the originator and prime mover behind Java, you would expect it to feature in many parts of the Sun site. So, for example, the Sun news highlights include many Java-related developments. The URL for the main page for specifically Java-related issues is:

http://www.sun.com/java

This page has links to a lot of Java-related topics and it also leads you back to the JavaSoft site.

A.1.3 Microsoft

The Microsoft home page URL is:

http://www.microsoft.com

Although late to join the Java fold, Microsoft now offer a range of products for developing and running applications written in Java.

The URL of the main page for Java-related issues is:

http://www.microsoft.com/java

This page has links to a lot of Java-related topics such as news, issues and trends, technical information and the Microsoft SDK for Java. There are also many related topics, which change frequently, such as information about bugs found in beta version of products which can be downloaded from the Microsoft site.

The URL for the main page about Java security is:

http://www.microsoft.com/java/security

This page at first appears to be for a user who knows very little or nothing at all about Java security, but there are some very good links to more technical information. We found that a more effective way to get the required information from the Microsoft site was to use the internal search function. Searching for Java security produced more than 50 hits, although a number of them were for material that is only available to members of the Microsoft Developers Network.

A.1.4 IBM

The IBM home page URL is:

http://www.ibm.com

There are many links from this page, including a fair proportion of Java-related pages. The URL of the main page for Java information is:

http://www.ibm.com/java

This page has a number of links to various pages but the easiest way to approach it is to link to the site index page:

http://www.ibm.com/Java/siteindex.html

This page lists all of the Java-related topics on this site in alphabetical order.

A.1.5 Reliable Software Technologies

RST performs research and consultancy in all aspects of the security, safety, and testability of computer systems. They work closely with academics, in particular the Princeton Safe Internet Programming team (see below).

http://www.rstcorp.com

A.2 Universities

There are many universities which maintain Java sites and Java Security sites; it would be an impossible task to list them all. For this reason, we have decided to concentrate on the universities who's pages we found most useful and informative. There is also a brief list at the end of this section which contains some other Java sites which you may find interesting.

A.2.1 Princeton

Princeton University is the leading center for Java security research. The main Java security page is:

http://www.cs.princeton.edu/sip

This page contains a lot of information and links about Java security.

The purpose of this site is to study the security of widely used Internet software, especially mobile code systems like Java, ActiveX, and JavaScript. They try to understand how security breaks down, and to develop technology to address the underlying causes of security problems.

This Web site has the following sections: news, people, partners, research, publications, FAQ and a miscellaneous section. There are also links to many publications about Java security

A.2.2 Yale

There are a number of Java security sites at Yale, for example:

http://pantheon.yale.edu/~dff/java.html

This site is mainly a collection of links to various Java security sites.

Another Yale site worth visiting is:

http://daffy.cs.yale.edu/java/java_sec/java_sec.html

This site gives a good breakdown of Java security and some good guidelines for security measures to take.

Finally:

http://pantheon.yale.edu/help/programming/jdk1.1.1/docs/api

This site gives a list of many topics, including some good Java security papers produced by the university.

A.2.3 Georgia Institute of Technology

This is the home of Mark LaDue, who has written a number of hostile applets, illustrating the capacity for cycle-stealing attacks in Java. His page of increasingly vicious attack applets is now hosted by Reliable Software Technologies Corporation:

http://www.math.gatech.edu/~mladue/HostileApplets.html

The second page of interest is:

http://voreg.cc.gatech.edu/gvu/user_surveys/survey-10-1996/graphs/author/Knowledge_Of_Java_Security.html

This page contains some statistics about how many professionals have Java knowledge all over the world. Well worth a look.

Finally:

http://shannon.math.gatech.edu/~mladue/java_was_1.html

This page is Mark LaDue's report on how the difference between the capabilities of Java and bytecode leads to some of the flaws in the Java virtual machine.

A.2.4 Others

The following pages are from other university sites which have some good information and links :

A page of information put together by Patricia Evans (a grad student at the University of Victoria):

http://gulf.uvic.ca/~pevans/java.html

David Hopwood, a student at Oxford, discovered some of Java's flaws that led to attack applets. His page has good information, though it is now aging:

http://ferret.lmh.ox.ac.uk/~david/java/bugs/public.html

A list of Java security resources provided by Steven H. Samorodin of the UC Davis Security lab:

http://seclab.cs.ucdavis.edu/~samorodi/java/javasec.html

Gene Spafford of Purdue University's security hotlist entry for Java security. A bit out of date, but the rest of the list is amazing:

http://www.cs.purdue.edu/homes/spaf/hotlists/csec-body.html#java00

A page at the University of Utah, devoted to Java Security. Includes pointers to talk slides, and a few pointers to related Web sites.

The URL for this site is:

http://www.cs.utah.edu/~gback/javasec

Compiling Functional Programs to Java Byte-Code, by Gary Meehan at the University of Warwick:

http://lite.ncstrl.org:3803/Dienst/UI/2.0/Describe/ncstrl.warwick_cs%2fCS-RR-334?abstract=

A research group at the University of Washington implementing a new Java security architecture based on factored components for security, performance, and scalability. See their Security Flaws in Java page:

http://kimera.cs.washington.edu

University of Arizona's Sumatra Project, research on mobile code. See especially the Java Hall of Shame:

http://www.cs.arizona.edu/sumatra

JAWS (Java Applets With Safety) is an Australian National University project using theorem-proving technology to analyze safety and security properties of Java Applets. Java down under:

http://cs.anu.edu.au/people/Tony.Dekker/JAWS.HTML

Appendix B. Signature Formats

Both fields and methods have signatures within the Java class file. They are a shorthand to describe the type (of a field) and the return type and parameters (of a method). Signatures are constructed using characters or strings to represent the various data types. The signature of a field is simply the character or string representing its datatype.

The signature of a method is a pair of parentheses enclosing a list of the characters or strings representing the datatypes of the parameters, separated by semicolons. The parentheses are followed by the datatype of the return type of the method.

Table 9 indicates how data types are represented by characters or strings.

Table 9. Data Type Representations in Method Signatures

Type	**Character or String Used in Signature**
long	J
byte	B
character	C
double	D
float	F
integer	I
object reference	L<classname>[a]
short	S
boolean	Z
array	[<datatype>

a. The class name here is the full name of the class with '/'s in place of '.'s

Table 10. Examples of Method Signatures

Signature	**Type**	**Description**
[C	char[]	An array of character
Ljava/lang/String	String	A Java string

Signature	Type	Description
[[java/lang/Object	Object[][]	A two dimensional array of objects
()V	void methodName()	A method taking no parameters and returning no value
([Ljava/lang/String;I)I	int methodName(String, int)	A method taking a String and an integer value and returning an integer.

Appendix C. The Bytecode Verifier in Detail

The first stage of the bytecode verifier process is the identifying of bytecode instructions and their arguments. This operation is completed in two passes. The first pass locates the start of each instruction and stores it in a table. Having found the start of each instruction, the verifier makes a second pass, parsing the instructions. This involves building a structure for each instruction, storing the instruction and its arguments. These arguments are checked for validity at this point. Specifically:

- All arguments to flow-control instructions must cause branches to the start of a valid instruction.
- All references to local variables must be legal. That is, an instruction may not attempt to read or write to a local variable beyond those that a method declares.
- All references to the constant pool must be to an entry of the appropriate type.
- All opcodes must have the correct number of arguments.
- Each exception handler must have start and end points at the beginning of valid instructions with the start point before the end point. In addition, the offset of the exception handler must be the start of a valid instruction.

C.1 The Data Flow Analyzer

Having established that the bytecodes are syntactically correct, the bytecode verifier now has the task of analyzing the runtime behavior of the code (within the limitations we examined in Chapter 6, "An Incompleteness Theorem for Bytecode Verifiers" on page 95).

To perform this analysis, the bytecode verifier has to keep track of two pieces of information for each instruction:

- The status of the stack prior to executing that instruction in the form of the number and type of items on the stack.
- The contents of local variables prior to executing that instruction. Only the type of each local variable is tracked. The value is ignored.

Where types are concerned, the analyzer does not need to distinguish between the various normal integer types (byte, short, char) since, as we discuss in "Java Bytecode" on page 69, they all have the same internal representation.

The first stage is the initialization of the data flow analyzer:

- Each instruction is marked as unvisited. That is, the data flow analyzer has not yet examined that instruction
- For the first instruction, the stack is marked as empty and the local variables corresponding to the method's arguments are initialized with the appropriate types
- All other local variables declared as used by the method are marked as containing illegal values
- The "changed" bit of the first instruction is set, indicating that the analyzer should examine this instruction

Finally, the data flow analyzer runs, looping through the following steps:

1. Find a virtual machine instruction whose "changed" bit is set.
2. If no instruction remains whose "changed" bit is set, the method has successfully been verified, otherwise turn off the changed bit of the instruction found and proceed to step 3.
3. Emulate the effect of this instruction on the stack and local variables:
    - If the instruction uses values from the stack, ensure that there are sufficient elements on the stack and that the element(s) on the top of the stack are of the appropriate type.
    - If the instruction pushes values onto the stack, ensure that there is sufficient room on the stack for the new element(s) and update the stack status to reflect the pushed values.
    - If the instruction reads a local variable, ensure that the specified variable contains a value of the appropriate type.
    - If the instruction writes a value to a local variable, change the type of that variable to reflect that change.
4. Determine the set of all possible instructions which could be executed next. These are:
    - The next instruction in sequence if the current instruction isn't an unconditional goto, a return, or a throw.

- The target instruction of a conditional or unconditional branch.
- The first instruction of all exception handlers for this instruction.

5. For each of the possible following instructions, merge the stack and local variables as they exist after executing the current instruction with the state prior to executing the following instruction. In the exception-handler case, change the stack so that it contains a single object of the exception type indicated by the exception handler information. Merging proceeds as follows:

- If the stacks are of different sizes then this is an error. Stop!
- If the stacks contain exactly the same types, then they are already merged
- If the stacks are identical other than having differently typed object references at corresponding places on the stacks then the merged stack will have this object reference replaced by an instance of the first common superclass or common superinterface of the two types. Such a reference type always exists because the type *Object* is a supertype of all class and interface types.
- If this is the first time the successor instruction has been visited, set up the stack and local variable values using those calculated in Step 2 and set the "changed" bit for the successor instruction. If the instruction has been seen before, merge the stack and local variable values calculated in Step 2 and Step 3 into the values already there; set the "change" bit if there is any modification.

6. Go to Step 1.

If the data-flow analyzer runs on the method without reporting any failures, then the method has been successfully verified by Pass 3 of the class file verifier.

Appendix D. What's on the CD?

The CD that accompanies this book contains a number of things:

The sample code
All of the samples contained in Chapters 2, 4, 7, and 9 are on the CD both as source Java and as compiled class files. There is also the DumpConstantPool application which we used to examine the applet files in Chapter 4.

The book itself in HTML
The complete book is on the CD in HTML format so that you can read it using your browser (because "you can't grep a tree").

Some useful links
There is a table of HTML links to Java and security Web sites which we found useful while creating the book.

VisualAge for Java Entry
VisualAge for Java is IBM's award-winning visual application builder environment. We have included the Entry version for Windows (95 or NT) on the CD. This has all of the function of the full professional product, except that it is limited to creating a maximum of 100 new classes.

NetREXX
REXX is a programming language used widely in IBM mainframe environments and OS/2. It offers powerful facilities, particularly in the area of data parsing, but at the same time it is very user-friendly. NetREXX is a version of REXX that incorporates object-oriented constructions and which can be used to generate Java source code or bytecode.

D.1 How to Access the CD

To access the contents of the CD, simply point your Web browser at file **index.htm** in the CD root directory and follow the links you find there.

Glossary

3270 Usually any of a family of block-mode VDUs including the IBM model 3270

AWT Abstract Windows Toolkit, the Java package for creating GUIs

CGI Common Gateway Interface, an interface that allows server-side executable code to be linked to be invoked as a URL.

CICS Customer Information Control System

CERT Computer Emergency Response Team. An organization that acts as a clearing house of information about security problems

CORBA The Common Object Request Broker Architecture, a standard for implementing a distributed object architecture

DES Data Encryption Standard, a bulk (symmetric key) encryption algorithm

DMZ De-militarized zone, used here to indicate the portion of a network surrounded by firewalls

DNS Domain Name Service

FTP File Transfer Protocol

GET An HTTP command which requests the server to send data to the client

Gopher An information service providing linked pages

HOD Host-On-Demand, an IBM 3270 terminal emulator

HTML Hypertext markup language

HTTP HyperText Transfer Protocol

HTTPS HTTP encapsulated in SSL protocol

ICMP Internet Control Message Protocol

IIOP Internet Inter ORB Protocol, a specification for the way that ORBs communicate

IP Internet Protocol

IPv4 Version 4 of Internet Protocol

IPv6 Version 6 of Internet Protocol

JCA Java Cryptography Architecture

JCE Java Cryptography Extensions (the parts of JCA that cannot be exported from the US

JVM Java Virtual Machine

KeyPair A matching pair of public and private keys, used for digital signatures and public key encryption

LAN Local Area Network, with typical bandwith greater than 4 M bits/second

MD5 A message digest (secure hash) algorithm from RSA Corp

MIME Multipurpose Internet Mail Extensions

NetBIOSLAN protocol generally used by PCs

ORB Object Request Broker, a program that provides services to enable the use of distributed objects

PC Personal Computer

POST An HTTP command which sends client data to the server

RC4 A bulk (symmetric key) encryption algorithm which allows variable key sizes

RMI RemoteMethod Invocation, a technique to allow Java on one system to access objects on another

RSA Rivest, Shamir and Adelman formod tho RSA corporation to market cryptographic software and algorithms, in particular the public key encryption mechanism that also bears their initials.

SHA Secure Hash Architecture

SNA System Network Architecture

SOCKS A protocol used to encapsulate other TCP protocols

SSL Secure Sockets Layer

TCP/IP Often used as a generic term for the suite of TCP, IP and related protocols

TCP Transmission Control Protocol

UDP User Datagram Protocol

URL Uniform Resource Locator

VDU Visual Display Unit

WAIS Wide Area Information Service

WAN Wide Area Network, with typical bandwith less than 4 M bits/second

WWW World Wide Web, usually refers to systems using HTTP

Index

Numerics

A

B

C

D

E

F

K

L

M

N

O

LICENSE AGREEMENT AND LIMITED WARRANTY

READ THE FOLLOWING TERMS AND CONDITIONS CAREFULLY BEFORE OPENING THIS CD PACKAGE, *JAVA NETWORK SECURITY.* THIS LEGAL DOCUMENT IS AN AGREEMENT BETWEEN YOU AND PRENTICE-HALL, INC. (THE "COMPANY"). BY OPENING THIS SEALED CD PACKAGE, YOU ARE AGREEING TO BE BOUND BY THESE TERMS AND CONDITIONS. IF YOU DO NOT AGREE WITH THESE TERMS AND CONDITIONS, DO NOT OPEN THE CD PACKAGE. PROMPTLY RETURN THE UNOPENED CD PACKAGE AND ALL ACCOMPANYING ITEMS TO THE PLACE YOU OBTAINED THEM FOR A FULL REFUND OF ANY SUMS YOU HAVE PAID.

1. **GRANT OF LICENSE:** In consideration of your purchase of this book, and your agreement to abide by the terms and conditions of this Agreement, the Company grants to you a nonexclusive right to use and display the copy of the enclosed software program (hereinafter the "SOFTWARE") on a single computer (i.e., with a single CPU) at a single location so long as you comply with the terms of this Agreement. The Company reserves all rights not expressly granted to you under this Agreement.

2. **OWNERSHIP OF SOFTWARE:** You own only the magnetic or physical media (the enclosed CD) on which the SOFTWARE is recorded or fixed, but the Company and the software developers retain all the rights, title, and ownership to the SOFTWARE recorded on the original CD copy(ies) and all subsequent copies of the SOFTWARE, regardless of the form or media on which the original or other copies may exist. This license is not a sale of the original SOFTWARE or any copy to you.

3. **COPY RESTRICTIONS:** This SOFTWARE and the accompanying printed materials and user manual (the "Documentation") are the subject of copyright. The individual programs on the CD are copyrighted by the authors of each program. Some of the programs on the CD include separate licensing agreements. If you intend to use one of these programs, you must read and follow its accompanying license agreement. You may <u>not</u> copy the Documentation or the SOFTWARE, except that you may make a single copy of the SOFTWARE for backup or archival purposes only. You may be held legally responsible for any copying or copyright infringement which is caused or encouraged by your failure to abide by the terms of this restriction.

4. **USE RESTRICTIONS:** You may <u>not</u> network the SOFTWARE or otherwise use it on more than one computer or computer terminal at the same time. You may physically transfer the SOFTWARE from one computer to another provided that the SOFTWARE is used on only one computer at a time. You may <u>not</u> distribute copies of the SOFTWARE or Documentation to others. You may <u>not</u> reverse engineer, disassemble, decompile, modify, adapt, translate, or create derivative works based on the SOFTWARE or the Documentation without the prior written consent of the Company.

5. **TRANSFER RESTRICTIONS:** The enclosed SOFTWARE is licensed only to you and may <u>not</u> be transferred to any one else without the prior written consent of the Company. Any unauthorized transfer of the SOFTWARE shall result in the immediate termination of this Agreement.

6. **TERMINATION:** This license is effective until terminated. This license will terminate automatically without notice from the Company and become null and void if you fail to comply with any provisions or limitations of this license. Upon termination, you shall destroy the Documentation and all copies of the SOFTWARE. All provisions of this Agreement as to warranties, limitation of liability, remedies or damages, and our ownership rights shall survive termination.

7. **MISCELLANEOUS:** This Agreement shall be construed in accordance with the laws of the United States of America and the State of New York and shall benefit the Company, its affiliates, and assignees.

8. **LIMITED WARRANTY AND DISCLAIMER OF WARRANTY:** The Company warrants that the SOFTWARE, when properly used in accordance with the Documentation, will operate in substantial conformity with the description of the SOFTWARE set forth in the Documentation. The

Company does not warrant that the SOFTWARE will meet your requirements or that the operation of the SOFTWARE will be uninterrupted or error-free. The Company warrants that the media on which the SOFTWARE is delivered shall be free from defects in materials and workmanship under normal use for a period of thirty (30) days from the date of your purchase. Your only remedy and the Company's only obligation under these limited warranties is, at the Company's option, return of the warranted item for a refund of any amounts paid by you or replacement of the item. Any replacement of SOFTWARE or media under the warranties shall not extend the original warranty period. The limited warranty set forth above shall not apply to any SOFTWARE which the Company determines in good faith has been subject to misuse, neglect, improper installation, repair, alteration, or damage by you. EXCEPT FOR THE EXPRESSED WARRANTIES SET FORTH ABOVE, THE COMPANY DISCLAIMS ALL WARRANTIES, EXPRESS OR IMPLIED, INCLUDING WITHOUT LIMITATION, THE IMPLIED WARRANTIES OF MERCHANTABILITY AND FITNESS FOR A PARTICULAR PURPOSE. EXCEPT FOR THE EXPRESS WARRANTY SET FORTH ABOVE, THE COMPANY DOES NOT WARRANT, GUARANTEE, OR MAKE ANY REPRESENTATION REGARDING THE USE OR THE RESULTS OF THE USE OF THE SOFTWARE IN TERMS OF ITS CORRECTNESS, ACCURACY, RELIABILITY, CURRENTNESS, OR OTHERWISE.

IN NO EVENT, SHALL THE COMPANY OR ITS EMPLOYEES, AGENTS, SUPPLIERS, OR CONTRACTORS BE LIABLE FOR ANY INCIDENTAL, INDIRECT, SPECIAL, OR CONSEQUENTIAL DAMAGES ARISING OUT OF OR IN CONNECTION WITH THE LICENSE GRANTED UNDER THIS AGREEMENT, OR FOR LOSS OF USE, LOSS OF DATA, LOSS OF INCOME OR PROFIT, OR OTHER LOSSES, SUSTAINED AS A RESULT OF INJURY TO ANY PERSON, OR LOSS OF OR DAMAGE TO PROPERTY, OR CLAIMS OF THIRD PARTIES, EVEN IF THE COMPANY OR AN AUTHORIZED REPRESENTATIVE OF THE COMPANY HAS BEEN ADVISED OF THE POSSIBILITY OF SUCH DAMAGES. IN NO EVENT SHALL LIABILITY OF THE COMPANY FOR DAMAGES WITH RESPECT TO THE SOFTWARE EXCEED THE AMOUNTS ACTUALLY PAID BY YOU, IF ANY, FOR THE SOFTWARE.

SOME JURISDICTIONS DO NOT ALLOW THE LIMITATION OF IMPLIED WARRANTIES OR LIABILITY FOR INCIDENTAL, INDIRECT, SPECIAL, OR CONSEQUENTIAL DAMAGES, SO THE ABOVE LIMITATIONS MAY NOT ALWAYS APPLY. THE WARRANTIES IN THIS AGREEMENT GIVE YOU SPECIFIC LEGAL RIGHTS AND YOU MAY ALSO HAVE OTHER RIGHTS WHICH VARY IN ACCORDANCE WITH LOCAL LAW.

ACKNOWLEDGMENT

YOU ACKNOWLEDGE THAT YOU HAVE READ THIS AGREEMENT, UNDERSTAND IT, AND AGREE TO BE BOUND BY ITS TERMS AND CONDITIONS. YOU ALSO AGREE THAT THIS AGREEMENT IS THE COMPLETE AND EXCLUSIVE STATEMENT OF THE AGREEMENT BETWEEN YOU AND THE COMPANY AND SUPERSEDES ALL PROPOSALS OR PRIOR AGREEMENTS, ORAL, OR WRITTEN, AND ANY OTHER COMMUNICATIONS BETWEEN YOU AND THE COMPANY OR ANY REPRESENTATIVE OF THE COMPANY RELATING TO THE SUBJECT MATTER OF THIS AGREEMENT.

Should you have any questions concerning this Agreement or if you wish to contact the Company for any reason, please contact in writing at the address below.

Robin Short

Prentice Hall PTR

One Lake Street

Upper Saddle River, New Jersey 07458